The Handbook
of Estate
Planning

The Handbook of Estate Planning

Third Edition

Robert A. Esperti
Tax Attorney, Lecturer, Consultant

Renno L. Peterson
Tax Attorney, Lecturer, Consultant

McGraw-Hill, Inc.

New York St. Louis San Francisco Auckland Bogotá
Caracas Hamburg Lisbon London Madrid
Mexico Milan Montreal New Delhi Paris
San Juan São Paulo Singapore
Sydney Tokyo Toronto

Library of Congress Cataloging-in-Publication Data

Esperti, Robert A.
    The handbook of estate planning / Robert A. Esperti, Renno L.
Peterson.—3rd ed.
        p.   cm.
    Includes index.
    ISBN 0-07-019684-2
    1. Estate planning—United States.   I. Peterson, Renno L.
II. Title.
KF750.E816   1991
346.7305'2—dc20
[347.30652]   90-24714

1 2 3 4 5 6 7 8 9 0   DOC/DOC   9 7 6 5 4 3 2 1

ISBN 0-07-019684-2

*The sponsoring editor for this book was William A. Sabin, the editing supervisor
was Frank Kotowski, Jr., and the production supervisor was Pamela A. Pelton.
It was set in Baskerville by McGraw-Hill's Professional Publishing composition
unit.*

Printed and bound by R. R. Donnelley & Sons Company.

For Liz and Karen

Contents

The authors are not engaged in rendering legal, tax, accounting, or similar professional services. While legal, tax, and accounting issues covered in this book have been checked with sources believed to be reliable, some material may be affected by changes in the laws or in the interpretations of such laws since the manuscript for this book was completed. For that reason the accuracy and completeness of such information and the opinions based thereon are not guaranteed. In addition, state or local tax laws or procedural rules may have a material impact on the general recommendations made by the authors, and the strategies outlined in this book may not be suitable for every individual. If legal, accounting, tax, investment, or other expert advice is required, obtain the services of a competent practitioner.

Introduction

Our objective in writing this handbook is to familiarize you with the estate-planning process; to impart a good understanding of that process; and to give you a comfort and security level that will motivate you to accomplish your planning objectives by seeking the assistance of estate-planning professionals.

We do not believe that you should attempt to plan your estate by yourself; estate-planning loners will generally not accomplish good planning results. A little bit of knowledge can be very dangerous with regard to the estate-planning process—dangerous if it is viewed as complete or ultimate knowledge. On the other hand, a little bit of knowledge can go a long way if it is used to initiate the selection and monitoring of good professionals to assist you in accomplishing your objectives.

How-to-do-it books may be fun to read, but fill-in-the-blank estate planning can be worse than no planning at all. Good planning necessitates a motivated and knowledgeable client who interacts with professional advisers to bring out the very best in them with respect to their knowledge.

Some people are unfamiliar with what kinds of professionals they should seek to assist them in planning their estates; others know what kinds of professionals they need but do not know how to go about selecting them.

We believe that every estate-planning team should consist of the following professional players:

An estate-planning attorney

An accountant who is well versed in tax knowledge and knows your affairs

A professional life insurance agent who knows the estate-planning process and the general techniques used within it

A financial adviser, if you have one

Today, attorneys are called upon to deal with an enormous volume of law created by an ever-growing and complicated society. In truth, most attorneys tend to get very good at dealing with selected areas of the law. They tend to specialize because of their ability to acquire extraordinary skills in specific legal areas.

In searching for an attorney to plan your estate, you should, in our opinion, always look for the specialist: an attorney who practices in the area of estate planning to the exclusion of most other legal areas. Attorneys who readily fall into this category are tax attorneys.

Some tax attorneys specialize only in the area of income tax planning; the majority spend a significant amount of their time in the estate-planning area as well. There are also nontax attorneys who, because of their clients' needs and because of their desire and experience, are excellent estate planners. They know a lot about tax too.

The problem most people have is where to find that specialist. Many attorneys do not advertise. We believe that people finding themselves in this predicament should ask other advisers for a referral or lead. Accountants, life insurance professionals, and financial advisers have usually had significant dealings with attorneys (both good and bad) and, based on their knowledge and experience, should be delighted to make a recommendation or two. If you do not have these other advisers, you should discuss the matter with the trust officials of your local bank's trust department. Trust officers are generally knowledgeable with respect to local estate-planning attorneys.

By law, and this is true in every state, the attorney is the only adviser who is licensed to write wills and trusts. This does not mean that the attorney should be used to the exclusion of the other advisers we have named. Attorneys are usually not licensed to practice accounting or sell life insurance; they are licensed to practice law. We believe this same concept applies to the other advisers as well.

We believe that our advice in the selection of an attorney applies equally well to the selection of an accountant, a life insurance professional, and other financial advisers. You should always select knowledgeable specialists with the assistance of your other advisers. Just because one of your current advisers is a friend or a relative or just someone you trust does not make that adviser an estate-planning expert. Do not be afraid to expand your planning team.

Professional advisers should be selected for the knowledge they possess within their disciplines. All your advisers should participate in the estate-planning process and should work well not only with you but with each other. In our opinion, there is no room for the professional loner regardless of expertise.

You should encourage all your advisers to work together harmoniously for your benefit. The estate-planning process should manifest the best ideas of each of the professional players and coordinate them into one overall plan that meets your objectives to your satisfaction.

Since *The Handbook of Estate Planning* was first published, numerous major pieces of tax legislation have been passed: the Tax Equity and Fiscal Responsibility Act of 1982, the Tax Reform Act of 1984, the Tax Reform Act of 1986, the Revenue Act of 1987, the Technical and Miscellaneous Revenue Act of 1988, the Revenue Reconciliation Act of 1989 and, most recently, the Revenue Reconciliation Act of 1990.

The Tax Reform Act of 1986, which we will refer to in this book as TRA 1986, is the most comprehensive tax bill in over thirty years and represents tremendous change in our federal tax laws. Each tax act since TRA 1986 has been aimed primarily at fine tuning and refining those changes made by TRA 1986. The Revenue Reconciliation Act of 1990 was signed by President Bush shortly before this edition was finalized for publication. We have highlighted what we believe are the major impacts on estate planning of this most recent law. The law is complex, and many of its provisions will undoubtedly need interpretation by the IRS, the courts, and Congress.

In addition to these changes in federal tax law, the courts and the IRS have been busy interpreting the federal tax laws we already have on the books. States continue to change their laws affecting death taxes and spousal rights. We have once again revised *The Handbook of Estate Planning* to help keep you and your advisers up to date on those changes in our laws that affect your estate plan.

Acknowledgments

We deeply appreciate the assistance of:

Eileen Sacco for her good humor and hard work on the original manuscript of this book.

Frederick A. Malsom for his prompting and assistance with regard to the English language.

Steven M. Laiderman, LL.M., with the law firm of Newman, Goldfarb, Freyman & Stevens, P.C., St. Louis, Missouri, for his technical revisions to the Third Edition of this book.

Lisa Kane DeVitto for her thoroughness and diligence in putting the Third Edition together.

The Handbook
of Estate
Planning

1

What Is Estate Planning?

"It's More Than Money"

It is people: spouses, children, grandchildren, favorite family members, and close friends; their security and prosperity without you. It is state and federal taxes: income, death, and gift. It is lawyers, accountants, insurance people, banks, and financial planners. It is society's rules along with the red tape and courts of law that accompany those rules. It is a world of advisers busily accomplishing things that most people do not understand. It is time and money!

Estate planning takes time: a little now or a lot later; time to identify and accomplish goals that are personally important; or time to react to a host of external forces that may have their own interests rather than those of your loved ones at heart.

Estate planning involves money, business, and finance. It involves dollars, lots of dollars, to create and maintain a lifestyle for your loved ones after your death. It involves the sacrifice of dollars to purchase life insurance or to invest in a portfolio, in lieu of your personal indulgence, with the sincere belief that you are creating security for you and your loved ones.

Estate planning is human ambition and the fulfillment of that ambition by acquiring and holding property. It is a life statement of commitment to others.

Estate planning is living planning. It is your attempt to use your resources to create an environment for yourself and others that will extend beyond your life. It is the ability to share your success with others. Estate planning allows you the opportunity to control your success both during life and on death.

We have always asked our clients, "What do you want done with your property and insurance after you're gone?" The responses have been different, but they all contained thoughts which could be summarized as follows:

> "I would like to give my property to whom I want, in precisely the way I want. Further, I wish my beneficiaries to receive my property when I wish them to receive it.
>
> "But, and this is very important to me, I want to save every last tax dollar, both state and federal, in accomplishing my objectives. Oh yes, I also want to avoid or, at the least, reduce attorneys' fees and court costs.
>
> "Lastly, I don't want myself or my family involved in a lot of red tape that prevents my objectives from being accomplished quickly."

You probably know what you want to do with your property both during life and on death. You are sensitive to the red tape imposed by society's rules. You do need professional help in accomplishing your planning objectives.

You are unique; therefore, planning for you must be unique. Planning, to be good, must fit you; it must be comfortable, like a favorite pair of shoes. You must understand the estate-planning process, for without understanding there can be no comfort. Planning without understanding results, more often than not, in uncertainty and anxiety.

Our main objective is to assist you in understanding the rules, to take the "black magic" out of planning and replace it with knowledge and comfort. We hope to expand your planning horizons.

Your understanding is our mandate. With the comfort of knowledge, you should be able to confidently seek out the professional advisers and products you need. You should have the ability to communicate your goals and objectives to your advisers. On completing this book, you should have a good grasp of the estate-planning process and the techniques it utilizes. You should be able to discern between the knowledgeable professional and the not so knowledgeable professional. We hope to give you enough understanding of the estate-planning process to enable you to participate in a meaningful dialogue with your advisers in accomplishing your estate-planning objectives.

We have heard many times, "Why do today what I can put off until tomorrow." In estate planning, tomorrow may instantly become today. None of us can, with certainty, predict the timing of our own deaths.

Death sneaks up on most of us and respects no time parameters. Statistically, there may be a tomorrow, but don't plan on it! Planning *now* is mandatory.

Estate planning is a process that begins within your life and can continue far after death. It is not unique or indigenous to any economic class. Its audience is America. Its players, Americans. How often we have heard, "Estate planning for me? Heavens, I don't need an estate plan! I have so little." Really? No loved ones, no disposition toward a favorite family member, close friend, or institution (charitable or otherwise)? No property, no insurance or pension plan? No personal possessions, mementos, or family heirlooms that require a loving pass-on? No debts?

In 1981, President Reagan and Congress passed a massive piece of legislation called the Economic Recovery Tax Act, which we will refer to as ERTA. ERTA had a profound impact on estate planning. The changes in the Tax Reform Act of 1984 and the Tax Reform Act of 1986 pale in comparison to those made by ERTA. Even today, ERTA represents the most important change in our federal estate- and gift-tax laws made in some forty years.

For those of you who have planned in the past, we have some good news and some bad news. The good news is that President Reagan and Congress have revolutionized our federal estate- and gift-tax laws. The bottom line is that the law is terrific for taxpayers. The bad news is that estate plans prepared prior to September 13, 1981, must be reviewed and may have to be redone in order to take full advantage of ERTA.

ERTA was not just another technical change in the law that added additional regulations and red tape. ERTA was the cutting edge of a tax revolution. It gave back a huge piece of America to Americans. TRA 1986 continues this tradition.

ERTA and TRA 1986 are massive pieces of legislation whose intent is easily understood. They reduce confiscatory taxes that have been an everyday reality for far too long and herald a new frontier in government's recognition of the role of the individual and the family.

The time for planning to take advantage of these laws is now.

2
Estate-Planning History

"A Simplified Version"

Primitive people did not recognize that land could be owned; the land belonged to all people. It was unthinkable that land could be transferred at all, much less on death.

Only personal property was possessed and owned by primitive people, and on death, our early ancestors either destroyed or buried such property with its owner.

When people began to recognize the value in their possessions, they began to become concerned with passing those possessions on death. Perhaps the earliest written evidence of the penchant for passing property on can be found in the hieroglyphics of the early Egyptians. Although our knowledge of these early wills is limited, we do know they passed property to select heirs.

In Babylonia, as a result of the Code of Hammurabi, property, with only a very few exceptions, had to pass to heirs on death. This was true under the laws of Solon in Greece also. Roman law, especially under Caesar Augustus, followed this practice as well. As a matter of fact, it would appear that Augustus was the inventor of the estate tax; he levied a tax of 5 percent on the value of all estates to help support his army.

Emperor Justin of the Byzantine Empire, long recognized as one of the greatest lawmakers of all time, created the Justinian Code. It was this code that prescribed the first formal requirements that attached to wills. The code also allowed a certain form of contract that is remarkably similar to modern day trusts.

Many of our current will and estate laws can be traced to both Rome and the Justinian Code. Rome extended its rule to most of the known world; its rule included creating a system of law for each territory it conquered, and Great Britain was no exception. Even though the Romans were pushed out of Great Britain by the Anglo-Saxons, much Roman law remained.

Up until the Norman conquest in A.D. 1066, the Anglo-Saxon law allowed people to pass title to most of their property through the use of wills on their deaths. Their laws even provided that in the absence of a will certain property would pass to heirs. All of this changed, however, after the Norman invasion in England and the advent of feudalism.

The foundation of the English feudal system was that the king owned all the land under his domain. Land was to be disposed of only by the king. Even though the king distributed land among his nobles, he still retained an interest called a military tenure. In fact, the nobles took the property given them by the king subject to their making continuing financial contributions toward the king's war efforts.

The king needed large armies that could only be raised by nobles owning large estates. To prevent the dilution of land into smaller parcels by inheritance, the English law prohibited land from being left by will. Such property passed automatically to the eldest living male heir (primogeniture). Primogeniture allowed wealth to accumulate in a very few hands. It also created a large caste of property-poor nobles and knights.

English feudal wills could, in the main, pass only personal property. There was a constant battle between the church and the king about who had the authority to administer these feudal wills. At first the king took on this task and charged for his services. This charge, or "herriot," covered his expenses of administering the will and created tax revenue for the king's coffers.

When the church began to administer these estates, it also charged a fee. It also inherited substantial property through deathbed persuasion and the bequests that resulted from that persuasion. The king feared the power the church was accumulating by its increased wealth, and the saga of their power struggle began.

Over the years, property vested in fewer and fewer hands because of primogeniture. Events, however, were to change this. Nobles wanted to control the passing of their lands. Primogeniture was too restrictive; it took the fun out of being rich.

Under the English feudal system, two courts and systems of law developed. The first was the system of the common-law courts. Common-law courts applied the king's laws strictly and without compassion. Participants began to appeal to the king for mercy and equitable relief. The second system came into being when the king appointed a chancellor to take charge of his royal courts of mercy or equity. Two court systems were emerging in tandem: common courts of law and royal courts of equity. Often these courts would conflict, but over time their functions became separated. Basically, the common-law courts would say what the law was, and the courts of equity gave relief to litigants under their rules. The law of trusts, as we shall see, grew out of the conflict and confusion between the two systems.

As we mentioned earlier, it was impossible, under feudal law, to dispose of land by will. The common-law courts had jurisdiction in this area.

During this time a new concept was developing that allowed a noble to sell property to a third person (not leave it but sell it while alive). Legal title would be in the name of that third party; however, the property was to be used for the benefit of another person named in the seller's will. This great legal scam to get around primogeniture, with all its restrictions, landed in the lap of the courts of equity. These courts developed a body of law that allowed the transfer of property to one person subject to somebody *else's* use or benefit. This was called beneficial ownership, the beginning of the law of trusts.

Land began to have two title holders: (1) the legal title holder, the person whose name appeared on the deed, and (2) the beneficial title holder, the person for whom the property was held. Can you see the law of trusts emerging?

By the early 1500s, it is estimated that over two-thirds of all land in England was held in the form of a "use" (trust). Uses (trusts) were handy devices. They could *deter* creditors, particularly spouses with claims, and they could also avoid the herriot (transfer fees) of the king.

Now the plot thickens. The king was not happy. Parliament, at the king's bidding, passed the Statute of Uses in 1535. This law attacked and attempted to prohibit these early trust devices. There were too many loopholes in the Statute of Uses, and Parliament acknowledged the public sentiment and passed the Statute of Wills in 1540.

The Statute of Wills, for the first time, allowed a person to pass title to real estate (real property) through a will. By the mid-1660s, all property was allowed to pass by will; and in the latter part of the seventeenth century, the last great statute in this area was passed: the Statute of Frauds.

The Statute of Frauds required that all transfers of land be in writing, signed by the transferor, and witnessed by a plurality of witnesses.

Most of the rules created through this historic process have been adopted in the United States and are referred to as our English common-law heritage. In most states, courts of law and equity have been merged into the courts we have today.

Out of this heritage came the idea and ability for government to tax property at the owner's death. In the late 1700s, England passed the Stamp Act. This Stamp Act required people to write their wills on paper printed by the government. The paper had stamps on it. Different paper and stamps were used depending upon the size of the estate. When the paper was needed because it was will-drafting time, it had to be paid for. When the decedent's estate was administered, the court would check the size of the estate against the stamps on the will paper to make sure that the proper tax was paid. They would also check to see whether any gifts were made in contemplation of death. These gifts were assumed to be death devices and would also be taxed. Thus the first gift-tax law came into existence.

The first American attempt at a federal estate tax was the Revolutionary War Tax passed in 1797. The purpose of this tax was to pay the war debt. This was adopted from the English Stamp Act, and the person who inherited the estate paid a stamp duty. This act was repealed in 1802 when the revenue was no longer needed. In 1826, the state of Pennsylvania adopted the first inheritance tax. The inheritance tax was based on the Revolutionary War Tax. Instead of taxing the estate of the decedent, it taxed the recipient of the inheritance. By the late 1800s, nine states had adopted an inheritance tax.

The second federal estate tax was passed in 1862. This also was a stamp tax to raise revenue for the Civil War; this tax was repealed in 1870. In 1898, the Spanish War Tax was enacted, which was a tax on personal property passing by will or otherwise; it was repealed in 1902.

The forerunner of our current federal estate tax was the German War Tax passed in 1916. This tax, like the others, was to raise revenue for the war. This tax, however, did not go away.

The federal estate tax was held constitutional by the Supreme Court of the United States. Article 1, Section 8, Clause 1, of the United States Constitution states as follows:

> The Congress shall have Power To lay and collect Taxes, Duties, Imposts and Excises, to pay Debts and provide for the common Defence and general Welfare of the United States; but all Duties, Imposts and Excises shall be uniform throughout the United States.

In addition, Article 1, Section 9, Clause 4, of the Constitution states as follows: "No capitation, or other direct, Tax shall be laid, unless in Proportion to the Census or Enumeration herein before directed to be taken."

This new federal estate tax was not a direct tax on property. As a matter of fact, the federal estate tax as it was then and is now is merely a tax on the transfers of assets from deceased persons to their heirs. Technically, it is not a tax against property. Thus, unlike the income tax, which to become legal, had to be added as a constitutional amendment, the federal estate tax did fit within the strict original confines of the U.S. Constitution.

The gift tax was a natural extension of the federal estate tax. When the federal estate tax began in 1916, it was constantly amended. There was an amendment in 1917, one in 1918, and a major amendment in 1926. In 1926, the gift tax was formally recognized. Prior to 1926, a gift in contemplation of death was not taxed at the same rate as the federal estate tax. It was found that much revenue was being lost because people were making gifts during their lifetimes and these gifts were free from tax. Thus, in 1926, the first gift tax was passed so that there would be a tax on all property that was transferred from the owner to another person without charging a fair market value.

It seems clear to us that most laws historically restricted ownership based on social policy, not revenue policy. In feudal times wealth was held in a few hands for purposes of control and transfer. With the modern concept of centralized government, the "holding together" of estates in the hands of a few was considered antidemocratic and was politically unpopular.

Redistribution of wealth came into vogue for a variety of reasons; it seemed appropriate to have more people own a share of the available wealth.

The United States enacted estate taxes to fund specific military escapades. However, according to President F. Roosevelt, the federal estate tax was based on "the very sound policy of encouraging a wider distribution of wealth," or, in other words, redistribution of wealth. President Roosevelt made this statement at a time most apropos: the introduction of another rise in the estate-tax rates in 1935.

President Roosevelt's words have stood for reality for a very long time; but, thanks to ERTA and TRA 1986, the pendulum has swung back in the opposite direction.

3
Title

"How Do You Own It?"

"I don't know how I own it" is an answer we frequently receive from our clients when they are asked in whose names their various assets are held. One of the major problems confronting estate planners is that people frequently buy and sell assets without the foggiest idea of how those assets should properly be held.

Not understanding how property should be owned makes estate planning a frustrating and impossible exercise. You cannot plan for property that you do not own; and if for some reason you do attempt to do planning with what you do not own (and this does happen), your attempt will be to no avail.

There are three often-used methods by which an adult takes ownership of property: "fee simple," "tenancy in common," and "joint tenancy with right of survivorship." We will explain each method.

The concept of fee-simple ownership is easy. To own something in fee simple is to completely own it by yourself. The fee-simple owner is a sole and absolute owner.

To own property in tenancy in common is to own it with one or more other people. As a tenant in common, you cannot be a fee-simple owner of the entire asset. An example of this form of ownership would be you and a friend owning a 100-page book. You own the book as tenants in common. Each of you owns 50 percent of the book; that is, each of you owns fifty pages. Each of you would be able, since you each own fifty pages of the book, to leave your half on death to anyone. Each of you while alive could give your fifty pages away to anyone. Each of you owns absolutely 50 percent of that book. Each of you is a tenant in common with the other.

There is no limit to the number of tenants who can own something with others in tenancy in common; 100 people could be tenants in common in the ownership of a 100-page book. Each would then own one-hundredth, or one page, of the book.

The only real problem occasioned by tenancy in common is the fact that if one of the tenants wants to sell his or her interest and if the buyer wants to know what it is that he or she is purchasing, the selling tenant in common would not know which of the 100 pages is owned. All the seller knows is that he or she owns one-hundredth of the book.

Of course, we very seldom see 100 tenants in common. Generally, we see two, three, or four people who have bought something together, with each owning a half, third, or quarter of the property. Should a proposed sale by one of the tenants pose a problem as to what pages that tenant actually owns, the local court will have to become involved. The court's solution is called "partition." Here the court takes the asset and makes an actual, physical division based on each tenant's percentage of ownership.

That technique does not always work too well. Does one tenant get every other page of the book? the front half? the rear half? Generally, it is better for the quarreling tenants to sell the book to a third person and divide the cash according to their percentage of ownership.

All in all, tenancy in common is a frequently used method of owning property. The important thing to understand about this method of owning property is that if you are a tenant in common, you absolutely own your percentage share in the property. Your percentage share can be sold or given away during your lifetime and can be left to your chosen beneficiaries at your death.

A potential drawback of this form of ownership is if the other tenants do not particularly like the person to whom the deceased tenant has left the percentage share in the property. We commonly refer to this problem as the "breaks of the game." If an individual chooses this form of ownership, that person's co-owners and beneficiaries may face co-owners they do not like.

The third form of ownership commonly used in the marketplace is joint tenancy with right of survivorship. In our experience, this method of taking title is greatly misunderstood by the public—very greatly misunderstood. In fact, it is a form of ownership that is extremely confusing.

Joint tenancy with right of survivorship is a great deal like tenancy in common, yet totally different in the results it manifests. For example, we again have two people, each of whom owns 50 percent of that 100-page book; now, however, they own it as joint tenants with right of survivorship. This method of ownership does not mean, like tenancy in common, that each of them owns 50 percent of that book; each of them does not own half of the book, or 50 pages. If they own the book in joint tenancy with right of survivorship, they each own *100 percent* of that book for purposes of title holding. Both of them own the whole thing? Yes, that is correct.

Joint ownership, or "joint property" as it is commonly called, is a *fictional* form of ownership created by our English common-law heritage. Fictional in that, yes, two or more people can own the whole thing. What occurs to breathe realism into this fictional method of owning property is the added survivorship feature. Remember the proper name of this method of ownership: joint tenancy with right of survivorship. The survivorship feature means that as each individual joint tenant dies, that person simply falls off the ownership charts. Upon death, title is in the hands of the surviving joint tenants. Each of the survivors now owns a much greater percentage of the property. Specifically, if there were three tenants and one died, the remaining two would own the asset. It is almost as if the deceased tenant never really owned it in the first place.

"My word," you say, "do you mean to tell me that if I own a mountain cabin with my brother in joint tenancy with right of survivorship, upon my death, my spouse and children have absolutely no right to that cabin? That it all belongs to my brother? That since I died, I am removed from ownership, and since my brother survived, it is all his? That my family has absolutely no rights to that cabin? Is that what you mean?" Yes, that is exactly what we mean. Surprised? Many of our clients certainly have been.

Joint tenancy with right of survivorship is an automatic method of planning property because this method of taking title functions as a mini-estate plan. It automatically passes ownership by law to the surviving tenants. Please realize that there is no reason to plan your jointly held interest in your will or trust. As long as there is a joint tenant that survives you, the passage of the asset is already planned. So, if you have the opportunity to buy into a 100-page book as a joint tenant with ninety-nine other people for the price of $1000, and the total value of that book is $100,000, it might not be a good bargain. On the other hand, if the ninety-nine other people are all eighty years of age or older and you are only twenty-one, that might suggest a good deal. As each joint owner passed away, the remaining joint owners would then own the book as ninety-nine joint tenants with right of survivorship; ninety-eight joint owners with right of survivorship; ninety-seven, etc., right down to the last one to survive, which, odds are, would be you. What a deal. What a crazy form of ownership!

Now, on the other hand, from a living point of view, let us assume that you are a joint tenant who wishes to sell your interest to someone else. You certainly could and, in most states, would not have to receive the permission of the other joint owners; but what if you, as the joint tenant, wanted to carve out your interest for your sole and personal use? You would have to go to the local courthouse and ask the judge to apply that old legal remedy of "partition." You would have to ask the judge to divide the property; or you could hire a lawyer to come up with a complicated and technical solution. Amazingly enough, jointly held assets, when viewed from a living point of view (without the survivorship feature), function just like assets held in tenancy in common. It is the survivorship feature that distinguishes the two.

There is another offshoot to joint ownership, a special kind of joint ownership called "tenancy by the entirety." It is used in some states by a husband and wife to hold real estate. For most practical reasons, it works the same as joint tenancy. The major difference between the two is that generally under tenancy by the entirety there is no right to split the property during marriage. For our purposes, think of tenancy by the entirety as joint tenancy. If you do own assets in tenancy by the entirety, see your attorney because your state's laws are probably unique.

Many times a client will ask, "What if I just put my name and someone else's name on a piece of property and don't specify whether it is tenancy in common or joint tenancy; which method have I elected, if any?" In our jurisdiction, that property would be held in tenancy in common. In others, it would be held in joint tenancy with right of survivorship. The answer, therefore, depends on the law of your state. Each state has its own laws. Do not assume anything—find out the correct answer from your advisers.

Always know how you wish to take title to assets and properly communicate that intent to others. Is it fee simple, tenancy in common, or joint tenancy with right of survivorship? Know what you are doing in this area, because taking proper title to property is very serious business, as you will see throughout this book.

Types of Title: A Summary

Fee simple

You own *all* of it.

You can:
  Give it away.
  Sell it.
  Leave it on death.

Tenancy in common

You own *part* of it.

You can:
  Give your part away.
  Sell your part.
  Leave your part on death.

Joint tenancy

You own *all* of it with someone else.

But you can:
  Give your interest away.
  Sell your interest.

You *cannot* leave your interest on death.

4

Jointly Held Property

"Common but Complicated"

For years, professionals have been taking pot shots at joint tenancy as an ownership technique. Even the *Reader's Digest* has vigorously attacked it as a trap or pitfall to avoid.

Historically, joint ownership has had some good attributes.

Joint tenancy is a convenient form of ownership. It is a form of ownership that has been encouraged in the marketplace by financial institutions, by merchants, and, to some extent, by professional advisers.

Joint ownership appears to be psychologically pleasing to people, particularly to married couples. Its very name implies "the two of us," a partnership, a marriage of title as well as of love. On the surface, at least, it has appeared as the right way to take title to property between people who care for each other.

Joint ownership creates, because of its survivorship feature, an instant mini-estate plan for joint owners. Remember Chapter 3, "Title: How Do You Own It?" If two people own a book jointly and one of them dies, the other continues to own the entire book. Remember? There is no need to pass title. By law, title simply remains with the survivor.

Jointly held property requires no will, trust, or other estate-planning device. It does not go through probate court on the death of the first joint tenant. In fact, this has been one of its main selling points: "If there is no probate, owning property jointly has got to be good."

Jointly held property has been most attractive among close family members. What the heck; easy to do; natural and loving in name (jointly); a mini-estate plan; and no probate court. What an estate plan!

Traditionally, however, there have been significant problems with this form of property ownership.

Jointly held property can pass property to the wrong folks, to the other joint tenant rather than chosen beneficiaries. On the death of a joint tenant there is absolutely no question as to where that property interest is going. It is going to the surviving owner by operation of law. On death, a joint owner cannot control the way the property passes nor the time of its passage.

Death has its own timing. Who outlives whom is an unknown. So are the results of owning property jointly. As we see it, it is one big roll of the dice. Assume the following fact situation:

> A widow with three adult children meets and marries a widower with one adult child. They combine their assets and title them jointly. One day later the widow dies.

What is the result of joint ownership in this situation? That is easy. The widower receives *everything*, the widow's children *nothing*.

Joint ownership only works if there is a surviving joint tenant. What happens if the joint owners die at the same time? If you don't know, that's all right because most people don't either. Most states have adopted the Uniform Simultaneous Death Act. Under this law, joint property generally is distributed in proportion to the number of joint tenants. Only four states, Alaska, Louisiana, Montana, and Ohio, have not adopted the Uniform Simultaneous Death Act. In addition, Puerto Rico has not adopted this act. Simultaneous death and joint ownership do not mix well. Remember the survivorship feature. If one owner outlives the other by one second, it all goes to the heirs of the one who survived by one second. It is because of the survivorship problem that critics allege that jointly owned property may go to unintended heirs.

Jointly owned property is generally beneficial to creditors of the owners. Property taken in both names is generally seizable on the default or misdeed of either owner. Either or each joint owner could lose ownership in the property, which is not good estate-creditor planning.

Historically, joint ownership oftentimes created unintended federal and state gift taxes. Many types of property placed in joint names created a gift equal to 50 percent of the fair market value of the property at the time it was placed in the names of the joint owners. The gift was *from* the person whose money was used to purchase the property, and the recipient of the gift was the other joint tenant.

Believe it or not, when a working spouse purchased property other than real estate and placed it in joint ownership with the nonworking spouse, a gift was made. After 1954, real estate put in joint ownership between spouses was not considered a gift, unless a gift *was intended*.

In 1976, however, Congress helped the married taxpayer. It said that the first $100,000 worth of gifts made to a spouse would be tax-free; the next $100,000 would be fully taxed; and half of everything over $200,000 would be taxable.

How many folks knew about the gift-tax consequences of taking ownership to property jointly? In our experience, very few. We have upset our clients when we discussed gift taxes and jointly owned property. Nonworking spouses became instant ERA supporters; and we did not blame them. Bread-earner spouses, concerned about past-due taxes they incurred but did not know about, went crazy; and we did not blame them.

Joint property gave us additional problems because often clients wanted to get out of joint tenancy so they could really plan their assets; as a result we needed to get the joint property back in the name of one or the other spouse. Guess what? If we put some types of property back into the name of the bread-earner spouse, the other spouse, under federal gift-tax laws, made another gift. More tax! If we put it all in the name of the non-bread-earner spouse, the other spouse would be taxed on the value of the additional half that passed to the nonworking spouse.

Two spouses acquired property in the marriage and put it in joint names. They created, without knowing it, gifts. They owed gift taxes that had never been paid. Interest accrued on those unpaid taxes—they were unknowing tax evaders. (It has been, and still is, illegal not to pay taxes when they become due.)

The sad thing was that we often could not do enough planning to spare our clients from this tax trap. Oh, we could get real estate back in the name of the bread-earner spouse all right without a federal gift tax because of an exception in the law; sometimes we used up part of their death-tax exemption; but that was about it. It was not pleasant, it was not fair, but it was the law of the land.

In 1976, Congress tried to solve the joint-tenancy gift problem as it applies to spouses. It was Congress's avowed purpose to simplify the rules.

Yet the Tax Reform Act of 1976 was more complicated than the law it replaced and barely changed the effect of the law it replaced. Joint ownership, as you have concluded by now, is complicated; and Congress's ignorance in this area was not unique.

We still have another hurdle to get over with jointly held property. There was, and is, a federal estate tax.

Federal estate-tax laws attempted to tax all the jointly held property in the estate of the first owner to die. When the remaining tenant died, it was taxed all over again. Can you imagine? Joint property was generally taxed twice—in other words, 200 percent taxable! There were some exceptions; but in our experience, they seldom seemed to apply to the situation at hand. Federal estate tax and joint property simply did not mix very well.

ERTA dramatically altered the federal estate and gift taxation of jointly held property between spouses. It did not, however, change quite so dramatically the rules of taxation of property held jointly between nonspouses.

Today, spouses who are citizens of the United States can acquire property jointly without incurring a federal gift tax. The law is absolutely clear on this point, and there are no limits to the amounts involved. Regardless of which spouse's funds are used, no federal gift tax will result from U.S.-citizen spouses taking property jointly.

The law states that unlimited tax-free gifts are allowed between U.S.-citizen spouses. This unlimited-gifts rule between U.S.-citizen spouses is referred to as an unlimited lifetime "marital deduction."

If the spouse receiving the gift is not a U.S. citizen, there is no unlimited lifetime marital deduction. There is instead an exclusion from the gift tax of the first $100,000 in value of gifts to the non-U.S.-citizen spouse. This limited exception for non-U.S.-citizen spouses is discussed further in Chapter 11.

With passage of ERTA, the federal government finally recognized husband and wife as one family unit for purposes of federal gift taxation. Interspousal property transfers, when made to a U.S.-citizen spouse, are no longer of federal gift-tax consequence. Do not, however, make the mistake of neglecting to check your state's gift-tax laws as they may apply to jointly held assets.

Many states do have gift taxes and tax jointly held property much like the federal government used to. States sometimes follow the example of the federal tax laws; and if they do, it will take time to get these state laws changed. Keep in mind, though, that there have been, and probably will continue to be, states that elect to go their own way in spite of what the federal laws say.

The law has not materially changed with respect to owning property jointly with people other than your spouse. The smart individual will continue to be wary and sensitive to potential federal and state gift-tax traps when putting property in joint names.

ERTA also dramatically changed the federal estate-tax rules with regard to jointly held property.

Under the law prior to ERTA, all joint property was taxed in the estate of the first joint owner to die. This was always so unless it could be proven that the other owner contributed funds toward the property's acquisition.

As to spouses, ERTA drastically changed the law. The estate of the first spouse to die will include only *half* the value of the jointly held property, rather than potentially all of it under the old law. When the second spouse dies, the estate will be taxed on the value of the entire asset. Why? Because of the survivorship feature. Jointly held property automatically belongs to the surviving tenant. If it all belongs to the survivor, it will all be taxed in the survivor's estate.

If, however, the surviving spouse is not a U.S. citizen, the estate of the first spouse to die will include the entire value of the property, unless the spouses acquired the property by gift or inheritance, or the surviving spouse supplied some or all of the funds to purchase the property. The estate of the first spouse to die will include only *half* the value of the jointly held property if the non-U.S.-citizen surviving spouse becomes a U.S. citizen before the date on which the estate-tax return is filed and if the surviving spouse meets certain residency requirements.

Spouses can leave everything they own, including property held jointly with spouses, to their spouses free of federal estate tax. (We will *really* get into this in more detail in Chapter 12, "The Marital Deduction: Federal Recognition of a Spouse's Efforts.") For now, just remember: there is no federal estate tax on property held jointly with a spouse when the first spouse dies.

Great care and caution must be used in creating joint ownership with nonspouses. Don't forget that the jointly owned property will always belong to the surviving owners. Here your estate might have to pay tax on the value of your interest in the property even though the property is going to a non-family member on your death. Remember that cabin owned jointly with your brother? He will get the cabin if you die first, and your estate may pay the federal estate tax on half its value.

Even with all the good news, the law creates another problem with property held jointly between spouses. It has to do with after-death *income* tax planning and a concept called "step-up in basis" rules.

These rules have always stated (except for a short interlude) that upon the death of a taxpayer, property in the estate gets a new cost basis for income tax purposes. Here is an example of this concept:

> Eileen owns but one asset at her death: one share of stock. She paid $1 for it. If she sold it for $10 while alive, she would have a $9 income-taxable gain. At Eileen's death, the share of stock was valued at $10 for federal estate-tax purposes. If her heirs sold it after her death for $10, there would be no income tax. If Eileen sold the stock one day before her death, however, $9 would be subject to income tax. You see, her cost basis in the stock would be increased (stepped

up), by operation of law, from $1 to $10—its date-of-death value. This concept professionals refer to as "step-up in basis."

In our example, if Eileen owned the stock jointly with her spouse and died, only half the stock would get a step-up in basis. If Eileen's spouse sold the stock after her death for $10, he would have a $4.50 income-taxable gain. His starting cost was $0.50 (half the $1 paid). His half of the gain would be $5 ($10 price divided by 2). By subtracting his cost of $0.50 from the $5, we have a $4.50 gain. He has no gain on Eileen's half because her half got a step-up in basis to $5.

Contrast the tax problem of Eileen's spouse with this fact situation:

> Eileen owns the stock in her name (not in joint names). Eileen dies and leaves it to her spouse. There would be no *federal estate tax* (spouses can leave everything tax-free to surviving spouses, remember?). The entire value of the stock gets a step-up in basis to $10. Eileen's spouse sells the stock the day after her death for $10. There is no income-taxable gain to Eileen's spouse.

Joint property does not get a 100 percent step-up in basis for income tax purposes but rather only a 50 percent step-up because only 50 percent is included in the estate of the first spouse to die. When the planning is for spouses, jointly owned property becomes unattractive in many cases. Untutored planning with jointly held property can create income tax pitfalls even when this planning appears proper.

For example, if the surviving spouse is not a U.S. citizen or if the property is not held between spouses, the step-up in basis generally will depend upon the amount each joint tenant contributed to obtain the property

Jointly held property, at least between spouses where the surviving spouse is a U.S. citizen, is now treated much more realistically; however, many of the drawbacks of this form of ownership still persist even today.

We have not recommended the use of joint ownership to our clients to any great extent in planning their estates. In spite of the many changes in our federal estate-, gift-, and income-tax laws, our advice continues to be the same: joint ownership is a potential planning pitfall that should be avoided in most instances; but, as between spouses, the results it creates can easily be corrected. A summary follows:

Good Features of Joint Ownership

Easy and convenient

Psychologically pleasing

Mini-estate plan

Not complicated on surface

No gift tax to U.S.-citizen spouse

No death tax on the death of the first spouse, if the surviving spouse is or becomes a U.S. citizen

Bad Features of Joint Ownership

Passes property to unintended heirs

Affords no planning opportunities

No control

Excellent for creditors

Gift taxes to nonspousal owners or non-U.S. citizen spouses

Loss of complete step-up basis

5
No Estate Plan?
"Big Brother Has One for You"

Many people die without an estate plan. They die without leaving a will or without a legal will or without accomplishing complete will substitute planning. Many people simply do not take the time to plan or are intimidated by the planning process itself. Others would like to plan but do not know how to go about it. Many folks just do not get around to it.

If you do not plan your estate, your state law will plan it for you. As we meet hardened nonplanners, we are tempted to say: "Worry not, plan not, if that is your choice, for Big Brother has a plan already made to dispose of your property."

Each of the fifty states has laws that prescribe in great detail what happens to a citizen's property if there is no will or will substitute. These laws are generally referred to as "Statutes of Descent and Distribution" or as "Statutes of Intestate Succession." These "Big Brother" laws will distribute the property of nonplanners to the state-sanctioned heirs.

Regardless of what Big Brother's plan is called, the plan is his, and the result can, at times, be most discomforting.

In order to illustrate how these laws work, let us examine the statutes of the state of Colorado and apply them to the following family situation:

> The deceased-to-be and his spouse are in their middle forties. They have one teenager and two small children. A paternal grandmother is part of the family. She has lived happily, from everyone's perspective, in their home for seven years and derives her support mainly from the deceased-to-be.

Now the unexpected happens. The deceased-to-be is deceased. A tragedy has occurred. There is no will, no plan. Wait, yes there is. The following is Big Brother's plan, reproduced with some fun and a little artistic license, and only a touch of exaggeration.

Big Brother's Will

Being of sound mind and disposing memory, we, the State of Colorado, hereby direct the passage of the property of the departed as follows:

Paragraph I

The surviving spouse shall receive $25,000. She will receive one-half of the balance of the property.

The last half of the property will be held for the decedent's children by the probate court of the county in which the decedent resided.

Paragraph II

The surviving spouse *may* be named personal representative [administrator] of the deceased spouse's estate. If she is named [and the court may name anyone it wishes], she will be responsible for administering and managing the estate during the probate process. All her actions will be subject to the scrutiny and approval of the court and its officials [civil servants].

Paragraph III

The surviving spouse will probably be named guardian of the children by the court. If named, she will be allowed to manage the children's property as its conservator for their benefit under the scrutiny of the court and its officials [civil servants].

Paragraph IV

The court may insist, of course, that a bond [they are not inexpensive] be posted to guarantee that if the mother exercises poor judgment in the handling of the estate property and loses it, an insurance company *may* replace it.

Paragraph V

The surviving spouse will be required to render periodic accountings to the probate court about most of her actions. The court shall have the right to ask questions about what she has done, and the court's determination with regard to the answers will be final.

Paragraph VI

The paternal grandmother is of no concern to the state and has no rights under this will.

Paragraph VII

When the children reach the age of majority [eighteen in Colorado], they shall be entitled to a complete accounting from their mother as to her handling of their property [every last dime]. Should the children be displeased with that accounting, they shall have the right to sue their mother thereon.

Paragraph VIII

Each child, regardless of his or her need, may receive only one-third of the property which did not go to the mother. Each child, upon attaining age eighteen, shall receive the balance of the property, if any, and will be on his or her own thereafter.

Paragraph IX

Should the deceased's spouse remarry, the new spouse may be entitled to all funds previously given by us to the deceased's spouse. The new spouse shall have no obligation to use any of said funds for the benefit of the deceased's children.

Paragraph X

Should the spouse of the deceased also rely on Big Brother's will, upon her death the local probate court shall decide who will raise the children.

Paragraph XI

The state, through the probate court and through a newly appointed personal representative [administrator], shall be in total control of administering funds. All decisions may be questioned by our loyal civil servants.

Paragraph XII

All property shall be subject to the control and resulting costs of the probate court. All costs shall be paid by the children's funds.

Paragraph XIII

Significant sums may be paid to our Federal Brother as estate taxes. No attempt shall be made to reduce said taxes.

Signed,
Your Munificent Legislature

Keep in mind that the oftentimes ridiculous results of each state's legislative wills could be avoided with a little planning, if only we could convince the hardened nonplanner to take a few hours to plan.

It is a mistake to believe that a state's will gives your property directly to the state. The state ends up with property only when there are no blood relatives alive to receive it. When this occurs, the property passes (escheats) to the state.

Another problem with legislative wills is which state's law is going to control the assets of the deceased nonplanner.

Each of our states has the right to control "real property" within its borders. Land and buildings are called *real* property. If our hardened nonplanner owns a cabin in another state, that other state's law and courts will control the disposition of the cabin. Attorneys call this "in rem jurisdiction," a not too difficult concept. States are jealous as to soil within their borders; their laws, taxation, and other matters apply to that soil.

Another problem our hardened nonplanner faces is which state's law will control his or her personal property. The state in which the nonplanner lived determines where the personal property will pass. Where did the nonplanner really live? Attorneys would ask, "Where was the person's 'domicile'?" Domicile is the chief, number one, absolute, real residence of a citizen. There can be only one domicile, and it is sometimes hard to establish. States fight over whose laws apply if domicile is not clear. The state that wins collects death tax on that personal property. Take the estate of Howard Hughes. It seemed that any state Howard Hughes ever lived in wanted to tax the whole estate. By the way, there is authority that concludes that more than one state may share in the tax feast if domicile is not absolutely clear.

The point of this chapter is that a state's will is always a poor substitute for your own. These state wills are not very personal but, when activated, do work.

Perhaps state legislatures, in their zeal to assist their nonplanning citizens, have given false security to too many people. Maybe each state's will should say: "If you don't plan it, Big Brother will take it and put it in the general fund." With this alternative facing people, maybe they would plan.

6
Wills

"What Are They?"

Generally, a will is a set of written instructions drawn under legal formalities that directs how a person's property will be disposed of on death.

"Last will and testament" is the legal label for "will." It is an old phrase meaning "I dispose of my personal property and real estate."

Wills do not have to be written. In some states, under certain circumstances, they can be verbal; however, for purposes of this book, wills do have to be written, carefully written.

Many clients want to know if they can write their own wills. The answer is: Sure, as long as you know what you are doing and follow all the formalities required by your state's laws; that is, if you want your will to work.

Wills are a special creation of society. The law of wills is fraught with technicalities and very formal procedures. Do-it-yourselfers, as a result, should leave the drafting to professionals. Very few of the home-drawn wills we have seen actually work or accomplish what the maker intended.

Most of the law of wills that we use today is very old and steeped in English tradition.

For many years common folks were unable to leave all their property to their loved ones. On their deaths, much of their property passed (escheated) to royalty. In A.D. 1540, the English Parliament passed some truly progressive legislation: the Statute of Wills. Essentially, the Statute of Wills allowed common folks the right, under a body of rules, to pass all their property to others on death.

The legislation was revolutionary and vast. The rules adopted were complex. The cases of law that followed, as a result of society's getting comfortable with the concept, made the law bigger and even more complex. Does this ring a familiar bell in terms of today's government, its rules, regulations, and growth?

A will can only control property belonging to its maker. There is, however, a noteworthy exception. If someone else left property for you to use during your lifetime and specifically gave you the right to dispose of it on your subsequent death, you would have a "power of appointment"; you would have the right to say in your will who gets that property.

A will controls the passage of property to others on its maker's death. A very small percentage of wills, in our experience, pass property left by another through a power of appointment.

Wills do not control property that goes to others by other planning devices or by operation of law. Jointly held property, for example, is not controlled by a will. Jointly held property automatically belongs to the other joint owners on death. The same is true for property owned in tenancy by the entirety. Life insurance proceeds are not controlled by a will if the owner names a beneficiary other than his or her estate. These other techniques are "will substitutes" and are discussed at length in other chapters.

For those who would like to expand their vocabulary, try these terms:

Holographic will	A will in one's own handwriting
Nuncupative will	Oral will
Joint will	A will with two makers to dispose of their property on the death of the second maker
Mystic will	A name one author has given to filling in a cheap, preprinted will, and then signing it
Codicil	An amendment to a will

As we have stated, homemade wills usually do not work or, at best, do not work very well. Oral (nuncupative) wills hardly ever work.

Joint wills can really create planning nightmares, especially in the area of taxation. In our opinion, they should be avoided. Mystic wills may be hard to resist. Send in your $5, fill in the blanks, and sign it. "We'll get around those scoundrel lawyers." Need we say more than "Good luck"?

A codicil is just an amendment to a will. If the desire is to alter one's will without doing the whole thing over again, one has a codicil prepared; but, and this is a big "but," codicils must be signed with all, and not less than all, of the formalities of a regular will.

Wills are public documents. Generally, a will's contents are not made public while the maker is alive. On the death of the maker, a will *has* to be filed with the local court and its contents made part of the public record; everyone and anyone can read it if they want to. Private business becomes public business. Not only is the will made public, but all assets and debts as well as the proceedings disposing of them are made public.

We do not think that taking one's family public is a very good idea. Anyone, with good intentions or bad, can know a family's intimate financial affairs. It does not seem to be a sound practice to us, but you be the judge.

Wills are not effective until the maker is dead. Most people would like a little current benefit from planning, especially in view of the energy required to plan in the first place. Wills provide no current benefits that we can think of, other than peace of mind, of course.

Wills simply cannot provide for the care of their makers. What if you get sick or for a period of time lose your ability to reason or conduct your affairs? Your will cannot help you.

A will valid in the state in which it was made is valid in other states. The only problem is, Will other states follow their laws or the law of the state under which the will was drawn? Unfortunately, the former is oftentimes the choice.

Assume John draws a will in Colorado, where he resides. Further assume that John and his family move to Michigan. John does not have his will rewritten. John dies a resident (domiciliary) of Michigan. Michigan's law, not Colorado's law, may control. The result can be, at times, disastrous.

We do not believe that wills are viable interstate planning tools. Clients move around. Twentieth century Americans are mobile; they seek opportunities and are too frequently relocated by their employers. Even deeply rooted, self-employed folks retire and are known to relocate to find that "better climate."

There is a need for interstate flexibility in estate planning. Wills do not provide it. The living trust does—but more on that later.

Wills must go through the probate process. In discussions with clients we have found that most clients have the notion that to prepare a will is to avoid the probate court. This is definitely not the case. The property that passes under your will must go through probate court.

Probate is the process of passing title from the will maker to others. With a will, the probate process will pass title the will maker's way. Without a will or will-substitute planning, the probate court will pass title to property the legislature's way. Either way, with or without a will, your property will go through probate. We discuss probate in Chapter 8, which is coming up. For now, please believe that probate can be a needlessly expensive and time-consuming process and that it *can* be avoided.

Use of a will guarantees probate. In the middle sixties, Norman F. Dacey wrote a national best-selling book entitled *How to Avoid Probate*. A lot of people bought that book. It seems to us that the proof of the pudding is in the eating: probate is to be avoided.

In our experience, clients have one universal question with regard to wills: "Now that I've got it, what do I do with it?"

First, sign only one original will. If you sign duplicates and one duplicate original is destroyed, it may, by operation of your state's law, destroy all. It is a good practice to sign only one original will.

Second, store your will in a safe place. Store your will where it can be easily found by others. Tell your family, both verbally and in writing, where that safe, easily found place is.

Many attorneys recommend that clients leave their original wills with them. We do not believe this is a good practice. Who says a law office is safe from vandalism, theft, or a well-intended, but fatal, housekeeping? A misplaced will among thousands of files may just be misplaced, but it is lost until found. Your will is of critical importance to you and your family, but only one will among many in your attorney's office.

Storing your will in a safe-deposit box may be prudent or not depending upon the state in which you live. If your state has a death tax and follows the practice of sealing safe-deposit boxes until the tax examiner is present to inspect the contents, valuable time can be lost when matters must be completed under the will, but there is no will available because your civil servant has not gotten there yet.

We could write a volume or more just on wills, but others have already done that; besides, we are not all that keen on wills anyway. They are all right and they do work; they have been around for hundreds of years; but they do have several features that we view as unattractive.

Wills

Are only effective on death

May *not* control all property

Involve complex legal rules

Are public

Are not viable interstate planning tools

Must go through probate

Should be stored properly

7
More On Wills

"They're Not All They're Cracked Up to Be"

In our experience, most clients and some professional advisers who do not specialize in estate planning equate the estate-planning process with the drafting of a last will and testament. They believe that estate planning is will planning.

In countless situations when we have asked the question, "Do you have an existing estate plan?" the response has been "Yes, I have a will, but it's out of date" or "No, I've never had a will."

The belief that estate planning and will drafting are synonymous is unfortunate and, in most instances, not correct.

A will is but one method of disposing of property upon death. In our experience people generally give little or no thought to other methods as they relate to the estate-planning process. These methods have crept into the economic marketplace as practical and quick solutions to passing property at death.

In order to illustrate the impact of these alternative methods of will planning, let us conjure up a meeting with a typical client and his adviser:

(Attorney, accountant, insurance professional, financial adviser, or trust officer/banker: CATHERINE)   *(Client: JOHN)*

CATHERINE: Well, John, before we can recommend an estate plan for you and your family, we need to know what you own and how you own it.

JOHN: What do I own? Well, Liz and I own our home. The deed is in both our names as *joint owners*. I hope that's okay because that's the way the realtor said it would be best.

Let's see, there're the savings accounts—four of them. One is in *both our names*, you know, jointly held, I guess. One's just *in my name*, a few dollars, that's all. The other two are with the kids, *one in my name with our son*, Robbie; the other is in our son Jamie's name, but *Liz and I are both on it* as well. The person at the bank said it would be better this way; something about our being custodians or something; but I think we're all on with the kids as joint owners.

CATHERINE: Are you sure exactly how the accounts read, John?

JOHN: (*With some irritation*) Not really, but there's not much there. We can check, I guess.

Then, we have the life insurance. There's my group at the office. That goes to Liz and then to the kids if she dies before I do. I've also got my G.I. insurance. That goes the same way. Oh, yes, and I also have two other policies. One's not too large, but it's permanent insurance and the other's in six figures. It's term. They go the same way.

CATHERINE: (*Patiently, but eager to get on with it*) What else do you have?

JOHN: Our checking, *one's joint; one's in Liz's name*. I've got my pension and profit sharing plan at the company. I signed a card at the personnel office. I think the proceeds go to Liz and the kids.

CATHERINE: (*Sensing that the client is starting to move a little faster*) What else do you own, John?

JOHN: We have the cabin. That's in our names with my brother and his wife; *jointly*, I guess. Some stocks, some *in Liz's and my name;* some we put in the kids' names; one's with my sister and *both names are on it*. That's about it.

CATHERINE: Any personal possessions, John?

JOHN: Oh, do we ever. Two cars in both names; furniture; furnishings, you know; my stamp collection, been collecting since I was a kid; clothing, you know, the usual stuff. I'll tell you, though, I don't know who owns it. I guess we both do.

CATHERINE: Thank you, John.

Now, let us backtrack. Let us go through John's assets to see how they are titled and whether or not John's new will can control them on John's death or whether they will go directly to others because John used an alternative method of planning.

Summary

Residence	Joint with spouse
Savings accounts	
no. 1	Joint with spouse
no. 2	John's name
no. 3	Joint with son
no. 4	Joint with spouse and son
Life insurance	All policies have named beneficiaries: spouse and children
Checking accounts	
no. 1	Joint with spouse
no. 2	Spouse's name
Pension and profit sharing accounts at company	Beneficiaries on cards: spouse and children
Cabin	Jointly between families
Personal possessions	
Cars	Joint with spouse
Other	Who knows?

As we review the summary of John's estate, we can quickly get to the bottom line. Those items that John owns solely in his name will be controlled by and pass under the terms of his will. The balance will automatically pass by contract or by operation of law:

All joint property will automatically pass to the surviving joint tenants. They will be the exclusive new owners.

All life insurance will go to the named beneficiaries under the terms of the policy and the beneficiary designations.

The pension and profit sharing proceeds will also go pursuant to those beneficiary cards John signed.

Checking account no. 2 is in John's spouse's name and, as such, cannot be controlled by John's will.

Our obvious point is that the only property that John's will can control would be one savings account and the personal property deemed to be owned by John at his death. Wills may not control the disposition of your property as much as you think (or would like to think).

If you are questioning the "whats" and "hows" of joint ownership or beneficiary designations, that is fine. We will cover these techniques in other chapters. For now, the important point to remember is this: A will is but one tool available to the client and the estate planner to dispose of property on death. *Will* planning is *will* planning and is only a part of estate planning. *Estate* planning envisions how those "other assets" will pass; how they will pay or avoid tax; to whom they will pass and how they will pass. These "other" planning techniques (we'll refer to them as will-substitute techniques) are of critical importance.

A will is but one golf club in the estate-planning golf bag, a club which should be used only in the appropriate situations to pull off the right shot.

8
Probate
"Red Tape That Can Be Avoided"

Probate is the legal process of passing ownership of property from a deceased person to others. Probate courts have been a part of our legal heritage for centuries.

Generally speaking, every county in every state in the United States has its own probate court. These courts are not always called probate courts — sometimes they are called surrogate or common courts. Regardless of their names, these courts all have the same purpose: passing ownership of property to the heirs of people who died with a will plan or with no plan at all.

In 1965, Norman F. Dacey, a nonlawyer, authored a national best-selling book entitled *How to Avoid Probate*. The book was 349 pages including 50 pages of text and approximately 300 pages of tear-out "how to do it" estate-planning forms. Mr. Dacey's thesis was that probate should and could be avoided. The book generated a new crisis in the relationship between attorneys and clients. It rocked the estate-planning community by savagely attacking, fairly and unfairly, in our opinion, probate lawyers.

Following Mr. Dacey's book, a bar-sponsored attempt to respond to his better allegations was launched under the direction of a noted attorney and law school professor, Richard V. Wellman. Professor Wellman then authored a Uniform Probate Code that could be used in all states.

The Uniform Probate Code addressed many of the deficiencies pointed out in the Dacey book. At least eighteen states have adopted that code in one form or another. Those states that have adopted either the uniform act or some of its concepts include Alabama (used the UPC as a guide for its law), Alaska, Arizona, Colorado, Florida (used the UPC as a guide for its law), Hawaii, Idaho, Maine, Michigan (used the UPC as a guide for its law), Minnesota (in part), Montana, Nebraska, New Jersey (in part), New Mexico, North Dakota, South Carolina, Texas (with significant variations), and Utah. Professor Wellman did a great service to the probate bar and the public; unfortunately, much of the probate bar rejected his work, as have thirty-two states. The public was not well informed. Some magazines, such as the *Reader's Digest*, did communicate Professor Wellman's work to the public. They also communicated Professor Wellman's defeat. However, it appears that as time passes, more and more states are embracing the concepts offered by the Uniform Probate Code.

Please understand that if you die with a will (testate), the property your will controls goes through probate. If you die without a will (intestate) and without alternative will-substitute planning, your property will go through probate.

Getting the dead citizen's property into the hands of his or her or the state's beneficiaries is but one part or function of the probate process; it is really only the end result of the probate process.

The probate agent is responsible for most of the work to be accomplished in this process. That agent will report and answer to the probate judge through the estate's attorney. The probate agent is given different names in different situations and in different states. Generally, this agent is called:

Executor (male agent named in a will)

Executrix (female agent named in a will)

Administrator (male agent named by the court when there is no will)

Administratrix (female agent named by the court when there is no will)

Personal representative (agent, male or female, named in those states that passed the Uniform Probate Code)

The agents, regardless of their titles, are responsible for doing the work in the probate process. They work for the court or judge. Probate is a complicated legal process; the estate or agent relies on an attorney for assistance in getting through the legal maze. At times, the attorney can and will do most, if not all, of the work, but in some probate proceedings, the attorney does very little work.

Both the probate agent and the probate attorney are entitled to compensation for serving in their prescribed roles. Their fee is usually determined by state statute, but may be reviewed and awarded by the probate judge.

Probate judges are generally nonpracticing or retired lawyers. They can be brilliant or not so brilliant. They can be industrious or lazy. They are, after all, people. Most probate judges, in our opinion, are overworked and underpaid. They preside over a red-tape system that is ancient, meticulous, and time-consuming. The probate bench attracts candidates who range from superb attorneys who are committed and self-sacrificing individuals (they could earn a great deal more in private practice) to ne'er-do-well attorneys who have become involved in local politics. Probate judges can be appointed or elected, depending on the laws of the individual states.

Most practicing attorneys handle probate estates. This is particularly true in rural areas and among those attorneys who conduct a general practice. In our experience, few attorneys turn away probate work. The nature of the work is time-consuming and most of the time not too intellectually difficult. The economic rewards can be all the way from ample to splendid, depending upon whose point of view is being considered.

Those attorneys who *specialize* in probate fall into one of two categories: (1) mature attorneys who harvest the will files they have built up over a lifetime of law practice and who comprise the bulk of the specialists and (2) attorneys who restrict their practice to after-death planning. These are usually estate and tax attorneys who specialize in reducing costs and taxes and assist heirs in making after-death decisions. Generally, the tax specialists did not plan the estates they represent, but rather probate work is referred to them because of their expertise. These individuals, although looked upon as probate lawyers, are, in reality, postmortem planners.

The probate process, although complicated and confusing to most people, can be reduced to the following:

Understand the will.

Ascertain heirs.

Locate and value all property.

Pay the agent and attorney.

Ascertain and pay creditors of the estate.

Resolve all controversy between the parties.

File all tax returns.

Distribute property.

Understanding the will is usually not difficult. Homemade wills and wills drawn poorly can spell trouble, however, They usually result in will fights that generate a great deal of time and dollar expenditure.

Ascertaining or finding heirs is usually not difficult. On the other hand, when one gets into the extended family (third cousin once removed), the time and difficulty of locating such an heir can run up the costs for probate. In fact, there are companies which provide services to attorneys strictly for the purpose of locating distant heirs.

Finding and valuing a deceased person's property is generally a total nightmare. It took the deceased a lifetime to accumulate wealth, and the "books" with regard to such were usually kept in his or her mind. The records of the property, if they exist at all, are in many places. Finding the property is time-consuming and requires a real detective job. Even the basic task of determining what the deceased owned, much less where it may be located, is enormous in the usual estate.

Valuing the property that is found is a major responsibility of the agent, probate lawyer, and court. The higher the value of the property, the greater the potential state and federal taxes will be. Both tax laws and estate laws require that the property be valued at its fair market value. There is no "black and white" in the valuation process for many assets (closely held stocks, real property, partnership interests, etc.). From the perspective of beneficiaries or heirs, property should be valued on the low side of the valuation spectrum. From the judge's perspective, it should be valued "fairly." What about the attorney's perspective?

The involvement of probate attorneys in the valuation of probate and even nonprobate property has been often criticized. To whom do the attorneys owe their duty? Should they attempt to assist the probate agents in the hiring of appraisers who will come in with low valuations? Is their duty to the courts and states? Must they insist on fair market value (real value)? After all, they did take an oath to uphold the law. What about their involvement? Do attorneys have a conflict of interest? Many critics take this position: if attorneys are being paid on a fee basis and the fee is a percentage applied against the value of the estate property, there is an inherent conflict. The higher the value of the estate, the higher the fee and the higher the tax. Is there a conflict? You be the judge.

Finding, sorting out, and paying creditors of the deceased and his or her estate can be frustrating. What is important to understand is that creditors get paid before beneficiaries. Problems involving creditors preclude beneficiaries from getting their money until those creditor problems are solved.

Probate agents and probate lawyers are generally, according to the laws of most states, "first-class creditors." They get paid off the top. In fact, they get paid before other creditors and always before the state or federal government. All states prescribe by law how these probate "officials" will get paid. Probate agents usually get paid on a percentage of the estate's value. Some states prescribe payment on a "whatever-is-reasonable" basis (what is reasonable depends on the judge's determination of reasonableness). Attorneys' compensation is prescribed by law also. Attorneys are usually compensated on a percentage of the estate's value or on a whatever-is-reasonable basis. Some jurisdictions, in practicality, leave attorneys' fees up to the judge. Depending on the judge and his or her relationship with the attorney, fees may be very high, reasonable, or very low. Again, this depends on whose point of view is being considered.

There is often controversy in the probate process. Potential heirs can get into some very interesting fights. The probate agent and the probate attorney can get into a dogfight with real or fake creditors. In fact, the agent and the attorney may fight with each other or even with the judge. The judge resolves all probate disputes. The estate of the deceased pays for most, if not all, of the cost of these fights. The cost of probate disputes is generally not inexpensive.

Ascertaining what taxes are due and paying them within the time periods prescribed by law would seem to be a relatively easy task. But do not forget the assets have to be valued before the taxes can be computed. Another problem usually associated with the probate process is converting those assets to cash to pay the taxes. What does and does not get sold can create some probate battles among all of the probate players.

Payment of death taxes to both the state and the federal government involves, in many situations, substantial after-death tax planning. Most probate attorneys are not tax attorneys; tax attorneys, as a group, comprise a small percentage of all attorneys practicing law. Many critics of the probate process highlight this lack of professional expertise.

The distribution of probate property can be easy or difficult. If minor beneficiaries are involved and trusts have not been created for them, the court will stay involved until the minors are adults; adult beneficiaries who are mentally incompetent bring about the same result, and again the court may stay involved for a very long time.

The probate process is complex and full of red tape. Its weaknesses can be summarized as follows:

Probate is public.

Probate is time-consuming.

Probate is expensive.

Probate puts the real control in the judge's chambers.

There are several ways that you may choose to avoid probate. Commonly used methods include:

Joint tenancy with right of survivorship

Properly designating life insurance proceeds

Properly designating beneficiaries of employee fringe benefits

Using payable-on-death (POD) designations for bank accounts in states that have adopted the Uniform Probate Code

Creating and funding a living trust

Joint Tenancy with Right of Survivorship

The survivorship feature unique to joint ownership automatically passes title to property upon the death of a joint owner. As a result, on the death of a joint owner, joint property does not go through probate. But remember, joint ownership has several drawbacks associated with its use which may outweigh its use solely to avoid probate.

Properly Designating Life Insurance Proceeds

Life insurance proceeds made payable either to adult beneficiaries or a living trust as beneficiary escape probate. If, however, you designate your estate as beneficiary, your insurance proceeds will go through probate. Do not make your estate the beneficiary of your insurance contracts.

Do not name minors as the beneficiaries of your life insurance proceeds. If this is done, the proceeds will end up in probate court. Minors need court supervision until they reach legal adulthood. Under state law, this can be eighteen or twenty-one years of age. Instead, leave your insurance proceeds to a living trust created for the benefit of your minor beneficiaries. If you do, your life insurance proceeds will avoid the probate swamp.

If your life insurance proceeds are left to a trust you created for your minor beneficiaries in your will (this is known as a testamentary trust), the probate court will become involved with the proceeds. Wills, and the trusts created in them, are always under the jurisdiction of the local probate court; this is particularly true when the trusts are created for minors.

Life insurance proceeds can easily avoid probate when properly designated.

Properly Designating Beneficiaries of Employee Fringe Benefits

Most Americans have significant sums due them or their beneficiaries resulting from employer-sponsored fringe benefits such as pension and profit sharing plans. To whom fringe-benefit funds are paid on the death of the employee-participant is determined by a beneficiary designation placed on a company form. Do not forget to fill in and sign the appropriate designation forms. If you do not properly fill them out and sign them, the proceeds will go wherever the retirement plan directs. This may be your estate; if so, the proceeds will go through probate. The same is true if you name your estate as beneficiary. Do not name minors as your beneficiaries because, just like life insurance proceeds, your benefits will be controlled by the probate court.

Always name adults or a living trust as your beneficiary and avoid probate. Remember to complete your company's forms properly; most companies have trained personnel to assist you.

Using POD Designations for Bank Accounts

Earlier in this chapter we discussed Professor Wellman's work in devising a national Uniform Probate Code. If you'll recall, eighteen states enacted their own version of his code:

Alabama	Minnesota
Alaska	Montana
Arizona	Nebraska
Colorado	New Jersey
Florida	New Mexico
Hawaii	North Dakota
Idaho	South Carolina
Maine	Texas
Michigan	Utah

If you live in one of these states, another method of avoiding probate may be available to you. This technique applies to savings and checking accounts as well as certificates of deposit. The owner, in setting up the account, instructs the bank clerk to type on the account a "payable on death" (POD) designation. The owner then names the person or persons to receive the account proceeds upon death of the owner and has those names typed on the account after the magic "POD" letters. It is as simple as that. These accounts *by law* will not go through probate. The POD is merely a beneficiary designation for these assets. If you live in one of these states, however, do not use this technique to leave the accounts to minor beneficiaries.

Creating and Funding a Living Trust

Living trusts are a complete will substitute. They have been around for hundreds of years; assets placed in a living trust have always avoided the probate process. They were created, in part, to do just that.

Using a living trust as a will substitute has certainly come of age. Traditionally, living trusts were only used by nobility. In modern times, they have been used mostly by the wealthy. Today, living trusts are being used, and should be used, by just about everybody.

Property placed in a living trust is instantly available for the use and benefit of the trust maker's beneficiaries. No matter how vast and diversified your holdings may be, the living trust can accommodate all of them in avoiding the probate process.

Every probate-avoidance technique other than the living trust has potential planning disadvantages. This does not mean that those other techniques cannot or should not be used. It does mean that the living trust can be used to avoid probate for all your property and that as a technique it has few, if any, disadvantages compared to the other techniques we have discussed.

We have two chapters on the living trust: Chapters 17 and 18. The first discusses what it is and how it works. The second describes how property can be put into the living trust (how the trust can be funded).

Planning to avoid probate involves a little bit of time, some financial housekeeping, and, regardless of the methods you elect to use, requires the following:

The collection of all assets and the papers that evidence title to those assets (deeds, stock certificates, partnership agreements, etc.). This means getting your affairs organized and all of the paperwork together in one place.

Reviewing with your advisers the way ownership has been taken to your existing assets.

Changing the way you own your assets in one of several ways we have discussed, so that upon your death your property will escape probate.

Probate itself, you will recall, involves the collection of assets and the passage of title to beneficiaries under the control and supervision of the probate judge.

Probate your own estate while you are alive. Organize your affairs and retitle your assets so that they will not go through probate on death. Most people know what they own and can generally find the paperwork that evidences their ownership quickly. Once that is done, the professional adviser can quickly recommend the right ownership techniques to get the job done.

9

The Federal Estate Tax

"The Final Sting"

Many years ago, we had as clients a married couple who were constantly complaining about the income taxes they were paying. One day, in exasperation, they said, "Well, the only good thing about our tax situation is that the feds aren't going to tax us anymore when we are dead." You can imagine their consternation when we told them that the federal government does have a death tax and would, in fact, take a very substantial percentage of their lives' work as a result of that tax.

Federal death tax has been, and continues to be, serious business. However, ERTA gave massive relief to all taxpayers from our federal estate-tax law's historically confiscatory structure and rates. It's very important for you to digest and understand the historical perspective in order to understand and appreciate the current law.

The U.S. government's death tax is properly called federal estate tax. Like all other taxes imposed by our system of government, this one began as a rather modest tax. First seriously imposed in 1916, it had a maximum rate of 10 percent.

It is interesting to note that by 1932 the maximum rate was 45 percent, in 1981 70 percent.

In 1976 Congress made an attempt to initiate reform in the death-tax area; the result was the Tax Reform Act of 1976. This legislation gave little to the taxpayer and, in fact, took away a great deal.

The Tax Reform Act of 1976 increased the size of nontaxable estate property from $60,000 in 1976 through a series of expansionary leaps to $175,625 in 1981. It attempted to simplify the rules with regard to the tax on joint property and resulted in making them more complicated, in our opinion. It took away the rules that favorably taxed property after death for income tax purposes. Here, because of the hue and cry of the American taxpayer, and a few dedicated advocates, Congress had to backtrack and reverse itself. Enough was enough, or, in this case, too much.

The Tax Reform Act of 1976 unified federal estate and federal gift taxation law. In effect, the reform act put the two together and charged identical rates. This law is still with us and is discussed in Chapter 10, "The Unified System: Robbing Peter to Pay Paul."

The Tax Reform Act of 1976 did a great deal for the coffers of the U.S. government; it did not do a great deal for its citizens.

Federal estate tax has two distinct features. First, federal estate tax can be described as an "everything tax." Yes, Uncle Sam taxes everything, including the proverbial kitchen sink. Second, this tax is a "top tax." Uncle Sam receives his tax before your beneficiaries receive anything.

Federal estate tax is not a tax levied against a deceased person or his or her property. It is not a people or property tax at all. It is a tax levied against the "right to transfer" property on death. We could write volumes on the various property interests that Uncle Sam taxes under the federal estate tax. Fortunately, that will not be necessary. What is important to remember is that federal estate tax is an everything tax and that it is paid before beneficiaries receive their share of the proceeds.

Uncle Sam will tax all the property owned in your name at your death. Uncle Sam will tax all the life insurance proceeds owned by you on your life. Uncle Sam has attempted to tax the total value of all assets held in joint ownership. Uncle Sam has even taxed property that was given away during lifetime if any of the income from that property was retained by the maker of the gift or if it was given away within three years prior to death.

We can play the game of *Uncle Sam Will Tax* until your eyes close and the book slides from your hands, but that would belabor the point. It would be easier to list what Uncle Sam does not tax. Federal estate tax does not apply to:

Money going directly to beneficiaries through an annuity purchased by your employer

Funds passing to beneficiaries pursuant to death-benefit-only plans created by your employer

Social security payments to your dependents

Insurance proceeds on your life if you did not own or have any control over those policies

Fifty percent of the proceeds from certain sales of stock to an employee stock ownership plan if the sale occurs before 1992 for persons that die before December 20, 1989

There are other property interests, although not many, that are not subject to federal estate tax; these other property interests are foreign to most people, and an understanding of them is not necessary to a general understanding of Uncle Sam's estate tax.

Can you believe that Uncle Sam taxes life insurance proceeds? This does not mean that Uncle Sam taxes the premiums paid for that insurance; it means that Uncle Sam taxes all the death proceeds whether they are paid in installments or in a lump sum to your designated beneficiaries. If you paid $1000 in premiums for a $100,000 life insurance policy, the proceeds of which go to your children upon your death, all $100,000 is subject to federal estate tax but not the federal income tax. Many people believe that life insurance proceeds are not taxed on death. Some states may not have a death tax on life insurance proceeds, but the U.S. government does.

Many people have also believed that jointly held property would be treated like tenancy-in-common property: that it would be taxed only to the extent of the owner's proportionate interest in that property. This, in the past, was not the case. The law was very explicit in the presumption that the first joint tenant to die was the owner of all the property and that the value of all that property was to be included in that joint owner's estate. Today, however, ERTA has made that incorrect conclusion a correct one as to spouses. Only the spouse's proportionate interest in the joint property is subject to federal estate tax on death, where the surviving spouse is a U.S. citizen.

Federal estate-tax rates, like the federal income tax rates prior to TRA 1986 and the Revenue Reconciliation Act of 1990, are progressive. The more a taxpayer owns, the more tax that taxpayer is going to pay; this should be a surprise to no one. Historically, the federal estate tax has redistributed wealth; it has been a tax targeted to take from the wealthy and redistribute that wealth to the not so wealthy.

For many years, and, in fact, up until 1976, the first $60,000 of estate value was not taxed. As a result of the Tax Reform Act of 1976, that amount went up in stages until it peaked at $175,625 in 1981. This tax-free amount is referred to as the exemption equivalent.

Perhaps $175,625 can be construed as the beginning of real wealth in contemporary America. Perhaps not. Remember, it does include life insurance proceeds and just about everything else a taxpayer generated or owned during life. What about inflation? In past years, $60,000 may have been a lot of money. What about the real value of $175,625 in 1981?

By passing ERTA, Congress raised the tax-free amount to $225,000 for individuals dying in 1982, and then continued to increase the tax-free amount annually until it reached its maximum of $600,000 in 1987. Do you think that this new amount represents true wealth and that estates in excess of it should be taxed to redistribute that wealth to the U.S. government?

Congress has traditionally taken notice of the family unit and has made some allowances for leaving property to spouses in the federal estate-tax laws. For many years, the law provided that spouses could leave one-half of their property free of federal estate tax to surviving spouses. This provision of the estate tax appeared to salve the congressional conscience. The Tax Reform Act of 1976 increased this spousal benefit to $250,000 or one-half of the estate, whichever was greater. The real change was adding a base of $250,000 that went tax-free to the surviving spouse.

The tax-saving spousal device we have been discussing is referred to as the marital deduction. Property accumulated by husband and wife that was left to the surviving spouse was taxed only when it exceeded $425,625 (the sum of $250,000 of marital deduction and the $175,625 exemption equivalent).

Whether or not this rather arbitrary marital deduction was a good deal was a matter of opinion. President Reagan was not of that opinion; nor was Congress. In passing ERTA, they believed that "if a little was good, more would be better." Today, the marital deduction applies to all property left to a U.S.-citizen spouse. Just think, a 100% marital deduction. But, no marital deduction is available if the surviving spouse is a non-U.S.-citizen spouse, unless the property passes to a "qualified domestic trust," or if the surviving spouse becomes a U.S. citizen within certain strict time limits and meets some residency requirements.

A qualified domestic trust is a special trust that ensures estate assets passing for the benefit of a non-U.S. citizen spouse are available to pay any estate taxes that may be due when the non-U.S.-citizen spouse dies.

The rules of federal estate tax are important to understand. To understand how property is valued for purposes of applying this death tax is equally important. Understanding a tax table is not too difficult. Arriving at the value of the property prior to applying that table is very difficult.

Uncle Sam's death tax is a tax based on the fair market value of the property in an estate. It is not a tax on the value of the property when it was originally purchased. It is a tax based either on the fair market value of the property at the date of the estate owner's death or the value of that property six months after the date of the owner's death. This latter date is referred to as the alternate valuation date. Uncle Sam gives beneficiaries a valuation choice. They can value the property at its death value or its value six months later. Your postdeath agent can only use the alternate valuation date if it will both reduce the value of your estate and reduce the federal estate tax due. Generally, due to inflation, property goes up in value, but not always. Valuation should be computed on both dates to see if there is any decrease in the overall value of property which would result in lower federal estate tax. Your postdeath agent must be careful, however. Your agent cannot pick and choose different dates for different assets. The date selected applies to all the assets.

If the value of property should go down after the six-month valuation date, the estate has no federal estate-tax recourse; the law provides no relief for this contingency.

It is important to recognize that the fair market value of property can be astoundingly high. Most of us want to know who determines the fair market value of our property. Does the family determine the value? the attorney? the agent of the estate? Does the Internal Revenue Service determine its value? The fair market value of the property in an estate will ultimately be determined by the courts if the postdeath agents and the Internal Revenue Service cannot agree on its value. The standard the courts will use is the price that a willing buyer will pay a willing seller, both having no compulsion to buy or sell and each being aware of all the facts surrounding the sale.

Most assets have a spectrum of value. A car, for example, that is two years old may range in value from $6000 to $10,000, depending upon who is selling and who is buying. Its value will also depend on the environment in which it is being bought and sold. This range in value is referred to as the "spectrum of value." Generally speaking, postdeath agents representing an estate should always shoot for the low end of the value spectrum when submitting valuations on a federal estate-tax return. At the same time, these agents should not underestimate the Internal Revenue Service (IRS). The goal of the IRS is to collect revenue. In zealously seeking to achieve their objective, you can be assured that, in many cases, the IRS will go for the highest value possible within the value spectrum.

Often this difference in approach leads to heated arguments and some rather spirited negotiations between the representatives of the estate and the IRS. The result of these negotiations is usually a settlement. Sometimes, however, both sides remain miles apart, and the courts are called upon to make the ultimate decision. Remember, the roles of the estate's agent and the Internal Revenue Service require that each lean to a different end of the value spectrum.

Some types of property are easily valued for federal estate-tax purposes. Property of this type would include:

Stocks that are publicly traded

Bonds

Savings and checking accounts

Certificates of deposit

Money market accounts

Treasury bills

Most property holdings are not easily valued. Property fitting this description would include:

Real estate

Closely (privately) owned business interests

Equipment and machinery

Personal effects

The best way to reduce federal estate tax is to reduce the value of the property subject to the tax. The job of the estate's agent is to keep that value down. The job of the IRS is to get it up. It used to be that there were very effective methods for reducing the value of certain types of property by passing their future appreciation to family members on a tax-free basis. These so-called freezing techniques have been significantly curtailed. Chapter 30, "Putting Your Estate in Cold Storage," explains what the federal government has done to make these techniques more difficult to use.

Since 1976, land (real property) used in farming or ranching can be valued lower than its arguable fair market value if certain requirements are met. This exception to the general rules of fair market value resulted from intense lobbying efforts on the part of farm and ranch associations. The exceptions to the general rule apply to their special interests and are covered in Chapter 36, "Special Use Valuation." These legal exceptions are fair in our opinion.

Another important aspect of federal estate-tax law is that it is not a tax that can be easily deferred to a time when payment may be convenient. With few exceptions, the Internal Revenue Code says that Uncle Sam's death tax shall be paid in cash nine months from the date of death. Cash is a method of payment that does not allow for postponement. The result of not paying federal estate tax promptly unless you have special approval from the IRS is that the property will be seized by the IRS, which will be more than happy to get what proceeds it can by means of a tax sale. The federal estate tax is a tough, no-nonsense tax.

Effective January 1, 1982, the federal estate tax became less confiscatory as to the property left by most Americans to their loved ones.

The current federal estate-tax provisions can be summarized as follows:

The federal estate tax only applies to estates valued in excess of $600,000.

The federal estate-tax rates begin at 37 percent and are a maximum of 50 percent beginning in 1993.

Spouses are able to leave property to their U.S.-citizen spouses free of federal estate tax.

Prior to ERTA, federal estate-tax rates started at 18 percent and progressed with the size of an estate to a maximum tax rate of 70 percent. Just think, 70 percent of a citizen's estate (life's work) could have been seized by the government under the provisions of the old law; that is a lot of tax regardless of one's political persuasion.

The old tax rates were closely patterned after the progressive income tax rates Americans lived with before TRA 1986. The concept behind these progressive rates was simple: the more successful a citizen was in accumulating property in a lifetime, the more responsibility that citizen had to share that wealth, through government, with others less fortunate. As property values progressively increased, the federal estate-tax rates increased as well until that magic 70 percent bracket was achieved. There was no doubt that federal estate tax was predicated on the redistribution of wealth. Our political leaders were attempting to build a great society using as fuel the efforts of that society's most successful citizens.

ERTA created a radical departure from traditional political practices with regard to who would pay to keep the government afloat. One of the ways ERTA recognized this was to dramatically alter the federal estate-tax structure.

ERTA was revolutionary in concept, but evolutionary with regard to the implementation of its concepts. As it turned out, Congress made ERTA even more evolutionary than everyone thought. ERTA called for the maximum federal estate-tax rate to be 50 percent in 1985. Congress has delayed the realization of the 50 percent maximum rate until 1993 (see Table 9-1). Only time will tell if we ever see the 50 percent rate.

For those fortunate to have very large estates, Congress has taken a large step backward. The maximum federal estate-tax rate is increased to 60 percent for the value of an estate that is between $10,000,000 and

$21,040,000 ($18,340,000 in 1993). This erosion of the maximum federal estate tax may well be advance warning of higher federal estate taxes for all Americans.

Simple arithmetic will illustrate the impact the post-ERTA brackets have on the estates of our more successful citizens. In order to gain a perspective on these brackets, some thought should be given to inflation and the impact it has had in assisting the government in the collection of its death tax.

Traditionally, inflation has been an invaluable tool to the federal government's tax collectors. As property values have gone up, tax revenues have gone up. Inflation has forced most Americans into ever-higher federal estate-tax brackets, just as it has forced most Americans into higher income tax brackets. ERTA was a dramatic attempt to reverse this trend. We believe this law has been a benefit to all Americans.

Under the old law, estates were subject to federal estate tax once they exceeded $175,625. This amount was called the "exemption equivalent." The exemption equivalent was raised to $225,000 in 1982 and reached its maximum of $600,000 in 1987, as illustrated in Table 9-2.

The exemption equivalent is really a deductible amount that until reached will result in no tax on the death of a property owner. If a citizen dies after 1986, that tax-free amount is $600,000; this amount is approximately $425,000 more than the maximum tax-free amount under the Tax Reform Act of 1976.

The increase in the exemption equivalent represents a magnificent benefit that has been given to all Americans. It particularly benefits those Americans whose accumulation of property does not exceed the exemption equivalent. A parent who left $600,000 to his or her children in 1981 would have lost $145,800 to federal estate tax. That same parent would lose none of the property to federal estate tax if he or she died in 1990. The comparison made in Table 9-3 should make our point.

Table 9-1
Reduction of Tax Rates

Year of Death	Maximum Tax Rate
1982	65% on estates over $4,000,000
1983	60% on estates over $3,500,000
1984–1992	55% on estates over $3,000,000
1993	50% on estates over $2,500,000

Table 9-2
Increase in the Exemption Equivalent

Year	Exemption Equivalent, in $
1982	225,000
1983	275,000
1984	325,000
1985	400,000
1986	500,000
1987 and thereafter	600,000

Table 9-3
Comparison of Taxes under the Tax
Reform Act of 1976 and ERTA, in $

Taxable Estate	1981 Tax	1990 Tax	1993 Tax
500,000	108,800	—0—	—0—
1,000,000	298,800	153,000	153,000
1,500,000	508,800	363,000	363,000
2,000,000	733,800	588,000	588,000
2,500,000	978,850	833,000	833,000
3,000,000	1,243,800	1,098,000	1,098,000
5,000,000	2,503,800	2,198,000	2,198,000

The cries of the traditional redistributors of wealth that ERTA is only for the rich and superrich do not hold up. Every American is entitled to that $600,000 benefit, and for those who do not create an estate of $600,000 there will be no tax.

Some critics of ERTA believe that the exemption equivalent will only keep pace with inflation. Even if inflation does increase over the years, however, there can be no doubt that the $600,000 exemption equivalent granted by ERTA is far better than the $175,625 Americans had before the law was changed. The old saying that it is unwise to "look a gift horse in the mouth" seems to be appropriate in responding to these critics.

The law now provides spouses with a massive benefit. Today, spouses can leave any portion or all of their property federal estate-tax-free to their U.S.-citizen surviving spouses. There is no federal estate tax on property passing between spouses on death. This is called the "unlimited marital deduction," to which we have devoted the entire Chapter 12, "The Marital Deduction: Federal Recognition of a Spouse's Efforts."

ERTA is revolutionary as it applies to marriage partners. For the first time in the history of our federal estate-tax law, our government recognizes a plain truth: The success created in the accumulation of property by husband and wife is the result of the joint efforts of both spouses. Government's recognition of this plain truth has been long overdue.

The financial security that ERTA provided has helped, and will continue to help, the family unit survive economically. We believe that because of ERTA, widows and widowers are much less dependent on children and government for their economic existence. Government has given back to the family what it has taken away for years; it has allowed spouses to keep what they have earned through a lifetime of sacrifice.

In our Chapter 12 on the marital deduction and Chapter 25 on how to plan under ERTA for a spouse, we really delve into the ramifications of this law.

In order to take maximum advantage of ERTA, significant planning must be accomplished in most cases. Many people must replan their estates immediately. Most estate plans that involved "tax planning" between spouses may have taken advantage of the old law but may not be able to take advantage of the new law without significant changes.

ERTA was passed August 13, 1981. It provided a transitional rule that states that any preexisting plan that involves federal estate-tax planning which was not amended after September 13, 1981, would continue to be governed by the rules under the old law.

Under the old law, the maximum marital deduction was the greater of $25,000 or one-half of the adjusted gross estate. Under current law, the marital deduction can be as much as 100 percent of the estate. Estate plans that planned for spouses before ERTA often used trusts giving the surviving spouse the maximum tax-free amount under the pre-ERTA marital deduction law. If these trusts were not amended after September 13, 1981, and a spouse died in 1982 or after, the surviving spouse (except in some isolated circumstances) only gets half the property tax-free instead of *all* of it tax-free.

Congress did not, in passing this transitional rule, want to upset the planning applecart by invalidating plans created prior to ERTA; but the fact is that most estate plans completed before September 13, 1981, may be inadequate or potentially obsolete. If you have such a plan, please get to your estate planner's office soon. The number of inadequate and obsolete plans still in existence, despite ERTA's passage several years ago, continues to amaze us. Remember, in order to take advantage of ERTA's marital deduction provisions, you must change your existing plan.

The Tax Reform Act of 1984 delayed implementation of the maximum federal estate-tax rates that ERTA lowered. Instead of the 50 percent maximum federal estate-tax rate being fully phased in by 1985, the 1984 maximum of 55 percent was frozen until 1988. Again, in 1987, the 50 percent maximum federal estate-tax rate implementation was delayed until 1993. In addition, Congress added a 5 percent increase in tax to phase out the benefit of the graduated tax rate and the unified credit for estate values in excess of $10,000,000 and up to $21,040,000 through 1992 and $18,340,000 after 1992. The unlimited marital deduction and the greater exemption equivalent have still left Americans better off after the passage of ERTA, despite the delays in the 50 percent maximum rate imposed by the Tax Reform Act of 1984 and the Revenue Act of 1987.

The Tax Reform Acts of 1984 and 1986 and the Revenue Act of 1987 made some changes in the federal estate-tax laws, but none that were as sweeping or as fundamental as those made by ERTA. As a result, the law changes promulgated by ERTA remain the backbone of our current law.

Federal Estate Tax

Taxes the right to transfer almost all property interests

Applies to the fair market value of property

Is paid before beneficiaries

Is generally payable in cash nine months from date of death

The Current Federal Estate Tax

Only applies to estates valued in excess of $600,000

Provides rates beginning at 37 percent with a maximum rate of 50 percent beginning in 1993

Allows spouses to leave property to each other federal estate-tax-free

10

The Unified System

"Robbing Peter to Pay Paul"

Prior to the Tax Reform Act of 1976, the federal tax law favored lifetime gifts over transfers upon death. The federal gift-tax rates were actually 25 percent less than the federal estate-tax rates.

Historically, a potential giver had a $30,000 lifetime exemption. This meant that in addition to the old $3000 annual exclusion, an additional $30,000 was exempt from federal gift tax. Gifts in excess of the annual exclusion and lifetime exemption were then taxed on a cumulative basis. (This means that as the total value of gifts grew, the federal gift-tax bracket at which they were taxed progressively increased.)

Upon death, there was a $60,000 deduction. Property in excess of $60,000 of value was taxed for federal estate-tax purposes, also on a cumulative basis. The federal estate- and gift-tax systems were essentially separate and nonrelated. The net effect of the unrelated systems was that a gift removed property from the highest-possible estate-tax rate to the lowest-possible gift-tax rates.

The 1976 Tax Reform Act unified the federal estate- and gift-tax systems. As a result of this unification of systems, no longer was there a $30,000 lifetime exemption and a separate tax rate for gifts, nor was there a $60,000 death deduction and a separate tax rate for estates.

Under the unified system, gifts and estates were taxed the same. Instead of a gift exemption and a death deduction, a single exemption was given to taxpayers to use, at their choice, either for lifetime gifts or at

59

death. This single exemption is called the exemption equivalent by estate-planning professionals. The maximum exemption equivalent prior to ERTA was $175,625.

ERTA continued the unified system concept. Under ERTA the exemption equivalent was gradually increased to a maximum of $600,000, as is shown in Table 9.2.

An example of how the exemption equivalent works is as follows:

> Ginny Monday, not married, makes $400,000 in gifts that are subject to federal gift taxation during her lifetime. Ginny dies in 1989. Ginny's taxable estate for federal estate-tax purposes, before her remaining exemption equivalent is applied, is $500,000. Since Ginny used $400,000 of her exemption equivalent to make her lifetime gifts federal gift-tax-free, her estate has only $200,000 of remaining exemption equivalent (her $600,000 exemption equivalent less the $400,000 she used during her life). As a result, $300,000 of Ginny's property ($500,000 taxable estate less the $200,000 of remaining exemption equivalent) is subject to federal estate tax.

The exemption equivalent can be confusing. The exemption equivalent relates to a tax credit. Tax tables used to calculate federal estate and gift tax use both concepts. We find that the exemption equivalent is easier to understand, but if your professional advisers use the unified credit concept, please understand that they are saying the same thing. The $600,000 exemption equivalent is the same as a $192,800 unified credit.

When deciding whether it is better to use the exemption equivalent during your life instead of at your death, the time value of money must be considered. A dollar in hand today is worth much more than receiving that same dollar in the future. You can invest a dollar today at 10 percent and next year have $1.10. But if someone promises to pay $1 in one year, you have lost that $0.10 investment. The same is true of the exemption equivalent while alive. If you give a highly appreciating asset away, you may avoid gift tax by using your exemption equivalent, thereby removing both the asset and its appreciation from your estate. The value of using your exemption equivalent is twofold: you can remove the asset and its appreciation from your estate and do it in terms of today's dollars.

Many estate-planning techniques involve the use of a gifting program and may take current advantage of the exemption equivalent. With proper professional advice you may consider beginning a gifting program. Do not be afraid, at the very least, to consider such a program.

11

The Gift Tax

"The Manner of Giving Is Worth More Than the Gift"

Like the federal estate tax, the federal gift tax is not a tax on property. It is a tax on the privilege of transferring property. How the transfer is made determines whether a gift has been made.

A gift is defined as any transfer of property for which the giver receives less than the full property value in return. To the extent the transfer is for less than full value, a gift has been made. Intent or desire to make a gift is generally irrelevant for federal gift-tax purposes. The mere act of delivering the property to its recipient is enough to create a gift subject to the federal gift-tax laws. Professional estate planners call the person who makes a gift a "donor" and the person who receives the gift a "donee."

It is apparent from the definition of a gift that an inadvertent gift can easily be made. For example, payment of someone else's expenses or debts is a gift, unless there is a legal obligation to do so. Forgiving a debt, putting property into joint tenancy, or purchasing something for the benefit of another can all be construed as making a gift.

If a gift is made, it may not necessarily be subject to federal gift tax. The Internal Revenue Code has, for many years, allowed a certain amount, called the "annual exclusion," to be federal gift-tax-free; that is, a giver could give to as many individual recipients as the giver wanted certain gift amounts each year federal gift-tax-free. Any amount given to a recipient in excess of the annual exclusion was subject to taxation. For many years, the annual exclusion was $3000 per recipient.

In 1982, the annual exclusion was finally and significantly increased — it is now $10,000 per recipient per year.

The annual exclusion is eligible for gift splitting. Gift splitting is a method by which spouses can combine their annual exclusions and make a joint gift. For example, a mother with three children could give $30,000 federal gift-tax-free to her children: $10,000 per child; however, if she decides to give an additional $30,000 to the children in the same year (a total of $20,000 per child) and her husband consents, then their combined annual exclusions can be used. All $60,000 ($20,000 per child) is federal gift-tax-free because of the annual exclusion and gift splitting.

Two things are important to remember about gift splitting. The first is that each spouse must consent to the gift, which is done by filing a federal gift-tax return. The second is that if a spouse consents to gift splitting, each spouse will use up part or all of his or her annual exclusion as to the recipient for whom the consent was given. Thus if an $18,000 joint gift is made to one child, each spouse uses $9000 of his or her annual exclusion for that child. Each spouse can only give an additional $1000 to that child in that year and qualify for the annual exclusion.

The annual exclusion only applies to a gift of a "present interest." The annual exclusion does not apply to a gift of a "future interest." A gift of a future interest is defined as a gift of property which does not give the recipient *immediate* use and benefit of that property. Two examples of gifts of future interest are gifts of life insurance policies and gifts to a trust where the trustee is not required to immediately distribute the property to a beneficiary. The only exception to the trust rule is a 2503(c) minor's trust, discussed in Chapter 16, "Trusts: The Estate Planners' Golf Clubs."

All gifts between spouses, where the spouse who receives the gift is a U.S. citizen, are federal gift-tax-free. If the spouse who receives the gift is a non-U.S. citizen, the gifts are subject to an annual exclusion of $100,00. Before you start making gifts to your spouse, however, you should know that there are some drawbacks associated with them.

To explain these drawbacks, we must review the rules of step-up in basis. All assets of a deceased person are valued at their fair market value upon the owner's death. The assets then receive a step-up in basis to fair market value. For example, if an individual purchased a painting for $1000 (cost basis) and its fair market value at death was $10,000, the painting received a new or stepped-up basis of $10,000. If the painting was sold by the estate for $11,000, only $1000 would be subject to federal income tax.

A lifetime gift does not get a step-up in basis. Had that same individual given the painting to a spouse prior to death, the surviving spouse would receive the deceased spouse's cost basis of $1000. If the surviving spouse sold the painting for $11,000, $10,000 would be subject to federal income tax. Thus assets that have a low cost basis are not the kinds of assets that you should be giving to your spouse, at least from a federal income tax perspective. Remember, all assets which go to a U.S.-citizen surviving spouse at death pass federal estate-tax-free and receive a step-up in basis.

There are many other considerations that you should examine when making gifts. One major consideration involves the removal of highly appreciating assets from your estate. The trick is, of course, picking assets which will actually appreciate in value. However, if a highly appreciating asset is given to your spouse and you die first, the asset with all its appreciation will not be subject to federal estate tax on your death; the asset and its appreciated value will be subject to estate tax on your spouse's death. If you give highly appreciating property to someone other than your spouse, you will remove both the asset and *all* its future appreciation to your estate—and your spouse's estate. If you give highly appreciating property to someone other than your spouse, you may pay federal gift tax on its value, as of the date of the gift, but neither you nor your spouse nor your respective estates will ever pay federal gift or estate tax on the appreciation of the property.

Another consideration in making lifetime gifts involves reducing federal income tax. If you own property which generates taxable income, you may wish to give the property to one or more family members who are, or will be, in lower federal income tax brackets. TRA 1986 has made this reason for making gifts less attractive, however. Since tax brackets are lower, reducing income tax has become less important. In addition, income from property and other passive sources received by children under fourteen years of age is taxed in the same bracket as that of their parents. Check with your tax adviser before attempting to use gifts to shift income to family members.

Prior to ERTA, any appreciation in the value of a gift which did not qualify for the annual exclusion and which was made within three years of the giver's death was added to the value of the giver's estate. As a result, the gift did not remove the appreciation of the asset from the giver's estate. Under ERTA, only the value of a few types of gifts, such as life insurance policies, made within three years of the giver's death is added back to the giver's estate. It is easier to make a gift and be secure in the knowledge that the appreciation in value of the gift has been removed from your estate because of the new law; gifting opportunities have been expanded.

Some states have their own gift-tax laws. Each state's gift-tax laws are unique, and a discussion of these laws is outside the scope of this book.

When making gifts, be sure to consider whether or not your state has a gift tax.

Lifetime giving is as much an art as a science. *How* you give something away may be as important as *what* you give away. The making of gifts can be critical to the estate-planning process and, like all other major estate-planning tools, should be discussed with the members of your professional estate-planning team.

Gifts for Tax Purposes

Can be made inadvertently

May not be taxable because of the annual exclusion

Can be "split" with a spouse

Are tax-free when made to a U.S.-citizen spouse

Do *not* qualify for step-up in basis.

12

The Marital Deduction

"Federal Recognition of a Spouse's Efforts"

The marital deduction is a tax concept which describes a tax-savings benefit given to spouses for purposes of federal gift and estate taxes. It is also used by many states for purposes of their death- and gift-tax laws. An understanding of the marital deduction is critical when planning for a spouse.

The Marital Deduction and Federal Gift Tax

Before 1976, when a spouse made a gift to the other spouse, exactly one-half of the value of the gift made was not taxed by the federal government. This was because of the marital deduction. The marital deduction provisions of the federal gift-tax law were a government-sponsored benefit made available only for gifts between spouses. These provisions always removed one-half of the taxable value of a gift from gift taxation. If a gift was made to a spouse (marital), half of that gift was deducted (deduction) before gift-tax calculations were made.

Congress changed the marital deduction rules in 1976 with the enactment of the Tax Reform Act of 1976. This act made the marital deduction more difficult to understand.

The Tax Reform Act of 1976 gave a greater marital deduction to married citizens who made gifts of smaller amounts of property to their spouses. This marital deduction allowed a married citizen to give up to $100,000 tax-free to his or her spouse. This was truly a gift by government to its married taxpayers; however, when the federal government gives, it also can take away, and that is precisely what happened on the next $100,000 of gifts made to a spouse. Under the 1976 law, all gifts made to a spouse over $100,000 but not greater than $200,000 did not qualify for or get the benefit of the marital deduction and were subsequently fully subject to federal gift tax. For gifts over $200,000 to a spouse, the marital deduction was just like it was before 1976; one-half the value of the property that was given was not subject to tax.

The real change brought about by the 1976 act was to benefit only those married citizens who gave less than $200,000 to their spouses. The change in the law did not benefit spouses making gifts in excess of $200,000; for these married taxpayers, the change was no change at all.

President Reagan and Congress changed the marital deduction rules again with the passage of ERTA. This act took effect on January 1, 1982 and provided a 100 percent marital deduction for all gifts between spouses. The Technical and Miscellaneous Revenue Act of 1988 limited the 100 percent marital deduction to spouses who are U.S. citizens. If the spouse receiving the gift is not a U.S. citizen, there is only a $100,000 annual gift-tax exclusion. Any gift, regardless of its value, made to a U.S.-citizen spouse is tax-free for federal gift-tax purposes. This is called the 100 percent or unlimited marital deduction. Now, regardless of how much a gift to a U.S.-citizen spouse is, the rules are always the same.

ERTA also applied the unlimited marital deduction provisions of the federal gift-tax law to married taxpayers living in community-property states (Arizona, California, Idaho, Louisiana, Nevada, New Mexico, Texas, and Washington). Prior to ERTA, married citizens residing in these states did not get the right to the federal gift-tax marital deduction with respect to their community-property interests. One-half of all gifts between spouses of community property prior to ERTA was subject to federal gift tax. ERTA and other recent tax acts now provide a 100 percent marital deduction for community-property gifts between married taxpayers, where the spouse who receives the gift is a U.S. citizen.

The Marital Deduction and Federal Estate Tax

Prior to 1976, all spouses could leave up to one-half of their property to or for the benefit of their surviving spouses free of federal estate tax.

This was because of the federal estate-tax marital deduction which evidenced, in our opinion, Congress's belief that both spouses had a hand in creating the wealth in the marriage (a concept long recognized in the community-property states). In order to qualify for the tax break created by the marital deduction, the following *minimum* rules had to be met:

> The surviving spouses had to receive at least annually all the income from the property that was left for their benefit. This meant that the spouses also had the right to require that the property be invested in income-producing assets.
>
> The surviving spouses had to be given the right to leave that property on their deaths to whomever they pleased. This right is called a "general power of appointment."

In order to qualify for the marital deduction, all that spouses had to give surviving spouses was the income from the marital deduction property and the right for the surviving spouses to leave that property on their subsequent death to whomever they desired.

The Tax Reform Act of 1976 changed the rules with regard to the federal estate-tax marital deduction. This legislation, like its federal gift-tax counterpart, was designed to favor the less successful citizen. It provided that the marital deduction would exempt from federal estate taxation the first $250,000 left to or for the benefit of a surviving spouse. It also provided that the marital deduction would be the greater of $250,000 or one-half of the deceased spouse's adjusted gross estate (property the spouse left *less* debts and expenses). That $250,000 was important: an estate left to a spouse up to $250,000 was tax-free; an estate up to $500,000 still gave a surviving spouse $250,000 tax-free; an estate over $500,000 was back to the older rules under which only half of the estate would be tax-free to the surviving spouse.

ERTA and other recent tax acts dramatically changed the marital deduction rules. The law now provides for a 100 percent federal estate-tax marital deduction, where the surviving spouse is a U.S. citizen, and changes the rights that a surviving spouse must receive in order to qualify the property as marital deduction property.

In order to qualify for the current unlimited federal estate-tax marital deduction, the following mimimum rules must be met:

The surviving spouse must be a citizen of the United States.

The property interest must be included in the value of the deceased spouse's estate.

The surviving spouse must receive, at least annually, all the income from the marital deduction property for life.

The surviving spouse must have the right to require that the property be invested in income-producing assets.

No person can have the power to give any part of the marital deduction property to anyone other than the surviving spouse.

The last three requirements are called "qualified income interests."

There is no longer a requirement that spouses have the right to leave the property on their deaths according to their wishes. A general power of appointment is no longer required. This represents a massive change in the federal estate-tax law. There is a requirement, however, that the marital deduction property generally be left intact for the benefit of the spouse to ensure that the surviving spouse will continue to receive income for his or her life. No person can be given the power to give the marital deduction property to others during the life of the spouse.

In order to qualify for the marital deduction, a surviving spouse only needs to receive a qualified income interest from that property. If income is not given for the surviving spouse's life, it is not a "qualified income interest" and *no* marital deduction will be allowed.

Estate-planning professionals describe this marital deduction requirement as "qualified terminable interest property." Most of the professional literature on the subject has nicknamed a trust used to provide the surviving spouse with income as a "Q-TIP" trust: *q*ualified *t*erminable *i*nterest *p*roperty trust. We believe that Q-TIPs are used for other purposes and prefer to refer to this trust as a spouse's trust or marital trust instead.

If you live in Arizona, California, Idaho, Louisiana, Nevada, New Mexico, Texas, or Washington (community-property states), you, too, get to take advantage of the unlimited marital deduction law. The pre-ERTA marital deduction law was not available to you because it was only a 50 percent deduction and you got that automatically because of your state's community-property laws. As a matter of fact, community-property states by their own laws automatically give the equivalent of a 50 percent marital deduction. The federal marital deduction was originally passed by Congress to give all states the benefits conferred to spouses by community-property states. But if you completed your estate plan prior to the passage of ERTA, you may have to replan to take advantage of the unlimited marital deduction.

In Chapter 25, we will discuss the planning opportunities available under the unlimited marital deduction. They are different—very different—from anything that has been done before.

In reviewing our discussion of the marital deduction, please remember that:

You can give or leave all or part of your property tax-free to your U.S.-citizen spouse.

Your U.S.-citizen spouse must receive, at least annually, all the income from the marital deduction property for life.

Your U.S.-citizen spouse must have the right to require that the property be invested in income-producing assets and no person can have the power to give any part of the marital deduction property to anyone other than the surviving spouse.

13

Community Property

"Maverick Law in Maverick States"

Forty-two of our states base their laws of property ownership on our English common-law heritage. Eight of our states base their laws of property ownership, as to property owned between a husband and wife, on a heritage of French and Spanish law. These states have community-property laws with respect to the ownership of property acquired during the term of a marriage. Each of these eight states has its own brand of community-property laws; but all community-property laws, regardless of a state's variations, must be differentiated from the law of the forty-two non-community-property law states. The community-property law states are:

Arizona	Nevada
California	New Mexico
Idaho	Texas
Louisiana	Washington

Wisconsin has adopted legislation that makes it very similar to a community-property state.

In reviewing the list of community-property states, you can see the historical influence of the Spanish and French tradition. The French brought the Napoleonic Code to Louisiana, and the Spanish tradition was adopted by the remaining seven states.

Community-property law manifests the social and legal belief that property acquired by spouses during the marriage should be construed as one total "community" of property. Regardless of how ownership is taken to that property, it belongs to a marital partnership. Each of the marital partners, as a fifty-fifty partner, owns 50 percent of the partnership property, or "community."

To facilitate understanding of community property, we will call the marriage the community partnership. The property that a husband and wife own before they enter into their community partnership is their separate property; it was acquired outside the community partnership and remains the separate property of each. This is also true of gifts or inheritances received by either spouse during the marriage. If that separate property is sold and the proceeds commingled with other community-partnership activities and investments, it generally becomes part of the community partnership's holdings.

Income that is generated from the community partnership's holdings is owned 50 percent by the community partnership's partners. From this perspective, community property should be very understandable and, in fact, very logical.

For purposes of community-property laws, how property is titled is irrelevant. All property acquired during the term of a marriage is property that belongs to the community partnership, and each partner has a 50 percent ownership in that property because both spouses are fifty-fifty partners.

The federal government had to recognize the right of each of these eight states to create its own unusual form of ownership between spouses because of the Tenth Amendment to the U.S. Constitution. As a result, the federal government had to structure its estate- and gift-tax laws so that they would apply fairly both to the citizens of the forty-two "normal states" and the citizens of the eight maverick, or community, states. A historical perspective of the government's rules in this area follows:

> Because a community-partnership partner owned half the marital assets, the federal government could only tax half the marital property on the death of either partner. In order to maintain fairness, Congress was eventually persuaded in 1948 to create the marital deduction for spouses who did not reside in community-property states. The marital deduction historically allowed spouses to leave half their property tax-free to their surviving spouses. This appeared to equalize the federal estate-tax treatment of marital property in all the states.
>
> Citizens of community-property states did not get the federal estate-tax marital deduction except with respect to separate prop-

erty; they did not need it because community-property laws already gave them the same benefit.

The federal government also gave citizens of the other forty-two states the right to exclude from federal gift tax the value of one-half of the gifts made between spouses. This was also fair because property acquired by community partners was acquired 50 percent by each of the partners without a gift because of state law.

Spouses in community-property states did not get the federal gift-tax marital deduction except for separate property; they already had it under their state's community-property laws.

ERTA provided for an unlimited marital deduction that allows a spouse to leave all his or her property tax-free to the surviving spouse; it also allowed a spouse to give property to a spouse during life free from all federal gift taxes. The Technical and Miscellaneous Revenue Act of 1988 restricts the unlimited marital deduction to U.S.-citizen surviving spouses.

Now citizens in community-property states get an unlimited marital deduction for both federal estate- and gift-tax purposes. This was a major change in the law. Individuals who reside in a community-property state must have their estate plans reviewed by their professional advisers. The additional benefits that are afforded married taxpayers residing in community-property states are enormous.

Remember, community-property residents who have already completed their estate plans cannot take advantage of the unlimited marital deduction for federal estate- and gift-tax purposes unless their pre-ERTA plans are changed. If you live in a community-property state, please seek out and meet with your professional advisers; there could be substantial tax savings available to you.

14
State Death Taxes
"States Need Revenue Too"

Every state has its own death tax in one form or another. Individual states take pride in their uniqueness, and this pride is certainly borne out in the manner in which individual states structure their death taxes.

All states' death-tax laws fall into one of three general death-tax patterns: states which collect their taxes directly from the federal government (gap-tax states); states which tax the estates of their citizens much like the federal government does (estate-tax states); and states that base their death taxes on the value of the property that passes to certain defined beneficiaries (inheritance-tax states).

To help your general understanding of state death taxes, the following is our classification of the states in terms of the three categories each state falls under, as of 1990.

Gap-Tax States

The federal government's estate-tax tables allow as a credit against federal estate tax certain dollar amounts that can be paid to the individual states instead of to the federal government. In essence, the federal estate-tax system provides for a little bit of revenue sharing with those states.

The federal estate-tax tables spell out what the tax will be, bracket by bracket, for different-sized estates. These same tables provide that

Table 14-1
State Inheritance-Tax Table

	Exemption, in $	Share in Excess of Exemption, in $	Tax, in $	Rate on Next Bracket, in %
CLASS 1 BENEFICIARIES				
a. Widows or *minor child*	10,000 each	0	0	2
		25,000	500	4
		50,000	1,500	6
b. Husband or adult child, grandchildren	4,000 each	100,000	4,500	8
		200,000	12,500	10
		500,000	42,500	15
CLASS 2 BENEFICIARIES				
Sisters, brothers, nieces, nephews	1,000 each	0	0	4
		25,000	1,000	6
		50,000	2,500	8
		100,000	6,500	12
		200,000	18,500	16
		500,000	68,500	20

CLASS 3 BENEFICIARIES

Uncles, aunts, and their descendants   500 each

0	0	6
25,000	1,500	9
50,000	3,750	12
100,000	9,750	15
200,000	24,750	20
500,000	84,750	25

CLASS 4 BENEFICIARIES

All others   0

0	0	8
25,000	2,000	14
50,000	5,500	20
100,000	15,500	30

a small percentage of the federal estate tax will be forgiven if that amount is paid to the state in which the deceased citizen resided pursuant to that state's death-tax laws.

Some states have structured their death-tax rates so that the tax they collect is exactly the same amount as the federal government will forgive in the federal estate-tax tables through the federal revenue sharing program. States whose death-tax laws are structured so that the states receive funds only from the federal estate-tax revenue sharing program are referred to as gap-tax states by estate-planning professionals.

In reality, these gap-tax states only receive death-tax revenues that would have gone to the federal government anyway but for the state gap tax. A portion of the federal estate tax is paid to the gap-tax state instead of all the tax being paid to the federal government.

While gap-tax states used to be in the minority, now the gap tax is used by more states than any other method for collecting state death tax.

The gap-tax states are:

Alabama	Idaho	Oregon
Alaska	Illinois	Texas
Arizona	Maine	Utah
Arkansas	Minnesota	Vermont
California	Missouri	Virginia
Colorado	Nevada	Washington
Florida	New Mexico	West Virginia
Georgia	North Dakota	Wyoming
Hawaii		

The District of Columbia also has a gap tax.

Estate-Tax States

Some states tax the estates of their deceased citizens under death-tax systems which are structured very much like the federal estate tax. These states apply their own unique tax rates and have their own unique sets of rules as to how their rates will be applied.

Estate-tax states also get the benefit of the federal estate-tax revenue sharing program. Unlike gap-tax states, these states not only get revenues under the federal estate-tax revenue sharing program but also collect substantial additional funds as a result of their death taxes. Their death-tax rates are always higher than the amount from the federal estate-tax revenue sharing program.

The estate-tax states are:

Massachusetts	Oklahoma
Mississippi	Rhode Island
New York	South Carolina
Ohio	

Puerto Rico also has an estate tax.

Rhode Island is phasing out its estate tax and in 1991 will be a full-fledged gap-tax state. Likewise, South Carolina is phasing out its estate tax and in mid-1991 will be a gap-tax state.

Inheritance-Tax States

States which fall into this category are states that apply their death-tax rates against the value of the shares that pass to certain defined classes of beneficiaries. Because the state death tax is calculated on the share that *each* beneficiary will receive or inherit, it is called an "inheritance tax."

Inheritance-tax states have different tax rates that apply to different kinds or classes of beneficiaries. Generally, however, the closer the beneficiary's blood relationship is to the deceased, the lower the inheritance-tax rate will be; spouses almost always pay inheritance taxes at the lowest tax rates. An example of an inheritance-tax table is shown in Table 14-1.

This inheritance-tax table illustrates how most state inheritance taxes are structured. Your review of this example should highlight the fact that the more distant a relative is to the deceased, the lower the exemption and the higher the tax will be.

Inheritance-tax states also receive funds from the federal estate-tax revenue sharing program. Many inheritance-tax states provide that if the amount of the inheritance tax due is less than the federal estate-tax revenue sharing amount allowed, then the inheritance tax due will be a minimum of the federal estate-tax revenue sharing amount. This assures that they will receive the largest amount of federal funds available.

The inheritance-tax states are:

Connecticut	Louisiana	New Jersey
Delaware	Maryland	North Carolina
Indiana	Michigan	Pennsylvania
Iowa	Montana	South Dakota
Kansas	Nebraska	Tennessee
Kentucky	New Hampshire	Wisconsin

Wisconsin is phasing out its inheritance tax and in 1992 will be a gap-tax state.

A few states also have their own gift taxes. Like state death-tax laws, gift-tax laws are unique in each state. As of 1990, Delaware, Louisiana, New York, North Carolina, South Carolina (until 1992), Tennessee, and Wisconsin (until 1992) have some form of gift tax. Puerto Rico and the Virgin Islands have gift taxes as well.

State death- and gift-tax laws change from time to time, so the lists of states in this chapter may not reflect the current law in your state. And, a detailed discussion of individual state death- and gift-tax laws is outside the scope of this book. Your state's gift- and death-tax laws should be discussed with your professional estate-planning team. The impact of your state's death- and gift-tax laws is important when you are planning your estate.

15

Step-Up in Basis at Death

"It Almost Pays to Die"

"Basis" is a word developed for federal income tax purposes. Basis, or "cost basis" as it is sometimes known, is the amount which is generally used to compute the taxable gain for federal income tax purposes on the sale of property.

A simple example of this principle is the purchase of the family car. If you pay $5000 for your car, $5000 is your cost basis in the car. Upon a sale of the car for $6000, the gain subject to federal income tax is $1000 ($6000 sales price *less* $5000 cost basis).

The federal estate tax is an everything tax, as we discussed earlier. At death, or six months thereafter, the fair market value of all the assets owned by the deceased person is determined by the agent of the deceased person's estate. The fair market value of all the assets, less debts and expenses of the estate, is then subject to the federal estate tax. The end result of the federal estate tax is that all the appreciation in value of the assets in the estate can be taxed. Unlike with the federal income tax, the cost basis is ignored.

Congress has generally recognized that there may be an inherent unfair federal income tax element of the federal estate tax. If all assets are subject to federal estate tax (everything tax) and after death the same assets are subject to federal income tax (sales price *less* cost basis), there is a great danger of double taxation. Appreciation (growth) of assets could be subject to the federal estate tax as well as the federal income tax. This inherent unfairness has been turned into a magnificent benefit for most estates.

Assets which are in the estate of a deceased person, whether the estate pays federal estate tax or not, take as their cost basis for federal income tax purposes the fair market value of those assets at date of death or six months after death, whichever valuation date is used. This step-up in basis means that the appreciation of assets in an estate is *not* subject to federal income tax.

For example, if the family car is purchased for $5000 (original cost basis) by the bread-earner spouse and, at the bread-earner spouse's death, it has a fair market value of $6000 (step-up in basis), the $1000 in appreciation is not subject to federal income tax. If the estate sells the car for $6000, there is *no* taxable gain.

The step-up in basis rules apply to *every asset in an estate,* and the rules apply whether or not any federal estate tax is paid. The step-up in basis rules, however, do not apply to lifetime gifts. A recipient of a gift has the same cost basis in the asset that the giver had. The federal gift tax is determined based on the fair market value of the asset given. Thus a gift tax may be paid on the lifetime gift, and when the recipient of the gift sells it, there may be federal income tax due. Double taxation is possible.

When lifetime gifts are contemplated, not only is the federal gift-tax effect important, but the federal income tax must be considered. For example, if an elderly taxpayer owns property with a low cost basis, lifetime gifts may not be wise. It may be better to have the individual retain the assets so that their basis will be stepped up at death. On the other hand, if the elderly taxpayer has assets with a high cost basis, it may be good planning to use these assets for lifetime gifts.

Married residents of community-property states have a distinct advantage over their non-community-property counterparts when it comes to step-up in basis rules. If a community-property spouse dies, *all* the community property may receive a step-up in basis, not just the interest of the deceased spouse.

There is a tax gimmick that should be avoided because it will not work. Prior to ERTA, gifts were often made to an individual who was dying. The dying individual would make a will giving the property back to the original giver at death. The result was that the original giver received a step-up in basis on the giver's original property. ERTA restricted this transaction. It will not work for any property given to the dying individual within one year of death when the property is left to the original giver.

The step-up in basis rules under our federal estate tax are of the utmost importance. Because of their far-reaching effects on estate planning, the step-up in basis rules should be discussed at great length with your professional estate-planning team.

16

Trusts

"The Estate Planners' Golf Clubs"

A significant number of estate-planning techniques are implemented in the form of a trust. There are trusts designed to accomplish a host of planning alternatives. Most professionals use a panoply of trust documents in accomplishing the objectives of their clients. An estate planner uses trusts like a professional golfer uses clubs. In our experience, however, very few clients we initially meet understand what trusts do, what they involve, and how they are structured. Trusts and how they are used are apparently seldom taught outside of the professional domain.

Many people, and this is understandable, believe that trusts are on the government hit list. They read in their daily papers or favorite magazines about antitrust lawsuits between government and big business.

Before explaining what trusts are, how they work, and what they accomplish, give us a chance to make some sense out of this antitrust nonsense.

We will start with John D. Rockefeller, Sr. Toward the end of the nineteenth century, Mr. Rockefeller was engaged in the capitalistic pursuit of controlling the petroleum marketplace. Regardless of your politics, Mr. Rockefeller made a pretty good job of it. One of the problems he faced, however, was that different states had different laws; and these legal impediments threatened to curtail his interstate growth.

With the help of his chief legal mogul, Mr. Dodd, Mr. Rockefeller signed a document called the "Standard Oil Trust." He transferred all his Standard Oil stock to his trust, and he then named trustees to run that trust. Using a bold common-law form of title holding, Mr. Rockefeller set the world of finance on its ear. Through the use of the

Standard Oil Trust, Mr. Rockefeller crossed state lines with impunity and an empire was established.

Monopoly resulted from this Standard Oil Trust because Mr. Rockefeller indeed controlled the petroleum marketplace. Government stepped in and passed antitrust laws. These laws were passed to curtail and regulate Mr. Rockefeller's monopolies and other monopolies throughout the American marketplace.

These laws were antimonopoly laws, not really antitrust laws; but because Mr. Rockefeller's legal genius, Mr. Dodd, chose to use an old form of ownership to effectuate his client's industrial dominance, trust became synonymous with and a symbol of monopoly. Even the *World Book Encyclopedia* defines trust as a "term used in economics to describe a large industrial monopoly." Estate planners have inherited a public that, too often, equates a trust with its Rockefellerian usage.

In estate planning, trusts enable people to pass title to their property to others either during lifetime or at death. When a person creates a trust and places property in a trust, the trust maker, in effect, makes a gift. Trusts enable their makers to make gifts to their beneficiaries and allow the trust maker to exercise significant control, on a prearranged basis, over the disposition of the trust property. In effect, trusts allow property to pass to others with "strings attached."

All trusts have the following characteristics:

A trust is created by a trust maker. Attorneys call the maker a settlor, trustor, creator, or grantor.

The person responsible for following the maker's instructions is called the trustee.

Trustees can be individuals or licensed institutions. The maker can also be his or her own trustee.

Trusts can be created by more than one maker. Joint makers are called joint makers or co-makers. Trusts can be operated by more than one trustee, so then you have co-trustees.

Trusts can be created for the benefit of the maker or for the benefit of other people. The people for whose benefit a trust is created are called beneficiaries.

Trusts can accomplish just about any objective of the maker as long as it is not illegal or against public policy.

Trusts cannot last forever unless the beneficiary is a legally recognized charity.

The beneficiaries who have the first rights to the trust property are called primary beneficiaries. If the primary beneficiaries die or become disqualified, due to the instructions given to the trustee by the trust maker, then the property will go to other named beneficiaries called contingent beneficiaries.

Trusts, to be effective, must be in writing. They must be signed by the maker, and if a living trust is used, it should be signed by the trustee, although the trustee's signature is not necessary to make a trust valid. If the trust document is not signed by a trustee, the trust is not void; it still exists.

The law has always stated that "no trust shall fail for lack of a trustee." The local court having jurisdiction over trusts will name a trustee if one is not named in the trust document.

The trust document is often referred to as an indenture or a trust indenture (historically, a deed to which two or more persons are parties).

Trust beneficiaries do not have to sign the trust document or will containing a trust.

Any number of separate trusts can be created in a single trust document.

When the maker puts property in a trust, the maker "funds" the trust.

Trust makers can be primary or contingent beneficiaries of their own trusts.

There are several different kinds of trusts that accomplish a host of estate-planning objectives. (Please refer to Figure 16-1.) All trusts can be categorized in one of two ways. A trust is either a living trust or a death trust. Living trusts are often referred to as *inter vivos* (Latin for living) trusts. Death trusts are called testamentary (from the Latin *testamentum*) trusts and are created in a person's will. They do not come into existence until the death of the will maker.

A living trust is always created during the lifetime of the trust maker. A living trust usually provides that the maker is to be his or her own primary beneficiary. Living trusts can also pass the trust property to the maker's beneficiaries on the maker's death. Because living trusts can pass property on the death of the maker, they are often referred to as will substitutes. We will discuss the living trust in greater detail in the following two chapters.

A death, or testamentary, trust can only be created in a valid will. These trusts are never created to benefit the maker. Death trusts are created by a will maker, and although they are created or drafted during the will maker's life, they are not operative until the maker's death. Death trusts have no life until the death of the maker.

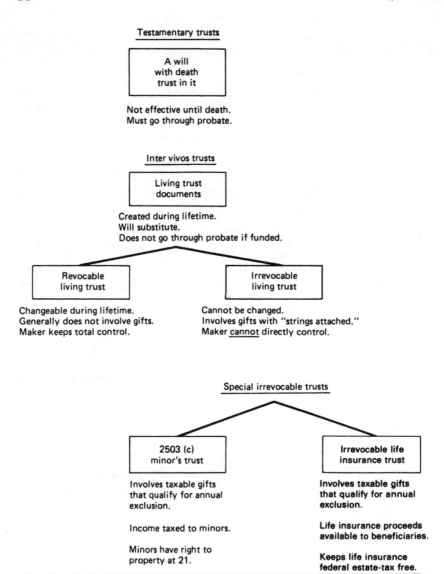

Figure 16-1. Different kinds of trusts.

Since a will goes through the probate process, the trusts—created in that will—will also go through the probate process. Testamentary trusts are involved in the probate process and are subject to the local probate court's direction and control (jurisdiction).

Both living trusts and death trusts represent massive tools to estate-planning professionals. They allow professionals to accomplish their clients' estate-planning objectives. You may recall from our discussion in Chapter 1, "What Is Estate Planning," that estate planning involves more than the outright passing of property from one person to another. People want to give what they have, to whom they want, in the way and when they want. They do wish to reduce taxes, attorneys' fees, and court costs to the greatest extent possible. These objectives are almost always accomplished through the utilization of various trust formats. Remember that trusts are gifts with strings attached: instructions and conditions given to the trustee as to the whom, how, and when of distribution of property.

Death trusts can always be canceled or changed by the maker, as long as the maker is competent, up until the maker's death.

Living trusts can be structured so that the maker can retain the right to change or terminate the trust while the maker is alive. Living trusts that give the maker the right to change his or her mind are called revocable living trusts. Living trusts that cannot be changed are called irrevocable living trusts; trusts created under this format can be altered only by court action. Neither the maker nor anyone else, for that matter, may alter these trusts.

When a trust maker creates a revocable living trust, a gift is not made. Since the maker has the right to change his or her mind about all the terms of the trust document, there can be no gift for federal or state gift-tax purposes. If, however, property does pass to others while the maker is alive (even though the trust is revocable), there may be a gift for both federal and state gift-tax purposes.

An important point to remember is whether a person gives property directly to others or gives property through the use of a trust, a gift will always result. Whether that gift will be taxed depends upon the amount of the gift and the circumstances surrounding how the gift was made.

When a trust maker funds an irrevocable living trust, a gift will always result. By creating an irrevocable trust, a trust maker gives up all control to the trust property *and* to the terms of the trust. Once the irrevocable trust is signed, a maker cannot change his or her mind or alter the terms of the trust.

By creating an irrevocable living trust, a trust maker makes a gift with strings attached. That is usually why these trusts are used. Irrevocable living trusts allow a person to get the use of property to others on a living basis pursuant to the maker's wishes and instructions to the trustee as to its use. Without the use of such a vehicle, gifts could not be made with instructions that would guarantee and control their use. Without the use of an irrevocable trust a gift made is a gift completed; the recipient can do anything with the property received.

Irrevocable trusts are commonly used in the following situations:

To own life insurance policies on the life of the trust maker. These trusts are designed to keep the insurance proceeds federal estate-tax-free on death and are discussed in Chapter 28, "The Irrevocable Life Insurance Trust."

To hold title to property given to minors so that the gift maker can exercise control over the property.

When a person wishes to make a gift to minors but wants to control the use of the property, a minor's trust can be created. A minor's trust is often called a 2503(c), or accumulation, trust. It is named after the Internal Revenue Code provision that gives the trust its existence.

When a minor's trust is created and property given to the trustee to manage and distribute to the minor beneficiaries according to the written instructions of the trust maker, the trust must be irrevocable. The income from the trust will be taxed for income tax purposes to the minor beneficiaries. Under prior law, this was an advantage because parents could give their children income-producing property and control the property by putting it into a minor's trust. This income would be taxed in the children's lower income tax brackets.

TRA 1986 greatly reduced this income tax advantage. Unearned income, including income from trusts, received by minors under fourteen years of age is now taxed in the same income tax bracket as is their parents' income. Even for minors who are over fourteen, there is not a great income tax advantage from using a minor's trust. Under TRA 1986, there are only two income tax brackets, one of 15 percent and one of 28 percent. For minors who are fourteen years of age or older, income tax can be reduced by having it taxed in a minor's 15 percent bracket, but since the difference in the brackets is only 13 percent, there may not be a great enough differential to justify using a minor's trust purely on income tax savings grounds. Since TRA 1986, minor's trusts are used mostly as devices to control gifts made to minors.

It should be noted that for these trusts to be effective, the trust maker should not be the trustee; the minor must have the right to the trust principal on attaining the age of twenty-one; and the income from the trust cannot be used to discharge a support obligation the maker of the trust owes to the minor beneficiary.

Trusts created under section 2503(c) of the Internal Revenue Code are often used to pass property to children or grandchildren subject to controls provided by the maker in the trust document. Minors' trusts should be carefully drafted by an estate-planning professional.

TRA 1986 eliminated the use of the ten-year, or Clifford, trust, a special kind of irrevocable trust. These trusts were used to make a gift of the income of property for a limited period of time, which could not be less than ten years. The maker of a ten-year trust would transfer income-producing property into an irrevocable trust for a minimum of ten years. During this period, the beneficiaries would receive and be taxed on the income generated by the property. When the trust ended, the maker would get his or her property back.

As of March 1, 1986, ten-year trusts were no longer allowed; the maker is now taxed on the income of these trusts. For ten-year trusts that were in existence on or before March 1, 1986, the beneficiaries are taxed on the income, but since TRA 1986 has reduced tax brackets and has eliminated most income tax benefits for children under the age of fourteen, even those ten-year trusts are much less effective.

There are many different kinds of trusts that professional estate planners use to accomplish the objectives of their clients. Estate-planning trusts are designed to allow people to pass title to their property to others either during lifetime or at death. In the chapters that follow, we will demonstrate how some of these trusts can be utilized to meet most estate-planning goals.

17

The Revocable Living Trust

"The Will Substitute That Has Come of Age"

We strongly believe that estate-planning professionals should use the revocable living trust as the main or foundation document to accomplish the majority of their clients' estate-planning objectives. The revocable living trust is a most attractive estate-planning device. It can be used instead of a will to accomplish the bulk of your estate-planning goals. Revocable living trusts have been used successfully for centuries, but their use as a total will substitute is a comparatively recent development. In our opinion, they have truly "come of age" and should be used by just about everybody.

Living trusts can be revocable or irrevocable (we discussed the difference in Chapter 16, "Trusts"); this chapter discusses the former, a trust that you can create and change at your whim while alive.

Here's a preview of the benefits that can be derived from the use of this very attractive estate-planning vehicle:

You can give what you own to whom you want and when you want subsequent to your death through the use of a revocable living trust. As the trust maker, you can spell out all your distribution terms and requirements as to how your property passes after your death.

A revocable living trust can control, coordinate, and distribute all your property interests while you are alive as well as on your death.

By using a revocable living trust, you can arrange for your well-being under your terms as you advance in years, become ill, or become mentally incompetent.

The use of a revocable living trust assures that your plans and affairs will remain private, rather than being made public, on your death or incapacity.

Revocable living trusts are easy to create and maintain during your lifetime.

It is not difficult for you to change or amend your revocable living trust at any time during your lifetime.

There are no adverse lifetime income tax consequences that result from the use of a revocable living trust.

Property that has been placed in a revocable living trust during your lifetime is not subject to and does not pass through the probate process on your death; it is probate free.

Continuity of cash flow and investments in your portfolio can continue uninterrupted by your death.

All opportunities of death-tax planning available through will planning are equally available through the use of a revocable living trust.

Revocable living trusts are legal in every state. Your trust can easily be moved with you as you cross state lines.

By using a revocable living trust, you can measure your postdeath trustees' abilities to manage your assets while you are alive.

Revocable living trusts are more difficult to attack, and usually less successfully attacked, by disgruntled beneficiaries than are wills.

If you choose to use a revocable living trust, you can avail yourself of all the benefits we have highlighted above. A detailed discussion of each of these benefits follows.

Property Distribution after Your Death

On and after your death, all property in your trust and the income that property generates will be distributed by the trustee according to your precise written instructions. Anything that can be accomplished through the use of a trust created by a will (testamentary trust) can be accomplished identically through the use of the revocable living trust.

Property in a revocable living trust can be left to the beneficiaries outright on your death or it can remain in trust and be distributed over a certain period of time to your beneficiaries. Several trusts can be created within a revocable living trust which will become operative for designated beneficiaries on your death. In fact, there is no limit to the number of separate trusts that can be created in a single revocable living trust. Each trust that is created within the trust document can spell out its individual terms with regard to the amounts to be distributed and the timing under which those amounts are to pass to your beneficiaries. Each of the trusts that are created in the trust document may have different terms and conditions as to the distribution of income and principal to your selected beneficiaries.

One Receptacle to Receive and Distribute All Property

Through the use of a single revocable living trust, you can control the distribution of all your property. This is true not only for the property you put in your trust while alive but also for other property which flows into your trust on your death. Proceeds from life insurance can be left to your trust if you name your trust as the beneficiary; the same is true with respect to your proceeds from pension and profit sharing plans. For that matter, any proceeds from third-party beneficiary contracts can be left to your trust if you simply make the trust the beneficiary of those proceeds.

Your revocable living trust can provide one receptacle to receive and distribute all your assets on your death. This should represent a major benefit to you.

Property that is not placed in the trust during your lifetime can still be put in the trust after your death through the use of a short, well-drafted will that attorneys call a "pour-over will." The provisions of a pour-over will simply state that any property you neglected to put in your trust will, nevertheless, pass to your trust (pour over to it) after your death. The pour-over will should always be used in conjunction with a revocable living trust. We often refer to these special wills as fail-safe wills; their use assures that any forgotten property will ultimately be placed in the planning pot to be controlled pursuant to your master plan.

It is important to understand, however, that property owned jointly cannot be put into a trust on your death. We have discussed this in several other chapters but say it again. Beware of jointly held property; you cannot control it on your death, and it may go to unintended heirs.

It Can Take Care of You Too

A revocable living trust can be designed so that it can provide for your care during your lifetime. In your revocable living trust, you can spell out in as much detail as you like how you wish to be taken care of with *your own* trust property in case of your incapacity, which could result from senility, accident, or illness. You can specify who your trustees will be if you become incompetent. You can also provide for the care of your loved ones should you lose control of your mental faculties.

The ability to provide for your care as well as the care of your loved ones during your lifetime is, in our opinion, one of the greatest attributes of a revocable living trust. Perhaps we can illustrate our point by asking you to recall Groucho Marx's last years.

Groucho, you will recall, like other older people, lost control of his mental faculties. Friends and family members, through attorneys and court proceedings, litigated who should take care of Groucho and his property. The sad plight of a great entertainer's final days was made public. Many of the costs that resulted were paid out of Groucho's estate. The entire affair could have been avoided if Groucho had planned for the contingency of his illness through the use of a revocable living trust.

A revocable living trust can avoid all the confusion and publicity occasioned by court proceedings that would otherwise come about upon your incapacity. Our point takes on even greater significance in light of the ability of modern medicine to keep people alive under almost unbelievable circumstances.

Some states, particularly Uniform Probate Code states, allow the use of a durable special power of attorney. This document allows you to give the right to someone you trust to place your property in your revocable living trust if you are unable to do so. It is durable in that, unlike general powers of attorney, its legality continues even if you are incompetent. By using this durable power of attorney as an addition to your revocable living trust, you can assure yourself that your property will be placed in your trust and used pursuant to your directions for you and your loved ones' benefit without costly court interference and publicity.

They Are Private

Unlike a will, revocable living trusts are private documents. They are not made public either while you are alive, at your death, or subsequent to your death. By using the revocable living trust, you can be assured that you will not be taking your affairs and your family's affairs public. We have read too many books that have exposed the affairs of great people to the public's scrutiny. The authors of these books had at their fingertips the probate court's records as to all the affairs of these people because they elected to use a will rather than a revocable living trust.

Revocable living trusts, their provisions and the property they control, remain the exclusive business of the beneficiaries for whom they were created; other than the trustee, the trusts are nobody else's business.

Easy to Create and Maintain

Revocable living trusts are easy to create. In our opinion, you should always seek out an attorney who knows estate planning, convey your wishes, and set a time for a future meeting to review your trust.

We do not believe that you should fill in preprinted forms sold in books. We do believe very strongly that you should be knowledgeable but that you should always seek the assistance of estate-planning professionals.

Once the attorney completes your plan, sign it if it meets your objectives. Unlike with a will, formalities of signing are almost nonexistent. That is all there is to it. Of course, the trust should be funded. That, too, is not difficult and will be discussed at length in our next chapter.

After creating your revocable living trust, you should check back with your attorney from time to time to make sure your trust has kept current with your objectives and new legal developments. Keeping current is important and can be accomplished through the use of a revocable living trust.

Easily Changed without Formality

In our Chapters 6 and 7 on wills, we discussed that wills have to be signed and executed, with a great deal of legal formality, and that codicils (will amendments) have the same formal requirements. This is not the case with revocable living trusts. These trusts need only your signature to infuse life into them. Likewise, trust amendments, regardless of their scope, require only your signature. Witnesses are generally not required, nor is the signature of the trustee (each state's laws are different in this area). There can be no doubt that you must know what you are signing when signing your trust or an amendment to it. Most states' laws are very clear on this subject. The point is that signing a trust amendment does not require a great deal of time or effort, and it can be accomplished with few legal formalities.

No Adverse Lifetime Income Tax Consequences

There are no adverse income tax consequences associated with the use of a revocable living trust during your life. Because the trust is revocable, the income generated by the property that is in the name of the trust is taxed to you and is reported on your personal income tax returns.

Before 1981, a revocable living trust which generated income had its own federal identification number and income tax return. For 1981 and after, this procedure has been eliminated. The result is that all income generated by the property that is in the name of the revocable living trust requires little extra effort by its maker.

Probate Free

Property that is in a revocable living trust will not, on your death, go through the probate process. Probate is a process that passes title to assets. Since the title to your property is already in your trust and since the trust does not die with you, there is no passing of title required; title has already passed during your life. The probate process is not applicable to trust property.

Total avoidance of probate is an enormous benefit to you and your beneficiaries. It represents a significant savings in costs, time, and court interference with respect to your affairs. Mr. Dacey wrote his national best-seller on this single benefit. Funded revocable living trusts avoid the probate process.

Continuity in the Handling of Your Affairs

Because there is no probate associated with revocable living trust property, you can be assured that a smooth and uneventful transition will occur with respect to your affairs on your death. Your beneficiaries automatically begin to receive income and principal on your death pursuant to the terms written in your trust document. This fluidity with regard to your affairs is of major importance because it reduces cost and does not create unnecessary change or crisis in the lives of your survivors.

Planning Opportunities for Death Tax

There are a host of techniques available that are used to reduce federal estate taxes by professional estate planners. In the main, these techniques have traditionally been implemented by planners through the use of trusts created by the client's will (testamentary trusts). A significant percentage of estate-planning professionals have used, and continue to use, the will as the vehicle within which they plan to reduce federal estate taxes.

Remember, every technique of federal estate-tax savings that can be implemented in a will can also be implemented in a revocable living trust.

Good in Every State

Every state's laws recognize the validity of a revocable living trust. A truly beneficial feature attributed to these estate-planning instruments is that they can cross state lines with their makers without any need to redrafting their terms to comply with local law.

You may change your domicile; many people do. They move around the country with increasing regularity. Their moves are usually associated with career opportunities or a better place to live on retirement. With each move the question is generally asked, "Do I have to redo my estate plan?" If a revocable living trust has been used, the answer is no. The state law under which that trust was prepared will still be the law that is used with respect to its legal validity. Most well-written revocable living trusts provide that the law with respect to the administration of the trust will be the law of the state in which the maker and trust reside from time to time.

Revocable living trusts can cross state lines much more easily than their will counterparts. This flexibility gives you the security and knowledge that you will not have to redo your estate plan every time you are transferred or move to another state. Any time you do move to another state, however, you should have your estate plan reviewed by an estate planner in that state, because additional planning opportunities may be available to you with regard to your new state's law. Remember, each state has its own system with respect to its death taxes.

Measuring Trustees during Life

Most trust makers elect to be their own trustees during their lives. Many of our clients elect to be their own trustees and name their spouses or close family members or friends as co-trustees. The advantage of the co-trusteeship is that on the incapacity or death of the trust maker, the co-trustee can continue the operation of the trust without the need to seek court assistance.

You may elect, however, to name the persons or professional institutions who will be handling your trust after your death on a right-now, or living, basis. If you decide to name your death trustees on a right-now basis, you will be able to observe their performance and abilities as they manage the trust property for your benefit. By using a revocable living trust, you are able to measure the performance of your after-death trustees while you are alive.

Difficult for Disgruntled Heirs to Attack

Most of you are aware of the horror stories associated with unhappy heirs attacking the will of a maker who did not leave those unhappy folks what they thought they had coming. Attacking a will is called a "will contest" by attorneys. Will contests, unfortunately, do occur too frequently. Wills are usually contested by family members who were "cut out" or who received less than their anticipated fair share of the maker's property.

Revocable living trusts are much more difficult for disgruntled heirs to attack than are their will counterparts. Revocable living trusts are private documents that are not involved in the probate process. They are not placed in a public forum that encourages debate and advocacy, as are their will counterparts. They are not subject to all the legal formalities that are associated with wills. Because there are fewer legal rules with regard to their creation, there are fewer legal opportunities to invalidate them. Our experience has driven this point home most convincingly. Our firm has prepared several thousand revocable living trusts over the years, and to the best of our knowledge, not one has ever been attacked, much less attacked successfully.

Criticisms of Revocable Living Trusts

The revocable living trust has so many attractive features unique to it that we cannot understand why it is not used more frequently as a will substitute by more professionals. Many professionals are suspicious of it because they do not understand it. Other professionals are critical of it and allege the following negatives with regard to its use:

It is difficult to establish and maintain.

It is expensive.

Significant savings on after-death income tax are lost because of its use.

Revocable living trusts are not difficult to establish. A professional estate planner can create them, at times, more easily than their will counterparts.

In our experience, they are not difficult to maintain. It is true that if you do create a revocable living trust, you will have to take time to organize your affairs and keep them organized within your trust's parameters. We believe that this is a positive feature that should encourage their use. Remember, what you do not do while alive, the probate court and your beneficiaries must do after you are gone. Please reread Chapter 8, "Probate," if you doubt our conclusion.

In our experience, revocable living trusts can cost more to create than their will counterparts. The increase in cost is due to an increase in work that is required of the planning professionals. When an attorney draws a will, that is all that is done, which is only a small part of the total estate-planning job. The attorney will finish that job when the will is taken through the probate process.

The attorney who utilizes a revocable living trust as an estate-planning vehicle has one fee. That fee is for both drafting the document and funding the document so there will be no probate process. Common sense and our experience would indicate a huge difference in cost. Generally, the fee for a will coupled with the cost of probate is enormous when compared to the cost of preparing and funding a revocable living trust.

Prior to TRA 1986, critics of the revocable living trust charged that its use reduced income tax planning opportunities after death. This criticism had some validity. When will planning is used, the income generated by the deceased person's property is taxed in the estate at the estate's income tax bracket. However, if that income is distributed to the beneficiaries, it is taxed in the beneficiaries' tax brackets. If the estate is in a lower income tax bracket than that of the beneficiaries, an income tax saving can result.

Revocable living trust income, both under prior law and under TRA 1986, not distributed to the beneficiaries of the trust will be taxed to the trust in its income tax bracket. Ultimately, however, because of a technical concept professionals call "throw-back rules," that income will be taxed to the trust beneficiaries in their income tax brackets. Probate estate income that is not currently distributed will be taxed at the estate's income tax bracket and is not subject to these technical throw-back rules. Thus an estate has an extra income tax bracket.

Under the Revenue Reconciliation Act of 1990, for tax years beginning in 1991 both estates and trusts are taxed at 15 percent, the lowest bracket, for the first $3,300 of income. Income between $3,300 and $9,900 is taxed at 28 percent, and for income over $9,900 the rate is 31 percent. The minimum and maximum amounts in each tax bracket are adjusted each year for inflation, beginning in 1991. Because of the small amount of income subject to the 15 percent rate and the 28 percent rate, the advantage of having some income taxed in the estate's income tax bracket is extremely small. Compared to the costs of probate, this potential tax savings is simply not relevant in most situations.

TRA 1986 gave some additional, but incidental, advantages to estates. These have to do with the tax year allowed and the estimated payment of income taxes. These provisions, which do discriminate in favor of probate estates, are also mostly window dressing and do not offer any real income tax advantages to estates, especially when to get them an estate must go through probate.

It is our belief that a revocable living trust should be used as a will substitute whenever *any* of its benefits are desired; the size of one's estate should not dictate its use. The revocable living trust should be used in the planning of most estates, regardless of their complexity.

Benefits of Revocable Living Trusts

Distribute property after your death

Create one receptacle for all your property

Take care of you

Offer privacy

Easy to create and maintain

Easily changed

No adverse lifetime income tax consequences

Probate free

Continuity in your affairs

Planning for death tax

Good in every state

Can measure trustees during your life

Difficult to attack

18

Funding a Revocable Living Trust

"Placing All Your Eggs in One Basket"

A revocable living trust can be unfunded, partially funded, or totally funded during the lifetime of its maker; it can also be funded on its maker's death. When estate-planning professionals refer to "funding," they are referring to property that has actually been placed in a living trust.

The advantages that result from funding a revocable living trust during the lifetime of the maker are profound:

Property that is in a revocable living trust does not go through the probate process on the death of the trust maker.

Property that is in a revocable living trust can be used to care for the trust maker and loved ones in the event of the trust maker's incapacity, without the intervention and control of a court.

To understand the funded revocable living trust, it is important to contrast it with its unfunded counterpart.

The Unfunded Revocable Living Trust

An unfunded revocable living trust is also referred to as an unfunded life insurance trust. It gets this nickname because there is no property placed in the trust when it is created except the *right* of the trust to receive the death proceeds of life insurance on the life of the trust maker. The trust is funded with only the expectancy of receiving those insurance proceeds. The expectancy of receiving insurance proceeds legally funds the revocable living trust in many states even though, in reality, nothing is in the trust at all.

In those states that require something more than a mere expectancy to establish the trust, professionals generally instruct their clients to place a nominal amount of cash in the trust, such as $10.

Either technique or both techniques used together still result in an unfunded living trust. Why do we go through this process? Because a trust must have some type of property to be valid for state law purposes. Both these techniques can do the job.

Advocates of the unfunded revocable living trust make the following points in defense of its use:

The trust can receive all life insurance proceeds as well as all other third-party beneficiary contract property. These include pension and profit sharing proceeds paid on the death of the maker.

The revocable living trust can be funded at a later time if the trust maker gives a "durable special power of attorney" to others. Durable special powers of attorney are discussed later in this chapter.

Since very few deaths result from accidental causes, most trust makers can generally predict or have notice of their impending demise, and as a result, trust makers can fund their trusts at that time.

In addition, a pour-over will can transfer property into the trust after the death of the trust maker.

There can be no doubt that an unfunded revocable living trust is far better than its will counterpart; however, when it is contrasted with its funded counterpart, it leaves much to be desired.

The problems usually associated with unfunded living trusts are as follows:

Some states do not recognize durable special powers of attorney. If a trust maker resides in such a state and becomes incapacitated, the property cannot be placed in the trust without costly and public court proceedings. In fact, there is no guarantee that the property will be placed in the trust at all.

If the trust maker dies accidentally or unexpectedly, the property will have to go through the probate process before it can ultimately end up in the trust. Thus a pour-over will guarantees probate on the assets it passes to the unfunded trust.

Funded Revocable Living Trusts

A funded revocable living trust, as its name implies, is a revocable living trust which has within it property owned by the maker. If you are wondering, "How can the trust have the property when the trust maker still owns it?" you are asking a very good question. The answer is that the property is titled in the trust's name; but the maker owns the right to use, possess, and enjoy the property. The maker owns the trust and is the beneficiary of the trust and, therefore, really owns the property.

Another way to explain this legal phenomenon is that the trust maker owns equitable title and the trust owns bare legal title. Equitable title is greater than legal title. Regardless of the explanation used, a revocable living trust that is properly funded leaves the ownership and control of the trust property in the hands of its maker.

Funded revocable living trusts have these advantages:

All property in the trust totally avoids the probate process on the death of its maker.

The trust assets are instantly available to the maker's beneficiaries pursuant to written instructions.

Should the maker become incapacitated or be adjudicated mentally incompetent, the trust property can be used to care for the trust maker and loved ones without the delays, expenses, and publicity associated with court proceedings.

Funded revocable living trusts take the guesswork out of probate avoidance and avoid the Groucho Marx problem. By funding a revocable living trust, the maker can be assured that the trust is being used for its highest and best use.

Estate-planning professionals use different techniques to fund revocable living trusts, but generally there are two major approaches:

Retitling all the trust maker's property in the name of the trust, for example, "Karen Smith as Trustee of the Karen Smith Trust."

Retitling all the trust maker's property in the name of an entity, called a "nominee partnership," which is a holding device for the trust.

Titling Property Directly in the Trust

In order to place property directly in the name of a trust, the property must be retitled in the name of the trustees of that trust, such as "Karen Smith as Trustee of the Karen Smith Trust." This form of trust funding certainly appears simple and, to most people, is very understandable. It does, however, create problems, some of which are:

> If real estate is transferred directly into the name of the trust, the entire trust agreement may have to be recorded under the laws of some states. This recording requirement can abrogate the privacy feature of the trust. Because of the growing acceptance of trusts, these filing requirements are becoming much less stringent. There are several alternatives available that avoid the necessity to record the full trust document.

> Publicly traded stocks and bonds that are titled directly in the name of a trust sometimes present logistical problems. When the stock or bond is sold, the transfer agent may require that it be provided with a complete and certified copy of the trust. The privacy feature of the trust can then be lost. Just as in real estate, there is much less likelihood of this happening today than even a few short years ago. Generally, only certain provisions of the trust will have to be disclosed, none of which deal with how the trust assets are ultimately to be disposed of.

> Safe-deposit boxes taken directly in the name of the trust present the same problem; a complete, certified copy of the trust may have to be kept on file in the institution where the box is located. This obstacle usually can be overcome by giving successor trustees signature authority on the box.

Titling property directly in the name of a trust can present some problems when the trust maker attempts to dispose of trust property. It is easy to put property directly in the name of a trust, but may be somewhat more difficult to get that property out of the trust. Some of those people with whom the trustees deal with regard to the trust property will want to assure themselves that the trustees do indeed have the right to dispose of the property.

People who deal with trustees may get sweaty palms because without a complete review of the trust document, they can never be sure that the trustee has the power to properly pass titles to the trust property. Most trusts are written in legal jargon, and that means that the wary buyer or transfer agent may want the services of an attorney prior to completing any transaction involving trust property.

One technique that is being used to reduce or eliminate problems associated with titling property directly in the trust is called an Affidavit of Trust or a Trust Certification. This is a short document signed by the trustees, and sometimes signed by the attorney who prepared the trust, that states the trust is in existence and that the trustees have the power to transact business on behalf of the trust. Certain provisions of the trust document are attached to the Affidavit or Certification including who the trustees are, their powers, and the signature pages of the trust itself.

In some communities, it may be more difficult to do business with assets that are titled in the trust name than it is in other communities. This should not deter most people from titling property directly in the names of their trusts. More and more, dealing with trusts and trustees is becoming familiar in the business world. If problems are encountered, there are usually alternate methods of funding that are effective and less likely to cause problems.

Using the Nominee Partnership to Fund the Trust

This is a method that we recommend to many of our clients in order to facilitate funding their trusts. It is a method which is easily accomplished and which facilitates commerce as trust makers buy and sell property during their lifetimes. It protects the privacy of the trust document and results in little additional expense to the trust maker or trustees. Most corporate fiduciaries have used this technique for years in dealing with property in their various trust accounts. Its simplicity in expediting the buying and selling of trust assets both within the home state and across state lines has facilitated its use.

The concept of a nominee partnership is simple: rather than put the assets directly in the trust's name, they are put in a holding vehicle created expressly for dealing with trust property. This holding vehicle is called a nominee partnership. The partnership holds bare legal title to the assets for the trustees of the trust. The nominee partnership generally does not own any property in its own right. Its terms provide that the partners deal with the trust property to expedite the buying and selling of trust assets.

The partners of the nominee partnership are totally responsible to the trustees and are usually the trustees. In fact, the partners of the nominee partnership and the trustees enter into a short agreement that makes it clear that the trust is the owner of the property and that the partners must abide by the trust's terms. Following is an example which will assist you in understanding this device:

Bill Wagner makes a trust. Bill and his wife Diana are the trustees. Bill and Diana Wagner are also partners in Bill and Diana Company, a nominee partnership. Bill funds his trust by retitling all his assets in the name of Bill and Diana Company. Bill and Diana, as partners in Bill and Diana Company, report to Bill and Diana, as trustees of Bill's trust. Bill and Diana, as trustees of Bill's trust, report to Bill, the maker of the trust. What a paper tiger!

But look what happened: Bill, as a partner in Bill and Diana Company, can buy and sell assets without saying, "Look at us, we're trustees."

Under our example, the fact that Bill is buying and selling property as a partner in Bill and Diana Company, a nominee for the Bill Wagner Trust, is of major consequence. Buyers and sellers are used to doing business with partners of partnerships; they are not used to doing business with trustees.

The benefits of a nominee partnership can be summarized as follows:

Trust documents stay private because the only document that needs to be recorded is the partnership agreement or a substitute agreement called a "trade-name affidavit." It is generally short and does not divulge any private matters.

Property can be bought and sold for the trust in the partnership name without buyers, sellers, and transfer agents getting sweaty palms.

Subsequent to the death of the trust maker, successor trustees can become successor partners so that the buying and selling of trust property will continue to be commercially expedient.

Nominee partnerships provide an excellent solution to the trust-funding problem. The only thing that a trust maker who uses this technique will have to learn to do is to sign his name "Bill Wagner, Partner," instead of "Bill Wagner, Owner." In terms of the world, Bill and Diana Company, a partnership, owns the property. In reality, Bill Wagner owns the property.

As we discussed in our previous chapter, there are no income tax consequences with respect to the use of a revocable living trust. If the nominee partnership method of funding is used, the partnership simply files an information tax return that says, in essence, "See Bill Wagner's tax return." This practice presents no problems. In our experience, the Internal Revenue Service does not raise an eyebrow when presented with these returns. It understands them and sees them frequently.

Other Methods of Funding a Trust

In some states, estate-planning professionals have additional techniques available to them to fund a revocable living trust. These techniques are generally used in addition to the nominee partnership and are used on a frequent basis. They are as follows.

Durable Special Powers of Attorney

A trust maker can give others the power to place the maker's assets into the maker's living trust. This power is given by using a durable special power of attorney. Unlike most powers of attorney, a durable special power of attorney continues even if the maker is incapacitated because of illness or injury. The durable power of attorney is "special" because it limits the power to this single function.

Unrecorded Deeds

In using this technique, the trust maker deeds real estate to the trustee or successor trustee of the trust, but the deed is not recorded until after the death of the trust maker. If the trust maker disposes of the deeded property during lifetime, the unrecorded deed is reclaimed and destroyed. If the trustee at death is a bank or nominee, the existence of the trust does not have to be revealed for title to the deeded property to pass to the trust. Some states have title standards specifically creating presumptions in favor of the validity of such transfers. The disadvantage of this form of funding is that it may be argued that no effective transfer took place when the deed was signed; however, if the trust maker's heirs and unsecured creditors are adequately provided for, it is unlikely that anyone would raise an objection. This is an excellent funding technique that can be used in those states that allow it.

After-Death (Postmortem) Assignments

Most of the Uniform Probate Code states provide that almost all property interests, with the exception of real estate, can be assigned by an owner to a revocable living trust but that the transfer will not take effect until after the owner's death. This technique, where permitted, allows a property owner to retain the use and control of property during lifetime and pass that property automatically to a revocable living trust on death. These assignments are not made public.

From a practical perspective, publicly traded stocks and bonds are not conducive to this technique. The New York Stock Transfer Association does not and will not apparently recognize this approach under its rules. As a result, individual stock transfer agents will not transfer the stock or bond that was assigned by use of this technique. The Stock Transfer Association is, in effect, ignoring the laws of those states that do allow this technique. We believe that the New York Stock Transfer Association should change its rules, but until it does, we recommend that our clients put their publicly traded stocks and bonds in a nominee partnership.

Postmortem assignments, where allowed, are extremely effective in transferring closely held (private company) stock certificates and partnership interests into a property owner's revocable living trust.

POD designations

Generally, Uniform Probate Code states allow the use of payable-on-death (POD) designations with respect to savings accounts, checking accounts, and certificates of deposit. In creating such an account, the owner simply designates a revocable living trust as the entity that will receive the account proceeds on death. When the owner dies, the account proceeds pass automatically to the trust without the intervention of the probate court.

Funding a revocable living trust is an important aspect of the estate-planning process. As you can see, there are many techniques available to fund your trust.

19
Trustees

"Modern Superagents"

The trust relationship necessitates three types of players: a trust maker; trust beneficiaries; and the person who runs the trust, the trustee.

A good synonym for trustee would be agent or, better yet, superagent. Our law refers to superagents as fiduciaries. The word "fiduciary" is used interchangeably with "trustee." Trustee is a word meaning "a person who runs a trust." Fiduciary comes from Roman law and means a person who has the same duties and responsibilities as a trustee.

Trustees in General

When a trustee is named, that trustee is given, both by the maker and by operation of law, massive rights and powers to be exercised on behalf of the trust's beneficiaries.

Trustees can be either individuals or properly licensed state and federal institutions. Individual trustees are usually family members, friends, or advisers of the trust maker. Institutional trustees are either trust companies or trust departments of commercial banks. Institutional trustees are often referred to as corporate fiduciaries.

Trustees, whether individual or institutional, must act in a fiduciary capacity. When acting in that capacity, trustees have the ultimate duty imposed by law as to relationships between people. When trustees make mistakes, and those mistakes are proven, they are liable to the beneficiaries for those mistakes. For a long time trustees' actions and liability for their actions have been measured by what attorneys refer to as the "reasonable-person rule." This rule asks the question, "Would a similar, reasonably prudent person acting in the same capacity, in the same or similar circumstances, have made the same judgment?" If the answer is no, trustees will be liable for the consequences of their actions.

The trend today, evidenced by both court decisions and legislative mandate, is to apply even tougher standards in the measurement of trustees' actions. In effect, the prudent-person rule is quickly becoming the prudent-expert rule. Clearly, a prudent expert makes no mistakes — or so it would seem. Philosophically, we take no position as to this trend. To know it exists and is being amplified is enough.

Becoming or naming a trustee is serious business. Trustees are fiduciaries; fiduciaries are superagents; and superagents are superliable for acts or failures to act that are not superbeneficial to beneficiaries.

Knowledge of the trustees' role and consequences of poor performance in that role should dissuade kind, but ill-prepared folks from acting as trustees. One does not accommodate a family member, friend, or client by accepting a trusteeship without opening his or her eyes about what a trustee is and does. If you have volunteered to be a trustee, please reexamine your decision.

The trustees' role can be a confusing one. Trustees are totally responsible for expert performance and judgment while following the written instructions of a trust maker for the benefit of that maker's beneficiaries. Trustees are responsible, as experts, for the preservation of the maker's property (principal), its growth with respect to income and capital appreciation, and its application to the beneficiaries.

People create relationships. Each relationship requires different expectations, duties, and results. Most relationships are not fiduciary relationships. They are business or personal relationships. Laws have been created to govern these relationships, and all of them fall short of the excellence required under fiduciary law.

In terms of practicality, however, trustees have only two major responsibilities: (1) they have an absolute mandate, by operation of law, to follow precisely the written instructions of a trust maker and (2) trustees have absolute responsibility to read between the lines and make judgment calls where there is no clear-cut alternative — and to be right in both. If trustees are called upon to make decisions which are too tough for them, they will ask a court to assist them. This is particularly true in a controversial environment.

Most clients view the trustees' role as primarily financial. After all, trustees are financial advisers, but not all trustees' decisions are financial. People decisions may affect financial decisions; thus our superagent needs to be supersensitive, indeed.

It is difficult to find competent and willing trustees on both a personal and an institutional basis because trustees must work superhard and are always held superaccountable for their actions.

In discussing the selection of an appropriate trustee with our clients, concerns center in the area of the trustee's knowledge of their families' affairs, investment performance, and the empathy that will potentially be accorded their beneficiaries.

A trustee's knowledge of the affairs of most trust makers is usually deficient. Our experience would suggest that people carry most of their affairs in their heads. Most spouses and children know too little about the family's economic affairs. We believe that you should fully brief your loved ones as to your financial affairs where possible and start now to communicate your affairs to your ultimate trustee.

As to investment performance, we often hear, "He's no good, he can't even handle his own money," or, "She's made a bundle for herself; she'll do all right for me." "What rate of return can he get?" "How effective will he be in making my principal grow?" "What guarantees do I get?" The answers to these questions are difficult.

Trustees cannot speculate with principal or the income it generates. This does not mean that assets cannot be sold or traded, nor does it mean that trustees cannot invest in assets which may go down in value, such as real estate, stocks, bonds, etc. It does mean that trustees must invest in proven investment areas on a conservative and cautious basis. It also means that they diversify, using good judgment in all cases, or not diversify if the assets they are given are profitable on a proven basis. It does mean that they must exercise prudent judgment.

Trustees should not knowingly (if they are aware of their liability) attempt to achieve a return predicated on speculative investment. Trustee speculators are liable for their losses. Speculation with regard to one's own funds may be all right; if losses are incurred, they may be earned back through labor and industry. If trustees speculate and lose, that is *not* all right; if trustees cannot pay it back, it probably cannot be replaced.

The trustees' investment approach should always be cautious. It should be prudent and relatively risk-free. There is little room for speculation in the trustees' portfolio.

Conversely, trustees have been known, on an all-too-frequent basis, to be too conservative in their investment strategies. The investment of funds at a below-market yield, both in terms of income and capital appreciation, can result in trustees being liable for lost opportunities. Safe investment is not necessarily "prudent" investment.

The accountability of trustees as to the empathy shown to beneficiaries is difficult to ascertain and difficult to measure. Regardless of whether individual or institutional trustees are selected, there are no guarantees that sound overall performance will result or that the beneficiaries will be satisfied with the trustees.

The point you should remember is that trustees have awesome power, accountability, and liability all wrapped together in their role as superagents.

Institutional Trustees

Now that we have discussed trustees in general, let's take a closer look at the role of the institutional trustee. Institutional trustees, often called corporate fiduciaries, fall into two separate categories: the full-time trust company and the trust department or trust division of a commercial bank.

Both the full-time trust company and the trust division of a commercial bank do precisely the same thing. They function as professional trustees. To discuss one is to discuss the other. How can they be the same if one is a separate professional trust company and the other is just part of a bank? The answer is fairly simple.

Originally, banks were banks, and trust companies were trust companies. Both existed side by side. Commercial banks accepted depositors' money and lent the majority of that money back to the public. Trust companies have historically managed trust assets for a fee.

They were separate entities, both serving the public in a different way. Each had its own building, ownership, and board of directors; each served the same local population.

A trend developed that resulted in the merging of the two institutions. The opportunity was taken to consolidate and reduce the overhead of the surviving institution and provide full-service banking.

This has been the trend for many years. Look around you. Many banks still have the title "and Trust Company" at the end of their names. At some point in time they acquired or created a trust company and brought it within the umbrella of the concept of "full-service bank."

Today, however, there are still trust companies which have elected not to merge or be acquired by a commercial bank. Nevertheless, trust companies and bank trust departments function the same way.

The first question every client asks when we discuss the institutional trustee is, "Does the bank lend my trust funds to bank customers?" The answer is, "Absolutely not." That is a bank function conducted with the money of the bank's commercial depositors. It does not occur with trust assets.

The trust division of the typical commercial bank is an entirely separate entity. Literally it is the successor of that historical trust company. Within a bank's trust division, assets are managed for beneficiaries of individual trusts.

An interesting note with regard to this dual relationship (bank and trust company) is that the commercial sector of the bank is 100 percent liable in terms of the fiduciary liability of their trust division. On the other hand, individual trusts are never liable for the acts or omissions of the bank with respect to the bank's banking function. This means that if the trust division makes a mistake, the beneficiaries *can* go against all the bank's assets. On the other hand, if the commercial sector of the bank makes a mistake, the bank's creditors *cannot* go against individual trust assets.

The institutional or corporate fiduciary is basically no different than any other trustee. It has the same duties, the same responsibilities, and the same opportunities to fail or succeed like any other trustee. As a practical consideration, however, it should be noted that the corporate fiduciary appears to have a *higher* duty or standard of care in administering and investing trust assets than a personal trustee. A judge or jury is more likely to measure the prudent-person standard on a tougher basis against the professional fiduciary than against a personal, nonprofessional trustee.

Trust divisions or companies are basically organized into distinct and separate areas.

The first we will call the administrative section. It contains the trust department's handholders, the people who work directly with the beneficiaries to accomplish their goals and objectives as well as those set forth by the maker of the trust. These men and women are usually attorneys, although there are many excellent trust officers who are not. They are people who tend to be public relations—oriented and who are extremely patient with beneficiaries.

In addition, most trust departments have an investment area. The people in this area assist the handholders in fulfilling investment objectives. They are usually trained in the investment of stocks and bonds.

Many trust departments are large enough to have an additional investment function called the real estate area. The individuals in this section obviously specialize in the purchasing and selling of real estate to meet investment objectives.

Apart from the account management and investment functions, most trust entities have a taxation section. The function of this area, as its name implies, is to consider all tax ramifications of investment decisions. Any time an asset is purchased or sold, the tax implications of the transaction should be analyzed.

Depending upon the sophistication of the institution in question, ad-

ditional services may be available to assist beneficiaries. Figure 19-1 illustrates a typical bank's organization.

When looking at these functions, administration, investment, and tax,
one may wonder how anything gets done. The answer is that all final
decisions are made by committee. Corporate fiduciaries work almost exclusively through the committee approach to problem solving. The advocates of this approach say every decision is examined and reexam-
ined, questioned and requestioned, before it is made. This process,
although lengthy, is supposed to be in the best interests of the beneficiaries. Conceptually, it should make for little or no error.

The opponents of institutional trustees cite this committee approach
as the horse-and-camel approach (the committee that decided to design
the horse and ended up with a camel instead). The criticism may or may
not be fair, depending on the institution and the types of decisions to be
made.

A sound critique of institutional trustees would attack their speed and
timeliness, not necessarily their ultimate conclusions.

One of the claims made by most financial institutions offering trust
services is that they provide *professional* advice. Opponents of institu-

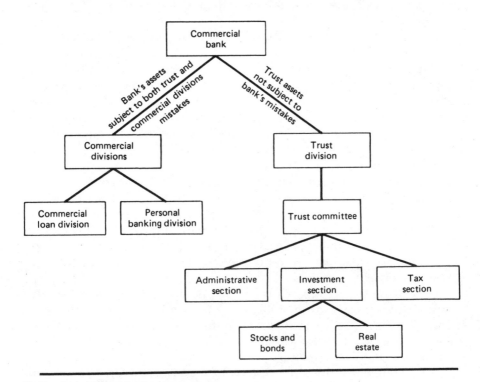

Figure 19-1. Typical bank organization.

tional trustees state that this is so much baloney. What they provide is nothing but cautious investment in stocks and bonds. Regardless of what assets are left in trust, these critics assert it will not be long before the institution will have sold the original assets and invested all the proceeds in a stock-and-bond portfolio. Critics also attack, with frequent justification, the investment abilities of these institutions.

These traditional claims may have some validity, although in the great bull market of the 1980s this complaint seemed to have disappeared. Even in the uncertainty of the 1990s banking climate, it appears that these institutions continue to hold their own. Financial institutions offering trust services have primarily centered their investment portfolios in stocks and bonds. They have done this in one of two ways. They either purchase stocks and bonds especially suited to a particular trust's objectives and held exclusively for that account or purchase and hold stocks and bonds through common trust funds. These are funds created within the trust department to meet broad-range investment objectives. These funds may be equity funds (funds that are supposed to grow over the years by way of capital appreciation) or they can be fixed-income funds (funds invested to provide current income). Another common trust fund that is frequently used is a tax-free fund. This fund is invested in securities, primarily municipal bonds, which will produce tax-free income.

By creating common trust funds, institutional trustees have attempted to offer diversification and lower management costs for many of their trusts that have common investment objectives.

Since one trust may be able to own relatively few securities due to the size of its principal, that principal can be pooled with the principal of other trusts by using a common trust fund. Each trust owns units in a common pool or fund which will own a diversified portfolio of stocks or bonds. This, proponents of professional trustees claim, provides a benefit for individual trusts at no additional fee and provides sound diversification.

Opponents of professional trustees assert that these common trust funds, as well as directly invested accounts, are nothing more than studies in carefully planned mediocrity—that, in fact, all investments are made in the same static pool of stocks and bonds selected by the institutions. Opponents claim that trust department employees are underpaid and that their collective investment decisions generally result in substandard performance.

Without taking sides, let us examine the real reasons for using a corporate fiduciary. First, and foremost, a corporate fiduciary is generally always collectible. Since a corporate fiduciary is backed by the entire institution's resources, if a mistake is made, there is a good likelihood that recovery will be made. This can be very comforting. If the institutional trustee makes a mistake, you can, with some security, rest assured that if proven wrong, the institution will return that which was lost as a result of its error. Most *do* have money. Also, keep in mind that the money which is being returned is not coming from other trusts but from that institution's shareholders.

Another reason that a corporate fiduciary is often selected is that it will not die or become mentally incompetent, sick, or senile. It is there day after day, year after year. The institution generally does not change. This is an important attribute of the institutional trustee.

Talk to the opponents of corporate fiduciaries, and you will find they believe most, if not all, corporate fiduciaries have a high turnover rate among their personnel. Opponents claim there is no continuity in the management of a trust account because of the high turnover and that turnover is high because institutions pay too little. Institutional trustees have been accused of underpaying talented people, which, in effect, makes them training grounds for talented youngsters and havens for others less blessed.

There is more than a little truth on both sides. The important thing to keep in mind is this: a trust instrument names the *institution* as trustee, *not* its employees. It is the institution which can boast when a good job has been done, and it is the institution which will pay if it is proven in error. Collectibility is of massive importance. That, in our opinion, is the ultimate justification for naming an institutional trustee.

Another factor emphasized by proponents of institutional trustees is that institutions are capable of objective, third-party decision making.

There is another side to this coin. Opponents of institutional trustees argue that third-party institutional objectivity does not exist. They claim that decisions are usually made by one or two employees who do not really care about the beneficiaries. Critics claim that relationships are distant at best and accountability for poor results is relatively nonexistent.

Institutional versus Individual Trustees

How do institutional trustees measure up against individual trustees? Before discussing this question, we would first like to outline the pros and cons of personal trustees.

Personal trustees are people. They have all the human strengths and weaknesses we all have. A personal trustee can be you or others you are close to. Tables 19-1 and 19-2 outline pros and cons attributed to different types of personal and institutional trustees.

These outlines of the relative pros and cons of individual trustees are

Table 19-1
Personal Trustees

Pros	Cons
FAMILY MEMBERS	
Family knowledge:	Indecisive and insecure
Personal	No track record or experience
Investment	Too emotionally involved
Business	Unskilled at business
Empathy, loving	People prejudiced
Bright	Uncollectible as to mistakes
Good common sense	
Personally involved	
FRIEND OR BUSINESS ASSOCIATE	
Family knowledge:	Human:
Personal	May embezzle
Investment	Speculate poorly
Business	Die
Empathy	Not enough time—a burden
Good business person	May play favorites
Good investor personally	Probably not collectible
Good common sense	
Tough, honest, hardworking	
PROFESSIONAL ADVISERS **(Attorney, CPA, Investment Adviser)**	
Family knowledge:	Human:
Personal	May embezzle
Investment	Speculate
Business	Be too conservative
Tough, honest, hardworking	Die
Trained professional	Not enough time
	May not be collectible
	Conflicts of interest
	Limited investment knowledge

Table 19-2
The Institutional Trustee

Pros	Cons
Professional	Dispassionate
Experienced	Ignorant of family affairs
Established track record	Poor investment performance
Collectible	High turnover among staff
Will always be there	Hard to reach
Not emotionally involved	Too conservative
Objective	Slow to act
Regulated	

obviously not all-inclusive. We are sure that you can add to each and encourage you to do so. Our outlines contain the essence of what clients and professionals have communicated to us about individual trustees over the years. You should contrast the pros and cons of an individual trustee with the pros and cons of an institutional trustee.

Practical Advice on Your Trustees

Our advice is that you should not pick a single trustee, whether an individual or an institution. Create combinations of trustees in your trust and provide a pattern for trustee succession. Planning for trustee succession involves stating what trustees you want to take over in the event previous trustees quit, die, or are fired. Providing for trustee succession is good business. It can provide for the use of personal and institutional trustees.

In your trust document, always spell out who has the authority to terminate a trustee. Trustees who are not doing the job to the satisfaction of the beneficiaries should be terminated. Many trusts we have reviewed do not provide for trustee termination. We believe this is a mistake. Poorly performing trustees who continue as trustees are a burden to beneficiaries. They are not easy to get rid of unless the document provides for their termination.

To remove a trustee without termination rights in the trust itself requires review and approval by a court of law. Generally, that court is the probate court. In our experience, using the court as a planning alternative is poor planning. There is no guarantee the court will agree with the unhappy beneficiaries. The legal process can be slow, expensive, and disappointing in the results it reaches.

The trust maker should always set forth those beneficiaries who may exercise the right to terminate trustees. For example, the termination rights may be given as follows:

> My spouse can fire the trustee at any time for any reason. After my spouse's death, a majority of the children may do so. If they are minors, then their guardian or a majority of their guardians can so fire the trustee.

Another might say:

> My spouse and my sister, if they agree, can fire the trustee at any time for any reason. If either dies, then the survivor along with my attorney can fire any trustee. If everyone is deceased, then a majority of my living beneficiaries can fire the trustee.

The important point to understand is that you should communicate your list of those individuals, in succession, who are to have the power to fire the trustee at any time and see that your instructions are placed in your trust.

Another major, and in our opinion mandatory, planning tool is for you to set forth whom you want to take over as trustee when a trustee is fired, quits, or dies. For example:

> If my sister is fired, quits, or dies, she shall be replaced by my friend, Fred. Likewise, if Fred is fired, quits, or dies, then First National Bank.

You can also provide for the appointment of trustees by giving others the right to select those trustees. For example:

> If my spouse quits or dies, my attorney, Ellen, may select a new trustee, either personal or corporate, but my attorney is not to serve as trustee. Should Ellen not be living, a majority of my children may select a trustee to replace my spouse, as long as their choice is made among institutional trustees with a capital and surplus of not less than $5 million.

There is no limit to the personal and creative choices you may make; just make sure that you think your choices out and see to it that your estate planner accomplishes your goals in this area.

When naming trustees for your trust, a good general rule is not to name your spouse as *sole* trustee. Give your spouse some help. If you desire, name an adult child of yours or, if you prefer, all your adult children. Perhaps you are close to another family member, business associate, or adviser. If you are, and feel good about it, name one or more as trustee with your spouse; just remember to provide for their termination and replacement.

If your planning situation dictates that there are no personal trustee candidates to assist your spouse, select an institutional trustee. There is nothing wrong with naming an institution as co-trustee with your spouse. In fact, our experience suggests that some clients prefer this approach. If you use this approach, always give your spouse the power to fire the institution and replace it according to your instructions.

You might want to combine the strengths of a personal trustee with the strengths of an institutional trustee. You may get the best of both worlds. You should choose your trustees based on your beliefs, prejudices, and particular situation.

Trustees' Fees

"Does a trustee get paid?" "How much do they charge?" These are questions clients commonly ask. Trustees are compensated. That there is no such thing as a free lunch applies in the trust business too.

Historically, trustees, especially professional trustees, charged an annual fee calculated on a percentage of the income earned by the trust property over the course of a year. This method is rarely used today.

Today most, if not all, institutional trustees charge and are paid pursuant to published fee schedules. These fee schedules generally are a percentage of the dollar value of the assets managed by the trustee. They are published to avoid any confusion that might otherwise arise between the trustee and the beneficiaries. The value that trustees apply their percentage fees to is the fair market value of the trust property as determined by the trustee. Institutional trustees almost always have a minimum fee that will be charged regardless of the value of the trust property. This minimum fee is not based on a percentage of the assets, but is a fixed amount.

Each institution, although independent, closely follows the fee structure of its competitors. Competition in the marketplace dictates this.

Institutional trustees generally apply their percentage fees on a sliding scale of asset value; for example, 1 percent on the first $100,000, ¾ of 1 percent on the next $400,000, and ½ of 1 percent on the balance. It is common in the institutional fiduciary world to reduce the fee as the value of the trust assets increases in size.

Institutional trustees vary in the amounts they charge if extraordinary management services are provided. For example, managing a closely held business interest may necessitate a special or negotiated fee.

Many institutional trustees do not publish special fees for special property in their fee schedules.

Our review of several published fee schedules would suggest:

Fee schedules are all pretty much the same. Shopping for trustees' fees may not be very productive.

Most, if not all, have a minimum fee.

Most use the percentage-of-value approach.

Most have sliding scales rather than escalating schedules.

The larger the institution, the more likely it is to charge differently for extraordinary services.

Many have termination fees.

The last entry in our synopsis suggests that many institutions charge termination fees; that is, they have language in their fee schedules setting forth additional charges which will be levied against the trust assets if the institution is fired or quits. These additional charges can involve hourly billing, percentage billing, or flat-fee billing to cover the costs of terminating the trust.

We strongly disagree with the institutional practice of charging termination fees. We do not accept the institutional arguments offered in their defense. If the trust is run properly, a great deal of time should not be required to turn over trust assets and records to another trustee. The time that is involved should be minimal and, in most cases, should have been covered by the ongoing fee.

Termination charges become a rear-end load. They might dissuade unhappy beneficiaries from terminating the trustee, but usually only result in bitter feelings, fee disputes, and arguments. These charges should be discussed with the institution from the outset and eliminated if at all possible.

On the other hand, we believe that most institutional trustees do not charge enough. Most fee schedules hover around 1 percent. That is not significant when compared with the trustees' duties and responsibilities.

We would prefer that institutional trustees raise their fees if that would result in increased competence, investment results, and service to those of our clients who have elected to name them as their trustee. Bluntly, we believe that institutional trustees do not charge enough to enable them to render the expert advice expected of them. It is difficult to provide top-notch advice without spending top-notch dollars on top-notch people.

Many of our clients question the fees of institutional trustees. Clients are too shrewd to believe that in the commercial marketplace they get a lot for little cost. Low rates generate suspicion as to promised results. There are, however, some institutions that are well operated and provide sound investment results. They provide one of the great bargains still around.

Personal or individual trustees are not sophisticated in the manner in which they charge fees. Many negotiate their fees. Many provide their services on a gratuitous or quasi-gratuitous basis. Some overcharge; but most do not charge enough.

Some states set fee schedules in their laws. Many trustees' fees are set by the court having jurisdiction over trusts. These courts are generally, but not always, probate courts. Fee disputes are ultimately settled by the judge of that court.

Trustees' fees are not, in general, a major concern to most of our clients. A trustee's performance is the major concern of all of our clients. Knowledge of trustees' fees, how they work, and what they are will assist you in selecting your trustees.

20
Getting Property to Minors

"Little Ones Are Tough to Give To"

If ever an estate-planning professional were to make a generalized statement, it would be, "Most people want their property to end up ultimately in the hands of their children and grandchildren."

Almost every simple will we have reviewed over the years has said, "I leave my property to my spouse. If my spouse does not survive me, I leave it equally to my children. If a child of mine dies leaving children, I want his or her share to go to his or her children, my grandchildren."

Almost every life insurance contract we have reviewed has named beneficiaries precisely like the simple will does: to a spouse, children, and grandchildren, in that order.

The purpose of this chapter is to discuss the problems associated with giving or leaving property to minor children and grandchildren. Under our system of laws, getting your property to minor beneficiaries is not easy.

Most states' laws define minors as persons who have not attained the age of twenty-one years. Some states have lowered that magic age to eighteen years.

Can you make an outright gift of property to your minor children or grandchildren? The answer is yes and no: yes, in that you can do anything you want; no, unless you follow the legal formalities that are associated under your state's law with the making of that gift. Under most states' laws, in order to make a gift of more than a nominal amount to a minor, you must do the following.

Set Up a Uniform Gifts to Minors
Act Account

These accounts are generally used in order to make a gift of stock, but in many states, they can be used for gifts of cash, other securities, and annuity contracts. An adult custodian must be named on the account with the minor. The custodian manages the account until the minor becomes an adult.

Create a Savings Account Trust

The savings and loan association law provides liberalized handling of accounts created in the name of a minor. These accounts can be established in the name of a minor, and the minor is entitled to make deposits or withdrawals in the same manner as an adult without any liability to the savings and loan association.

Establish a Totten Trust

There is an account that can be established with a commercial bank or savings and loan association called a "Totten trust." An account of this kind is created by registering the account in a form such as "John Jones in trust for Mary Jones." In those states that recognize this technique, it is usually presumed that the account belongs to the adult person named as trustee unless it can be shown that the trust was intended to be irrevocable. On the death of the adult trustee, the account proceeds would belong to the minor beneficiaries but would be controlled by the local probate court on behalf of the minor until he or she reached adulthood.

Fund a Living Trust Created for the
Benefit of the Minor Beneficiary

A living trust that is used to give property to minors is called a 2503(c) trust. It is named after the Internal Revenue Code section that allows the income from the trust to be taxed to the minor beneficiaries. Since TRA 1986, however, this income tax saving benefit is not as significant. The lower tax brackets make the potential savings negligible. In fact, there is no income tax benefit at all for children under fourteen years of age under the so-called Kiddie Tax provisions introduced by TRA 1986.

Petition the Local Court, Usually the
Probate Court, to Authorize a Custodial
Relationship

Here the court will name an adult custodian who will manage the property under the court's direction and supervision until the minor becomes an adult.

The techniques that we have discussed represent, in the main, the alternatives available to you when you want to give property to your minor children and grandchildren. If you think these living techniques are complex, can you imagine how difficult it is to get your property into the hands of these minors on your death?

If your will leaves property directly to minors or if your insurance proceeds are to be paid directly to minors, we can assure you that your minor beneficiaries *will not* directly receive anything. Every state in our country will require that those funds receive the supervision of a court-directed custodianship. The court that will supervise all matters relating to these funds will generally be the local probate court.

If you did not name a guardian for your minor children in your will, the probate court will select their guardian on its terms — not yours. If you have more than one child, the court could name a separate guardian for each child. Each court-appointed guardian will be totally responsible for all his or her actions to an already overburdened and extremely busy probate judge.

If you were prudent and named your choice of guardian in your will but, nevertheless, left property directly to minor children, the court will have to supervise the distribution of that property. The probate judge will appoint a custodian to administer your children's property. The custodian who is selected may be an adult person or a licensed institutional trustee. The person whom the judge selects will be responsible to the judge on an ongoing basis for all acts with respect to the children's property. The custodian may be the same person who has been named as the children's guardian.

A court-imposed conservatorship that results from leaving property directly to minors on death has, in our opinion, the following drawbacks:

All your property and all the conservator's actions with respect to it are made public.

The court will require that a bond be posted for each year of the conservatorship and that it be paid for from the children's funds. The cost will be approximately 1 percent of the fund value each year.

The conservator will have to keep detailed records of all his or her transactions and will have to show those records to the court. This takes time and costs money.

The conservator will be paid out of the children's funds.

The conservator is usually required to use the services of an attorney in working with the court; attorneys' fees will be paid out of the children's funds.

The conservator whom the court appoints may not be experienced in the investment of funds and may not have the best interests of the children at heart.

Leaving property directly to minors on death involves a great deal of red tape; it depersonalizes the planning process and can create confusion and insecurity in your loved ones. It also can create substantial expenses and unreasonable delays.

In talking with both parents and grandparents, we are convinced that they have very definite feelings with respect to how they want their children and grandchildren raised and economically provided for after their deaths; and yet so many people leave most of what they have directly to their minor children and grandchildren with the belief that somehow their property will miraculously be used to care for them. This assumption is a mistaken one.

Any parent or grandparent who wishes to leave property to minor beneficiaries should always seek out a professional estate planner to accomplish their wishes through the creation of a properly drawn trust. Through the use of such a trust, the following is accomplished:

Parents and grandparents can give what they have to minor beneficiaries in the way they want and when they want those beneficiaries to receive it; they can control the disposition of their estates and create unique planning solutions to accommodate unique planning objectives.

They can select the children's guardians and the person or persons who will invest and control the purse strings with respect to their property.

They can avoid the active control and intervention of the probate court and keep their affairs and those of their beneficiaries out of the public eye.

All expenses that result through a conservatorship can be avoided; the only expense would be the trustees' fees.

Our chapters on trusts and planning for children should offer more than a glimmer of hope to parents and grandparents who want to plan properly for loved ones who are underage.

21

Planning for Children

"Beliefs and Caring Can Survive Death"

In discussing estate planning with our clients who have minor children, we have learned that most parents have very strong and definite ideas as to how their children should be raised and provided for. Our clients have manifested significant concern with respect to who would raise their minor children and how those children would be economically provided for if neither parent were alive. As a result of thousands of such discussions, we have learned that parents of minor children are concerned, and perhaps even a touch paranoid, with respect to what could happen to their children if neither parent were alive to care for them. Their fears and insecurities with respect to the reality that would follow a catastrophe have, in the main, been well-founded.

The responsibility that a professional estate planner has in assisting these parents in planning for their children in the event the unspeakable occurs is awesome. The aftermath of planning in this area involves far more than mere economics. Planning for minor children involves creating an environment that will allow underaged loved ones to experience both love and the care that goes with it and the economic security that will provide more than the necessities of life as they grow to adulthood. The thought and sensitivity required to plan properly for potential orphans should not be taken lightly by any parent or professional adviser.

In this chapter, we will discuss the techniques that you can use to provide a substitute lifestyle for your minor loved ones should a catastrophe occur. It is important that you understand that your beliefs and wishes can become reality after your death if you take the time to plan properly.

Selecting the Guardian

It is mandatory that you take the time to select and name the person or persons whom you wish to raise your children in your absence; these persons are called "guardians of the person." Under the laws of most states, these guardians are named in a will. When a revocable living trust is used, the guardians should be named in the pour-over will that accompanies it.

Many of our clients become exasperated when asked, "Who do you want to raise and care for your children in your absence?" In attempting to respond, they can generally think of no one who, as a replacement parent, would do as good a job as they. Several names are usually discussed, and all are usually discarded because of one deficiency or another. Oftentimes the result of this process is no result at all. The parents, in frustration, come to the conclusion: "We don't have anyone who could raise our children as well as we would."

Our advice is always, "We understand, but please, after giving it much thought and after discussing it with your spouse, give us the best of the worst." You must select your children's guardian because your choice, regardless of its drawbacks, will, in all likelihood, be far better than the choice of the probate judge. If you do not name a guardian, the court will. The selection of a guardian is a painful process that must happen. In going through the process, you should always:

> Provide for a succession of guardians in your will. There is no guarantee that any guardian will be alive when needed or that your chosen guardian will agree to serve. Always spell out your first, second, and, if important to you, third choice of guardians in your will.
>
> Always discuss the situation with the guardians you would like to name before you name them. Be sure that they will, in fact, serve if named.
>
> Share your estate plan with the guardians you have named so that they will know and understand what they may be getting into.
>
> Select your guardians on the basis of their beliefs, morality, and lifestyle, not necessarily on their ability to manage a financial portfolio. Management of the children's funds will not necessarily be the responsibility of the guardians. Others can be named to manage the

children's property as trustees. If you choose, however, the guardians and the trustees can be the same.

If you elect to name a married couple as guardians, use both their full names in describing them in your will. If you use a "Mr. and Mrs." designation, there could be a different "Mrs." at the time they are needed.

In most states, the guardians who are selected and named in a will do not serve automatically. The probate court judge must, after independent inquiry, approve and name the guardian who will ultimately serve. In some states, the parents' choice is presumptive; in others, it is not. Regardless of the laws of the state in which you reside, always manifest your choices in your will and give the judge some help and direction.

Leaving Property to Children

Do not leave your property or insurance proceeds directly to your minor children. We have discussed the problems that occur when this is attempted in Chapter 20, "Getting Property to Minors: Little Ones Are Tough to Give To."

Always use a trust vehicle in leaving your property to minor loved ones. As we discuss in our chapters on trusts, you may elect to use either a trust in your will (testamentary trust) or a revocable living trust. We strongly believe that good planning dictates that the revocable living trust be used for all the reasons we discussed in our chapters on it.

By using a trust, you can spell out in great detail precisely how you wish your children to be taken care of and when you wish them to receive the balance of your property. You can also name the individuals or institutions you would like to have manage the property for the benefit of your children. These trustees or financial guardians can and will work closely with the personal guardians in following your instructions in providing for your children's well-being. The rest of this chapter will describe many of the techniques that are used in a trust by professional estate planners to care for minor children.

When Should the Property Be Divided among the Children

Many wills and trusts we have reviewed on behalf of our clients divide the property up into equal, but separate, shares for each child immediately upon the death of the maker. This technique appears to manifest the maker's intent to treat one's children equally, and as a result, each child has a separate trust share that can only be used for that child's benefit.

We believe that planning of this sort is ill-conceived and does not accomplish what the parent had in mind. Under this technique, what happens if one or more of the children have extraordinary needs for funds because of sickness or other unforseen emergencies? The answer is that once their individual trusts are depleted, they will become wards of the state. This would be true even though their brothers or sisters still had significant sums remaining in their trusts which they did not need.

A better technique, in our opinion, is to leave all your property in a common trust for the benefit of all your children for their health, support, maintenance, education, and general welfare. Once all your children become adults, whatever is left can be divided equally among them and given to them or placed in a separate trust for each of them to be distributed in accordance with your wishes.

The statement that "there is nothing so unequal as the equal treatment of unequals" would certainly seem to apply here. In reality, most parents, while they are alive, care for their children based on need rather than on a basis of "this is your share and that is your share." If a child needs medical care, parents pay for it without giving other healthy children the same amount to put in their bank accounts. The resources of the parents are used to care for all the children based on the needs of those children, not on a dollar-for-dollar accounting parity; after death, this reality should be no different.

Because of the 1976 Tax Reform Act, many parents elected to leave their property to their children in a separate trust or share for each child immediately upon the parents' deaths. This was done because of the orphans' exclusion provisions of the act, which stated that if a separate share was created for a minor orphan, it would be federal estate-tax-free to the extent that it equaled $5000 times the number of years the orphan was under the age of twenty-one. ERTA revoked this provision of the federal estate-tax law, and we are glad it did. Too many parents accomplished very poor people planning to take advantage of the small tax savings the orphans' exclusion provided.

When the common trust for the children is divided into shares is a matter of individual preference. Many of our clients believe that it should be divided when the youngest child attains the age of twenty-three or even twenty-five years of age. One technique that we find particularly intriguing divides the common trust into separate shares when the youngest child attains the age of twenty-three or, in the alternative, upon graduation from college, whichever happens first. When you choose to divide the common trust is your decision. The important consideration in your estate plan is to make sure all your children are provided for while they are minors and that they are provided for from all your resources.

One of the questions that this technique frequently raises is, "Do my older children have to wait until their youngest brother or sister reaches that magic age before my adult children can get some of their money to invest in a business or for any other good purpose?" The answer is no, if the trust document is carefully written. Instructions can be given to the trustee to advance money to any older child for the purposes which are enumerated in the trust instructions. In advancing the money, the trustee should be instructed to first be sure that enough common trust funds will be left to feed, clothe, educate, and care for the minor brothers and sisters. A provision can also be included in the trust document to provide that upon ultimate division of the common trust into separate and equal shares for each of the children, any amounts advanced to adult children will reduce the amount of the shares the adult children actually receive.

The choices that are available to you are limited only by your imagination. If we have spurred your thinking, we have accomplished our purpose.

When Should Property Be Distributed to Children

Many of our clients believe that when all their children have reached adulthood, the property in the common trust should be given or distributed to them outright. This approach is all right but may not be as sound as some other alternatives that can be used.

Wealth is a strange phenomenon; it is a concept that is relative to the perception of the wealth holder. Whether one's wealth is acquired quickly or over a long period of time appears to be relevant when a person makes the judgment as to whether or not one is indeed wealthy. Most of our clients are wealthy when measured against world or national averages; yet with few exceptions, they do not view themselves as financially secure and are prudent, and relatively conservative, in their lifestyles because they are concerned with the need to always have enough for the tomorrows in their lives.

Whether or not a young adult will exercise good judgment with regard to inherited property is always in doubt; however, there can be little doubt that most young adults do not have the experience or maturity to handle what are to them large sums of money. People do make mis-

takes, and generally the frequency of their mistakes is tied directly to
their experience or lack of it. Property that is left to a young adult all at
one time is frequently lost through poor investment or spent as if there
would be no tomorrow. Parents know too well what tomorrow may
bring and are generally very concerned about when and how their children receive their funds.

Parents who are concerned about when their children will receive
their funds usually provide for a pattern of distribution in their trust
documents. They provide that when the youngest child attains a magic
age, the common trust property will be divided equally among their
children. Rather than giving it to them outright, however, it is placed in
each child's separate trust to be distributed in accordance with the parents' wishes. How that property is distributed and when it is distributed
always depends on the wishes, beliefs, and prejudices of the parents.
While the property is in the child's trust, however, the trustee will always be instructed to care for the child with both the income and principal of the trust in accordance with the written instructions of the parent. Following are some distribution techniques that are selected with
regularity by many of our clients.

The first technique is to distribute the trust proceeds in two distributions, such as:

> The child will receive the trust proceeds in two distributions. These
> distributions will be half at twenty-one and half at twenty-five; or
> half at twenty-five and half at thirty; or half at thirty and half at
> thirty-five.

Regardless of the ages used, the concept is to ease the child into the
money—to provide that if a mistake is made with the first half, time and
experience will be on the child's side when the second half is received.
This technique also manifests the belief that there is a certain age below
which the child should not have the opportunity to exercise judgment
with regard to the inherited funds. The advantage of this technique is
that there will always be two or more distributions. This distribution
method should enable the child to learn from previous mistakes.

The problem with the multiple-age technique is that if the child is already over the last distribution age specified by the parent, the funds
will be received at one time. Many people believe that age does not a
wise person make, but, rather, experience. These people obviously
would not use this approach.

For those parents who do not like a distribution pattern predicated
strictly on age, they could use a pattern of distribution similar to the
following:

The child will receive half the funds upon attaining a minimum age or, if over that age, immediately on the death of the parents. The balance of the trust fund would be received five, ten, or fifteen years later.

The advantage of this technique is that there will always be two or more distributions. This distribution method should enable the child to learn from previous mistakes regardless of age.

Many of our clients prefer that their children receive their property in three or more distributions, which may be tied to certain ages or time intervals. Some parents like a plan of distribution which uses both time intervals and attained ages.

The concept of these parents is that by spreading out the distributions, each child will gain more experience and wisdom with every additional distribution. The disadvantage attributed to this approach is that the child will have to wait too long to receive the funds and will think that the deceased parent was not confident of the child's abilities or was trying to exercise control from the grave. An example would be:

One-fourth at twenty-five or one-fourth immediately if the child is over twenty-five on the death of the parent, with additional equal distributions every five years thereafter until all the trust principal has been distributed.

Some of our clients create uneven distribution patterns such as one-third of the property at twenty-five and the balance at age forty.

A few of our clients elect not to make outright distributions of their property to their children. These parents usually instruct the trustee to care for their children from their respective separate shares of both the income and principal of their trusts in accordance with the terms of the trust and provide that on the child's death the balance of the trust will go to that child's children. If that child has no children, it will go to the trusts created for the child's brothers and sisters.

The important point for you to recognize is that you can control how you wish your property to pass to your children. When you think about your preferences of distribution, you should know that you can also create different patterns of distribution for each of your children. For example:

To my sons, one-half of their share at twenty-five or immediately on my death if they are over twenty-five, and the balance five years later. To my daughters, one-fourth of their share at twenty-five or immediately on my death if they are over twenty-five, another fourth five years later, and the balance of the trust property is in trust for the lifetime of each of my daughters.

Parents who select this pattern of distribution believe that a daughter may need more protection in our society than a son. If that is their belief, this pattern might satisfy this concern. Obviously, this concern could be directed at sons and, if so, the pattern is reversed.

Please understand that you can leave your property equally to your children and, through the use of trusts, create different patterns of distribution with regard to each child's individual share. This technique is of major importance when planning for handicapped or disadvantaged children. Disadvantaged children may never have the ability to handle their own affairs; they may require lifetime care with respect to the property in their trusts. Trusts can be tailored to fit the needs of any child.

Most parents know their children, and all parents know their own minds; they should plan accordingly.

Planning for Children

Select a guardian for your minor children

Leave your property in a trust for your children, not outright

Use a common trust for minor children

Divide your property when all your children are adults

Make several distributions to your children

22
Per Stirpes versus Per Capita

"Serious Latin"

In reviewing estate plans with clients over the years, many of our clients have asked, "What does *per stirpes* mean?" or "What does *per capita* mean?" For years we have vowed that if we ever wrote a book on estate planning, we would explain these important words to our readers.

Per stirpes and per capita are Latin phrases, either of which can almost always be found in a will or trust. The use of the words "per stirpes" and "per capita" by an attorney provides a precise way to create a property distribution pattern. In using them, an attorney can cut the use of words considerably.

To explain their meaning in English is both frustrating and difficult. But, briefly and broadly, here we go:

> Per stirpes means "by roots or stocks; by representation." This distribution pattern means that beneficiaries get what their immediate ancestors had, or were to receive. Some professionals use its English name "by representation."
>
> Per capita means "by the head or polls; according to the number of individuals; share and share alike." This distribution pattern means that all beneficiaries are counted, irrespective of generation, and their number divided into the property at hand, with each beneficiary receiving a resulting equal percentage interest in the prop-

erty. Some professionals use its English name "share and share alike."

Please look at Figure 22-1. You will notice that we have created the same family tree twice. If the father, Jim, and his son, John, were both dead, notice how differently Jim's property would be distributed under each method.

Under the plan that used a per stirpes pattern of distribution, Jim's son, Herb, received one-half of his father's property, and Herb's nephew, Dick, and niece, Jane, each received equal shares of the half that was to pass to John; Dick and Jane each received one-half of what was supposed to pass to their father, John.

Under the plan that used a per capita pattern of distribution, Herb, Dick, and Jane each received the same distribution, one-third of Jim's estate.

If Dick died in the same accident that took his father's, John's, life and Dick had no children, the result under both distribution plans would be the same; Jim's son, Herb, would receive half of Jim's property and Jim's granddaughter, Jane, would receive half of Jim's property.

If Dick died in the same accident that took his father's, John's, life and left two living children, the result each plan would provide would be dramatically different.

Under the per stirpes plan, Herb would receive one-half of his father's, Jim's, property, or $50,000. Herb's niece, Jane, would receive one-half of the property that was to pass to her father, John, or $25,000. Herb's greatnephews, Chip and Dale, would each receive one-half of the $25,000 that was supposed to pass to their father, Dick, or $12,500 each.

Under the per capita plan, Jim's son, Herb, would receive one-quarter of his father's property as would Herb's niece, Jane, and greatnephews, Chip and Dale. Under the per capita method, they each would receive the same amount, $25,000.

These results can be illustrated as shown in Figure 22-2.

It is absolutely critical that you understand these distribution concepts and that you understand what Latin and English words go with each. If your attorney does not use the right words to accomplish your desires and you do not catch the mistake, your property will go in the wrong amounts to your beneficiaries.

People involved in planning their estates should understand the results that each distribution pattern creates. Other than your review, there may be no checkpoint that will ensure that the right words have been used. Mistakes in their use cannot be corrected after death.

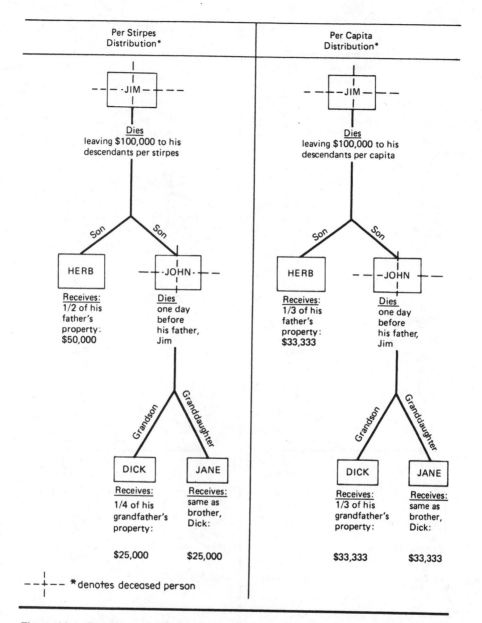

Figure 22-1. Per stirpes distribution and per capita distribution (illustrated through grand-children).

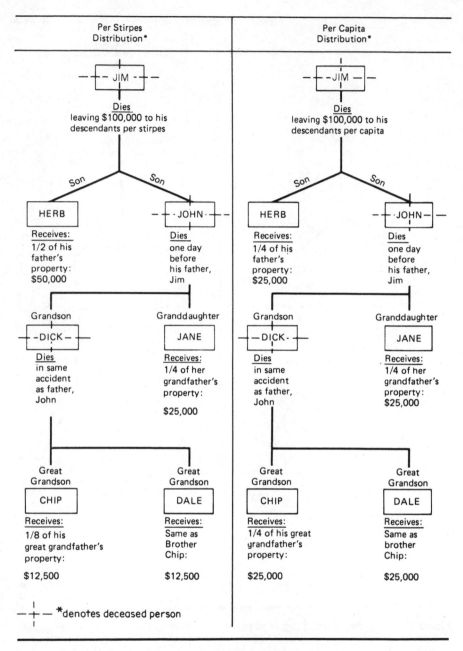

Figure 22-2. Per stirpes distribution and per capita distribution (illustrated through great-grandchildren).

We have listened to clients describe how they wish to distribute their property on death. We have also reviewed the existing wills and trusts of these same clients and have discovered that the wrong words were used. This does not happen often, but it can and does happen unless you know your Latin, or at least four words of it.

23
Generation Skipping
"A Dying Art"

As property passes from one generation to the next, it is subject to the federal estate tax. Before 1976, it was possible, however, to avoid the federal estate tax when property passed to subsequent generations. This avoidance of federal estate tax was usually accomplished by the use of a generation-skipping trust.

A generation-skipping trust allows the maker of the trust to skip federal estate tax as property passes from generation to generation. Here is how it works:

The maker of the trust creates a trust which receives the assets at the maker's death.

The trust provides that the maker's spouse receives all income from the trust. The spouse receives principal from the trust if needed.

At the death of the trust maker's spouse, the trust maker's children receive all the trust income. They, too, can receive principal from the trust if they need it.

Upon the deaths of the trust maker's children, the principal of the trust passes to the maker's grandchildren.

Alternatively, the trust maker could, at the death of the trust maker's spouse, provide that the trust property go directly to the trust maker's grandchildren, bypassing the trust maker's children completely.

Generation-skipping trusts have historically accomplished three basic objectives:

Provided support for the maker's spouse, if any, and children, if the maker so chose.

Prevented the maker's spouse and children from "wasting" the maker's property. The property was controlled by a trustee.

Limited federal estate tax to payment on the maker's death and on the deaths of the grandchildren. (The maker's spouse and children paid *no* federal estate tax on the generation-skipping property on their deaths.)

While generation skipping was not restricted to the use of a trust or for the benefit of family members, generation skipping became very popular, especially among the very wealthy. The federal estate-tax savings from generation to generation was significant. Because generation skipping was considered a tax loophole for the rich, its use was severely restricted by the Tax Reform Act of 1976.

The Tax Reform Act of 1976 subjected generation-skipping assets to federal estate tax on the deaths of the beneficiaries of the generation-skipping trust. For example, upon the deaths of a trust maker's children, the trust assets would be added to their federally taxable estate. The 1976 act treated generation skipping just as if the property had passed through each generation's estate.

Because the generation-skipping provisions of the Tax Reform Act of 1976 were so complex, they were virtually unenforceable. TRA 1986 repealed the 1976 law and replaced it with an only slightly less complex law. This new generation-skipping law generally became effective on October 22, 1986. It provided special rules that make generation-skipping taxes paid under the Tax Reform Act of 1976 subject to refund.

The generation-skipping tax under TRA 1986 subjects to tax almost all transfers of property from an individual in one generation to a person or persons at least two generations below the transferring individual's generation. The simplest example of a generation skip is a gift made by a grandparent to a grandchild. The generation-skipping tax can apply whether this gift is made during the grandparent's lifetime, at death, or by a trust or other method which delays the gift until some future time. Thus not only are the traditional generation-skipping methods covered by this tax, but so are all other methods which have the effect of skipping the federal estate tax in one or more generations.

Under the generation-skipping tax, everyone has $1,000,000 with which to generation-skip. For example, a husband and a wife each have a $1,000,000 exemption. A husband and a wife can, if they so choose, treat a generation-skipping transfer by one of them as being made one-half by each of them.

The $1,000,000 exemption applies to lifetime generation skips or those occurring at the death of the trust maker. The $1,000,000 can be allocated to one generation-skipping transfer, or it can be allocated in any manner the trust maker chooses among several generation-skipping transfers.

If a child of a trust maker dies before a generation-skipping transfer is made, then any transfers to that child's children by the trust maker are *not* considered to be generation-skipping transfers. From 1986 until 1989, there was a special $2,000,000 exemption per grandchild for generation-skipping transfers made directly from a grandparent to grandchildren, whether or not the children's parents were alive or not.

The generation-skipping tax is due either when property is received by the recipient of the generation-skipping property, when the recipient has the right to the property (even when it is in a trust), or when a direct skip is made from a grandparent to a grandchild. The applicable tax rate is the highest federal estate tax rate: 55% through 1992 and 50% beginning in 1993.

For those who want to pass more than $1,000,000 to their grandchildren, or $2,000,000 if they are married, there are some planning techniques that are available. For example, certain gifts of life insurance allow the generation-skipping tax to be leveraged. By making gifts of life insurance premiums, at worst, the amount of the premiums reduce the $1,000,000 exemption. At best, the premiums do not even reduce the $1,000,000 exemption. The following example shows how this leveraging can work:

> Charlotte McCarthy's grandchildren buy a $1,500,000 life insurance policy on her life, naming themselves as the beneficiaries. Each year, Charlotte gives her grandchildren enough money to pay the premiums on the life insurance, but does not require them to pay the premiums. Since the gifts to the grandchildren are gifts of a present interest and are in amounts less than $10,000 per year, there are no adverse federal gift-tax consequences. The gifts do not reduce Charlotte's $1,000,000 generation-skipping exemption because they are direct gifts to Charlotte's grandchildren. On Charlotte's death, the $1,500,000 in life insurance proceeds that pass to her grandchildren is not included in her estate for federal estate-tax purposes. In addition, *none* of the $1,500,000 counts toward her $1,000,000 generation-skipping exemption. Therefore, she still can leave another $1,000,000 to her grandchildren free from the generation-skipping tax.

The generation-skipping tax is aimed at wealthy individuals who want to pass a substantial amount of property to younger family members without paying federal estate tax when intervening generations of family members die. While this tax has made it more difficult to generation-skip, some methods still exist to maximize the amount that can pass from grandparents to grandchildren or great grandchildren. However, generation-skipping only affects those taxpayers who have large estates. For most of us, generation-skipping is a dying art.

24

Disinheriting a Spouse

"Spouses Have Rights Too"

In planning estates over the years, we have often been asked, "What happens after my death if I disinherit my spouse?" "If I disinherit my spouse, can my spouse contest my will or trust, and get my property?" The answer to both questions is that in all states, with the exception of Georgia, disinherited spouses will have the right to receive some of the property that was *not* left to them.

We must stress that each state has its own unique laws with respect to a surviving spouse's rights in the property of a deceased spouse. Most states give a surviving spouse the right to receive far less than half the deceased spouse's property.

In whose name ownership to property is taken can become of critical importance on the death of a spouse, because ownership rights not established during life will not be meaningfully restored on death under the laws of most states. Even in those states with laws that are liberal in bestowing rights to a surviving spouse, the rights are usually limited to a spouse's receiving a maximum of one-half of the deceased spouse's property.

Prior to ERTA, many husbands and wives were persuaded to leave up to one-half of their property to their spouses in order to maximize federal estate-tax savings. In order to qualify for the marital deduction, a surviving spouse had to be given at least the income from half the deceased spouse's property and the right to leave that property to anyone he or she chose. The requirements that a spouse had to be given the right to dispose of half the estate on his or her subsequent death brought about many a tear and much anger. Every spouse wanted to reduce federal estate tax by qualifying his or her planning for the marital deduction. But many spouses sacrificed the great tax benefits of the marital deduction because they knew or suspected that half their property would pass to their spouses' loved ones on the spouses' subsequent deaths. This was particularly true when each spouse had children from a prior marriage or when there were no children.

As a result of ERTA, your spouse no longer has to be given the right to leave half your property to whomever your spouse wants. The marital deduction requirements under ERTA have absolutely removed this planning impediment.

For those of you who are getting excited about the potential opportunity to disinherit your spouse and still obtain the federal estate-tax savings resulting from the marital deduction provisions of the federal estate-tax law, *be careful.* Your spouse, after your death, will still have all the rights given under your state law to "elect" against your will and perhaps even your trust.

Accomplishing your estate-planning desires, if you choose to disinherit your spouse totally or partially, can be determined only after you are aware of the rights your state gives your spouse after your death. After you finish this chapter, you should read the introduction to Appendix C and find your state's law with respect to your and your spouse's rights. It is important that you read the introduction to the appendix because it will familiarize you with the terms you will need to understand as you read your state's law. A knowledge of your state's law will also enable you to better apply the techniques of spousal planning that we discuss in Chapter 25, "Planning for a Spouse."

There are two techniques generally used to allow spouses to assure themselves that their spouses will not successfully elect against their wills or trusts. The first technique is called a premarriage contract. Attorneys refer to this contract as a premarital, or antenuptial, contract. The second technique is called an after-marriage contract and is referred to by attorneys as a postnuptial agreement.

A premarriage contract is used by persons who wish to marry but who also wish to establish their right to leave their property to their loved ones prior to taking their marriage vows. The right of potential spouses to enter into premarriage contracts is recognized in every state. Premarriage contracts have been in use for centuries and are used more than

ever today, particularly in second marriages. In order for these agreements to be valid, the following requirements usually must be met:

Each party must be bound to the agreement and consent to it.

Each party must totally disclose all assets.

The agreement must be in writing.

Both parties must understand what they are signing.

Premarriage contracts make it possible for the spouses to protect the
inheritance rights of their respective children by prior marriages and, as
a result, prevent strife over the disposition of their estates. The laws of
all states definitely favor these contracts if they are properly prepared.

After-marriage contracts can also be used to set forth the spouses' inheritance wishes. They are not legally recognized to the extent that
premarriage contracts are. The laws of each of our states are unique as
they apply to the after-marriage contract. Most states that recognize
these contracts require that:

They are negotiated in good faith and are reduced to writing.

There is complete and frank disclosure of all the economic facts of
each party.

The provisions must be fair and reasonable.

The circumstances leading up to the signed agreement must be free
of fraud, duress, and undue influence of any kind.

After-marriage contracts are looked upon with suspicion by courts
and, as a result, must be entered into very carefully. Because of this suspicion, the requirements of an after-marriage contract, where permitted, are much more complicated and rigorous.

Given a choice between signing a premarriage contract or an after-
marriage contract, you should always opt for the former; they are valid
and binding if fair and fairly made and have always been favored in the
laws of most states.

Second marriages offer the most troublesome of estate-planning chal-
lenges. The trouble arises because many people have children from
their first marriage and want to assure that all or most of their estate
goes to those children. Alternatively, if there are children from one,
two, or more marriages, making sure the children and the current
spouse are all taken care of can be very difficult. Mickey Rooneys and
Elizabeth Taylors are hard to plan for.

The best way to plan for a second marriage is through the use of a premarriage contract. Most problems of who gets what can be solved. If a premarriage contract was overlooked, an after-marriage contract may solve the problem.

What happens if neither the premarriage nor after-marriage contracts can be used? Spouses in a second marriage have rights too. As a matter of fact, absent those contracts, their rights are exactly the same as a *first* spouse's rights given under your state's law. Please refer to Appendix C for your state's law with respect to your spouse's rights.

When you are planning your affairs, whether you are married or are contemplating marriage, remember: Spouses have rights too!

25

Planning for a Spouse

"An Incredible Number of Choices"

Planning for a spouse under the old federal estate-tax law was fairly simple. Under the pre-ERTA rules, the maximum marital deduction was the greater of $250,000 or the value of half the estate of the deceased spouse. It is important that we illustrate the planning basics under the old federal estate-tax law so that you can truly understand the planning alternatives available to you since ERTA was passed. For purposes of comparing different planning techniques, we will assume an estate of $1,200,000.

Before 1982, a $1,200,000 estate left outright to a surviving spouse resulted in $145,800 of federal estate tax on the death of the first spouse. On the death of the second spouse (assuming for simplicity's sake no appreciation in the value of the property left to that spouse), there would have been an additional $321,022 federal estate tax. This can be diagrammed as shown in Figure 25-1.

In making federal estate-tax calculations, the exemption equivalent (unified credit) must be used. In our calculations it is included.

Before 1982, that same $1,200,000 estate could have been planned so that the total federal estate tax resulting from both spouses' deaths would have been reduced from $466,822 to $291,600, a savings of $175,222.

The typical planning strategy that accomplished this massive tax savings prior to ERTA was to create two separate trusts that came into existence within the overall master trust document on the death of the

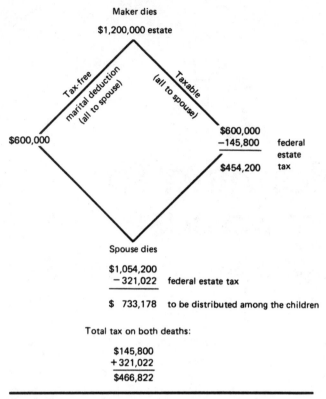

Figure 25-1. Outright to spouse—pre-1982.

trust maker. The first separate trust received the maximum marital deduction amount; it was called the marital trust. The marital trust was only for the surviving spouse. The terms of this trust had to provide the surviving spouse with all the income and the right to leave the trust property on death to whomever that spouse desired (general power of appointment). The principal of that trust could be used by the surviving spouse whenever the spouse desired or only in the discretion of the trustee of the marital trust. The principal of this marital trust did not have to be distributed at all. The maker of the trust had the right to give as much or as little of the principal of the marital trust to the spouse as the maker desired.

The family trust, or second trust, was created to receive the balance of the estate funds (in our example, $600,000 as well). The income and principal of this family trust generally were left in trust for the benefit of the surviving spouse and the children of the trust maker. The trustees were instructed to care for the needs of the spouse first and, after those needs were met, then the children. Many times, the spouse and a close friend or adult family member were named as co-trustees of the trusts, and the spouse was given the right to fire the other trustee as long as a replacement trustee was named.

The proceeds that went into the family trust were subject to federal estate tax on the death of the first spouse. In our case, the family trust would have incurred $145,800 in federal estate tax, the same amount of federal estate tax as in Figure 25-1. On the death of the surviving spouse, however, the family trust proceeds would *not* have been subject to federal estate tax and would have passed federal estate-tax-free directly to the beneficiaries of the family trust. In our situation, these beneficiaries would be the maker's children. Since the surviving spouse did not own the family trust property under the rules of the federal estate-tax law, the family trust proceeds were not included in the surviving spouse's estate.

On the death of the surviving spouse, the proceeds of the marital trust would have been subject to federal estate tax in the amount of $145,800. As a result of this two-trust planning, the total federal estate tax that would have to have been paid on both spouses' deaths was $291,600. This result is illustrated in Figure 25-2.

Professional advisers call this two-trust planning the "marital deduction trust planning." Before 1982, it was generally used to save federal estate taxes when the estate of a married couple exceeded $425,000, as discussed in our chapter on federal estate tax.

By using this planning approach, the trust maker could reduce the federal estate tax that would result from both spouses' deaths. The marital deduction trust technique both saved tax and allowed the trust maker to determine where one-half of the property ultimately passed. It also created substantial after-death income-planning opportunities for the maker's beneficiaries. Under the old law, the maximum income tax on trust income paid to a beneficiary was 70 percent. If all of a spouse's property was left to a surviving spouse, as illustrated in Figure 25-1, the surviving spouse would have received all the income from the property, potentially placing that spouse into the 70 percent income tax bracket.

Under the two-trust plan, the income from the family trust could be distributed by the surviving spouse as trustee, with the approval of the co-trustee, directly to the other beneficiaries. When the children and grandchildren received the income, they were more likely to be in an income tax bracket that was far lower than the surviving spouse's bracket. Because of this difference in income tax brackets, substantial income tax could have been saved in caring for the family's needs. Two-trust plans were the tax-saving vehicles to use because they saved both federal estate tax and income tax.

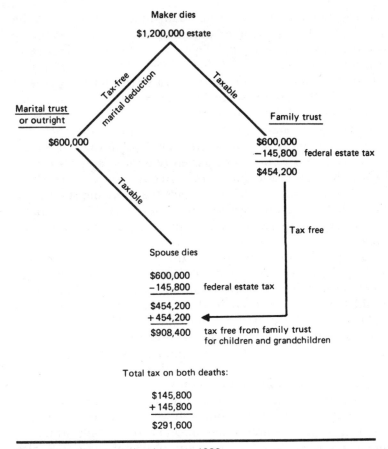

Figure 25-2. Two-trust planning—pre-1982.

Before we discuss how these techniques are used, let us spend a little more time on how they were structured for the maker's spouse and children prior to ERTA.

Time, space, and your understanding do not require that we discuss all the historical variations that were possible under these two-trust plans. In order to illustrate these concepts, we will discuss two planning alternatives. The first alternative assumes that a trust maker wants to save federal estate tax, but in so doing wants to benefit children and grandchildren with the family trust rather than the spouse (Figure 25-3). The second alternative is to save federal estate tax and give the spouse as much control and use of the family trust as possible (Figure 25-4).

In Figure 25-3, the first alternative, you can see that the surviving spouse would only receive income from the marital trust and the right

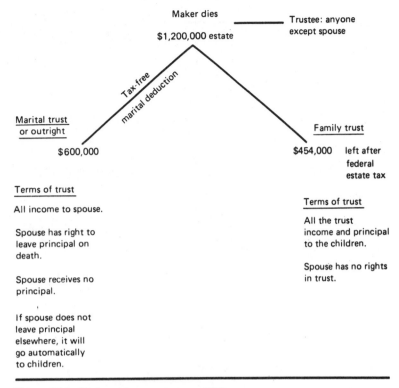

Maker dies

$1,200,000 estate

Trustee: anyone except spouse

Tax-free marital deduction

Marital trust or outright

$600,000

Family trust

$454,000   left after federal estate tax

Terms of trust

All income to spouse.

Spouse has right to leave principal on death.

Spouse receives no principal.

If spouse does not leave principal elsewhere, it will go automatically to children.

Terms of trust

All the trust income and principal to the children.

Spouse has no rights in trust.

Figure 25-3. Minimum to spouse—pre-1982.

to leave the principal of the marital trust to that spouse's chosen beneficiaries. A potential problem resulting from this technique is that the surviving spouse might be able to use state spousal rights to "elect" against the entire estate. (Remember Chapter 24, "Disinheriting a Spouse: Spouses Have Rights Too"? If not, a quick rereading is recommended. This concept will be of critical importance as we discuss the planning opportunities now available.)

In order for the trust maker to prevent the spouse from electing against the two-trust plan, the maker generally modified the terms of the marital trust to give the surviving spouse the minimum benefits that the surviving spouse would receive under the state's law.

Figure 25-4 will illustrate the *maximum* amounts and benefits a trust maker could leave to a surviving spouse under the pre-1982 two-trust plan.

Here, the surviving spouse certainly controls and benefits from the property in both trusts. The marital trust principal can be used by the spouse for any purpose. The family trust principal is primarily for the benefit of the surviving spouse if needed, as determined by the spouse

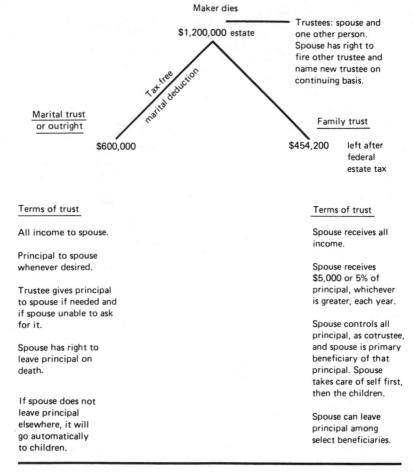

Figure 25-4. Maximum to spouse—pre-1982.

in the co-trustee's role. If the co-trustee disagrees with the spouse about the spouse's determination of need, the spouse can fire the co-trustee and select a more willing co-trustee. The children can also be taken care of by the spouse as co-trustee under the same terms.

In our opinion, when a trust maker wishes to maximize the benefits for a surviving spouse, the family trust should always provide for the distribution of income from the family trust according to the trustees' discretion. If the surviving spouse does not have to receive the income from the family trust, it can be given to the children, who may be in lower income tax brackets; however, the family trust can provide that the spouse could always pay the income to the spouse if needed.

The two-trust planning format continues to be used under the provisions of ERTA by professional estate planners to reduce federal estate taxes on the deaths of both marriage partners. It is also used, in some cases, to provide for after-death income tax planning.

When discussing the planning alternatives available to you, we will assume, for purposes of our illustrations, that death occurred after 1986. You may recall in Chapter 9, "The Federal Estate Tax," that under ERTA the exemption equivalent increased each year until it reached its maximum of $600,000 in 1987. The exemption equivalent represents that amount which can be left federal estate-tax-free to nonspouses and non-U.S.-citizen spouses.

Before discussing the planning opportunities available since ERTA, it is important to understand that the marital deduction is unlimited when property is left to U.S.-citizen spouses. There are special rules for property that passes to spouses who are not U.S. citizens. These complex rules are outside the scope of this book. For purposes of the figures in this chapter, all references to spouses are to surviving spouses who are U.S. citizens.

You could, if you desired, leave all your property outright to your spouse and be assured that your estate would pay *no* federal estate tax on your death. The discussion which follows is directed to those who desire to reduce federal estate tax for both you and your spouse. If you have already created a two-trust plan, please remember that if your plan was completed before September 13, 1981, it is obsolete if you wish to take advantage of the expanded marital deduction. The unlimited marital deduction will not be available to you unless you replan.

Figure 25-5 illustrates the federal estate-tax consequences of leaving all your property directly to your spouse under the provisions of ERTA.

The result, under our illustration, of leaving your entire $1,200,000 estate to your spouse is the payment of $235,000 of federal estate tax. Contrast this with the result that would occur under the traditional two-trust plan, illustrated in Figure 25-6.

By using a two-trust plan, there would be *absolutely* no federal estate tax on the death of either you or your spouse on a $1,200,000 estate. The two-trust plan would save $235,000 of federal estate tax.

Right now you may be asking yourself, "What should I do if my estate is less than $1,200,000?" The answer depends on whether your planning motive is to give your spouse the maximum benefits from and control over your estate (Figure 25-7) or whether your motive is to give your spouse the least benefit from and control over your estate (Figure 25-8).

Figures 25-7 and 25-8 are illustrations that can accomplish both these aims and still reduce federal estate tax.

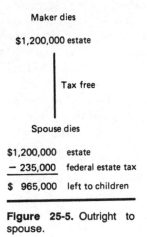

Maker dies

$1,200,000 estate

Tax free

Spouse dies

$1,200,000   estate
− 235,000   federal estate tax
$ 965,000   left to children

Figure 25-5. Outright to spouse.

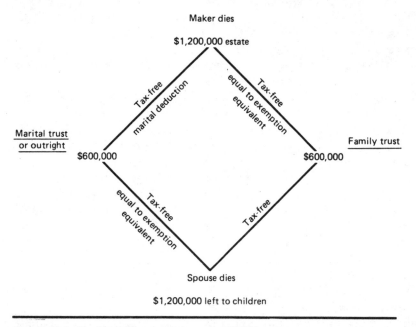

Maker dies

$1,200,000 estate

Tax-free marital deduction

Tax-free equal to exemption equivalent

Marital trust or outright

$600,000

Family trust

$600,000

equal to exemption equivalent Tax-free

Tax-free

Spouse dies

$1,200,000 left to children

Figure 25-6. Traditional two-trust plan—post-ERTA.

Let us assume an estate of $800,000 in each of the illustrations.

You can see the dramatic difference each of the illustrations provides to the surviving spouse. In both illustrations there will be *no* federal estate tax on the death of either you or your spouse, unless the marital share grows to exceed the exemption equivalent.

In Figure 25-8, our minimum-to-spouse diagram, the only right your

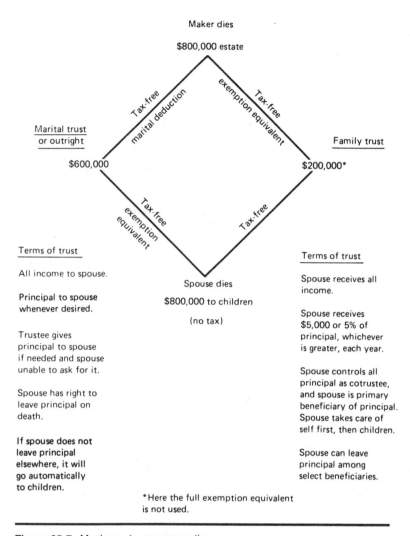

Maker dies

$800,000 estate

Tax-free marital deduction

exemption equivalent Tax-free

Marital trust or outright

$600,000

Family trust

$200,000*

Tax-free exemption equivalent

Tax-free

Terms of trust

All income to spouse.

Principal to spouse whenever desired.

Trustee gives principal to spouse if needed and spouse unable to ask for it.

Spouse has right to leave principal on death.

If spouse does not leave principal elsewhere, it will go automatically to children.

Spouse dies

$800,000 to children

(no tax)

Terms of trust

Spouse receives all income.

Spouse receives $5,000 or 5% of principal, whichever is greater, each year.

Spouse controls all principal as cotrustee, and spouse is primary beneficiary of principal. Spouse takes care of self first, then children.

Spouse can leave principal among select beneficiaries.

*Here the full exemption equivalent is not used.

Figure 25-7. Maximum-to-spouse motive.

spouse has is the right to the income from the $200,000 in the marital trust. Do not forget, however, that your spouse under state law may have the right to elect against your plan. Good planning for estates under $1,200,000, when a spouse is to receive minimal benefits, would be to create a marital trust that would equal but not exceed the spousal rights accorded that spouse under state law. For example, assume you died a citizen of a state which provides that if your spouse and children survive you, your spouse would be entitled to one-third of your estate.

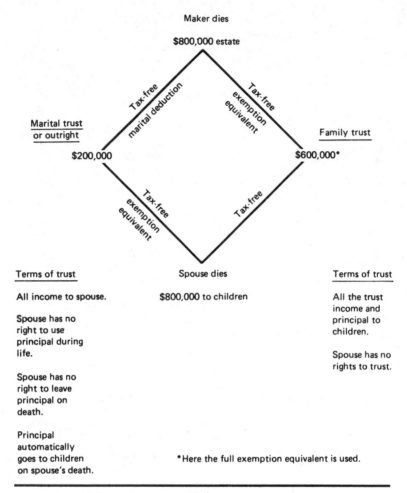

Figure 25-8. Minimum-to-spouse motive.

A plan that would accomplish your objectives and not be inconsistent with state law could be illustrated as shown in Figure 25-9.

For estates of $1,200,000 or less, the planning variations are almost endless. If your estate is under $1,200,000, please understand that you can accomplish your planning motives and always keep your estate free of federal estate tax on the deaths of both you and your spouse. How your objectives will be accomplished will be determined through the advice and counsel of your estate-planning professionals.

If your estate is less than $600,000, you may be tempted to do nothing with respect to planning your estate. This may not be a wise deci-

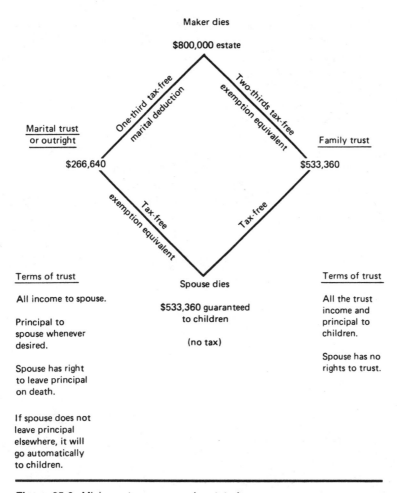

Maker dies

$800,000 estate

One-third tax-free
marital deduction

Two-thirds tax-free
exemption equivalent

Marital trust
or outright

$266,640

Family trust

$533,360

Tax-free
exemption equivalent

Tax-free

Terms of trust

All income to spouse.

Principal to
spouse whenever
desired.

Spouse has right
to leave principal
on death.

If spouse does not
leave principal
elsewhere, it will
go automatically
to children.

Spouse dies

$533,360 guaranteed
to children

(no tax)

Terms of trust

All the trust
income and
principal to
children.

Spouse has no
rights to trust.

Figure 25-9. Minimum to spouse under state law.

sion. In addition to the many nontax reasons that require estate planning, you should not ignore inflation and what it may do to the value of your estate. It is important to remember the impact that growth may have on the value of your property.

If your estate has a value in excess of $1,200,000, the planning opportunities that are available to you are staggering. Planning your estate in order to minimize federal estate tax on your death and the death of your spouse will always depend on your planning objectives. Let us first compare the old two-trust plan with a new two-trust plan. The old plan, you will recall, put half your property in a marital trust and the balance in the family trust. A new two-trust plan would first put the exemption equivalent ($600,000 for our purposes) in the family trust and the balance in the marital trust. If we use a hypothetical estate value of $3 million, the old two-trust approach would generate a total federal estate tax on both spouses' deaths of $726,000.

This can be illustrated as shown in Figure 25-10.

Contrast the old plan with a new two-trust plan under ERTA, shown in Figure 25-11.

If you used the ERTA plan, the children would have lost an additional $58,000 to federal estate tax on the death of your spouse over what they would have lost had the old two-trust plan been used.

The old plan may look better at first. Under the old plan, $363,000 of the total federal estate tax was paid on the maker's death. Under the ERTA plan, no federal estate tax is due until the maker's spouse dies.

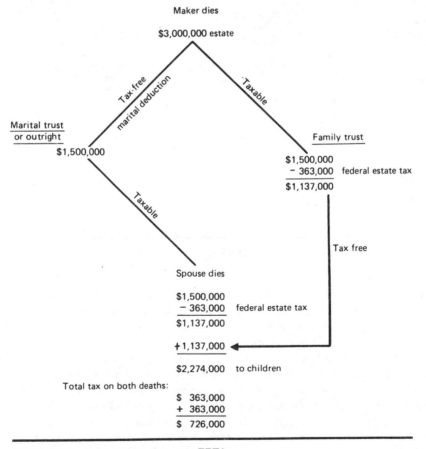

Figure 25-10. Old two-trust plan—pre-ERTA.

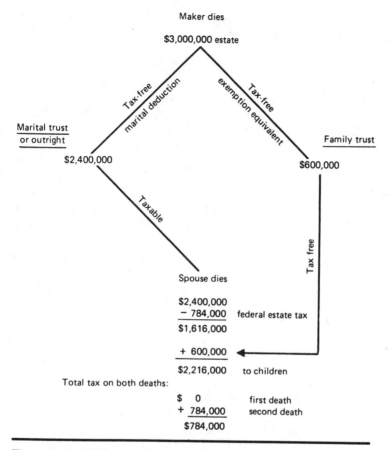

Figure 25-11. ERTA two-trust plan.

Therefore, under the ERTA plan, there is $363,000 available to invest until the spouse dies. The value of deferring the federal estate tax until the second death could be significant.

Whether or not one should use the deferral technique as opposed to staying with the traditional two-trust approach depends on a host of economic considerations, such as:

Life expectancy of the surviving spouse

Projected inflation and real growth rates

The liquidity of the estate

The projected income tax brackets of all beneficiaries

The asset mix of the estate

The projected reduction of the estate for the needs of the beneficiaries after the maker's death

Under ERTA there is no requirement that you give your spouse the right to leave your property on your spouse's death. Because of this change, three major planning formats come readily to mind as alternatives that can now be used. They can best be explained through the illustrations in Figures 25-12, 25-13, and 25-14.

You have probably noticed that the federal estate tax for each plan is not shown. The federal estate tax on each is identical. A total tax of $784,000 is due on the death of the spouse in each example.

In reviewing the three alternatives set forth in Figures 25-12, 25-13, and 25-14, we believe that Figure 25-14 reflects the planning desires of most of our clients. It is an ideal alternative to maximize the benefits a spouse will receive but, at the same time, assure the maker that at least half the estate will go directly to the children on the second spouse's death.

In Figures 25-12, 25-13, and 25-14, for non-community-property states, the total value of the estate, $3,000,000, represents the value of the property owned by one spouse in his or her name. In Figures 25-12

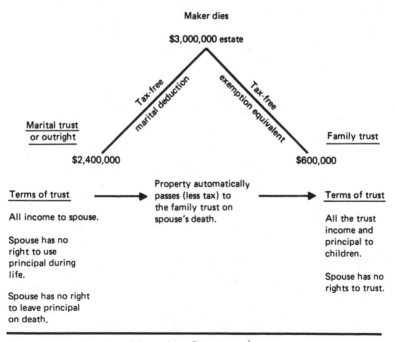

Figure 25-12. Plan 1—minimum benefit to spouse.

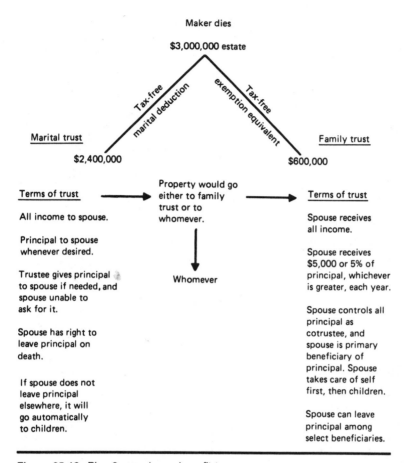

Figure 25-13. Plan 2—maximum benefit to spouse.

and 25-13, in a community-property state, the $3,000,000 is one spouse's share of the community property plus any sole and separate property owned by that spouse. In Figure 25-14, in community-property states, the $3,000,000 is the total value of the community property. The $1,500,000 allocated to marital trust 1 is the surviving spouse's share of the community property.

For those of you who are concerned about your state law and the rights your spouse has under it, the plan shown in Figure 25-15 should be of interest.

In a non-community-property state, when a married couple owns most or all of their property in the name of only one spouse, or in a community-property state where a spouse has the majority of his or her property as sole and separate property, another technique can be used

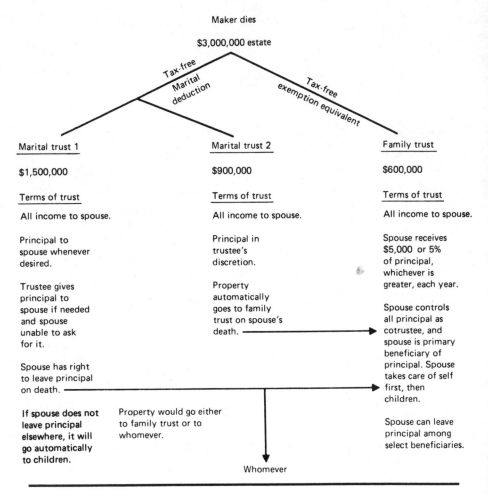

Figure 25-14. Plan 3—maximum benefit to spouse with children guaranteed at least half your property.

to reduce federal estate tax under ERTA. In using this technique, the asset-owner spouse gives property federal gift-tax-free to the other spouse, who must be a U.S. citizen. The value of the gift should equal $600,000, the full exemption equivalent. If the spouse already has $600,000 worth of property, a gift is not necessary. If the spouse then dies first, an amount up to the $600,000 exemption equivalent will not generate federal estate tax. If this property is left in a family trust for the benefit of the asset-owner spouse and children, there will be no federal estate tax on the death of the asset-owner spouse. If this technique

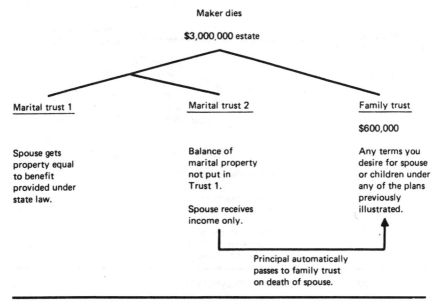

Figure 25-15. A compromise under state law.

is not used and the non-asset-owner spouse dies first, that non-asset-owner spouse's exemption equivalent is lost. The loss of the exemption equivalent could cost as much as $300,000 in additional federal estate tax on the death of the asset-owner spouse. The bypass trust technique is used when both spouses own property at least equal to the exemption equivalent. This technique is illustrated by Figure 25-16.

Now that the gift-to-spouse technique has been illustrated, we will compare the federal estate-tax result when it is not used and when it is used. Please refer to Figures 25-17 and 25-18.

Without using the gift technique, federal estate tax is $1,083,000. Using the gift technique generates only $784,000 of federal estate tax. The difference is a whopping $299,000!

The gift technique that we have illustrated uses a "bypass" family trust. Not only does it save federal estate tax on the second spouse's death, but the bypass trust also gives substantial control of the property to the asset-owner spouse as a trustee. As a trustee, the asset-owner spouse can control both the income and principal of the bypass family trust. By naming a co-trustee serving with the asset-owner spouse, the income from the trust principal can be paid to both the asset-owner spouse and children for income tax savings, as we discussed earlier. In using this planning technique, the asset-owner spouse should always be given the right to terminate and replace the co-trustee.

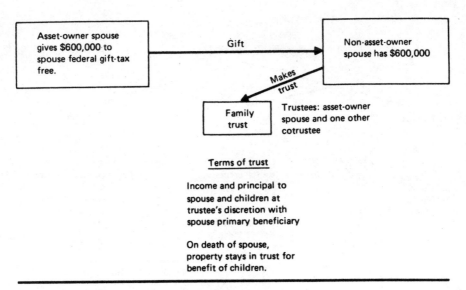

Figure 25-16. Gift-to-spouse technique with bypass trust.

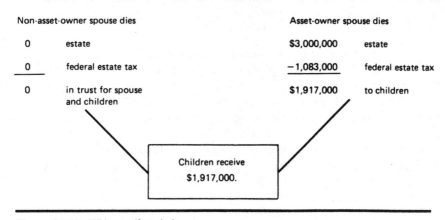

Figure 25-17. Without gift technique.

When using the bypass trust technique, remember that the exemption equivalent is $600,000.

But what if each spouse has assets in excess of the exemption equivalent? If bypass trust planning is used, federal estate tax will be generated.

For example, if each spouse has an estate of $800,000 and the first spouse to die has a bypass trust, the results shown in Figure 25-19 occur.

What is the result if the first spouse to die uses two-trust planning in such a way to maximize tax benefits? Figure 25-20 will show you.

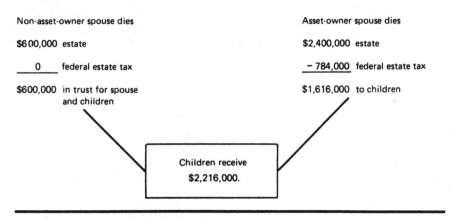

Non-asset-owner spouse dies

$6 00,000 estate

    0   federal estate tax

$600,000 in trust for spouse
          and children

Asset-owner spouse dies

$2,400,000 estate

 − 784,000 federal estate tax

$1,616,000 to children

Children receive
$2,216,000.

Figure 25-18. With gift technique.

Spouse 1 has $800,000 and dies first:

Family trust

$800,000   estate
−600,000   exemption equivalent

$200,000   taxable estate

$ 75,000   federal estate tax*

Spouse 2 has $800,000 and dies second (remember,
all of Spouse 1's property went to the family trust):

Family trust

$800,000   estate
−600,000   exemption equivalent

$200,000   taxable estate

$75,000   federal estate tax*

*The total federal estate tax on both deaths is
$150,000−$75,000 on each death.

Figure 25-19. Bypass trust when over exemption equivalent.

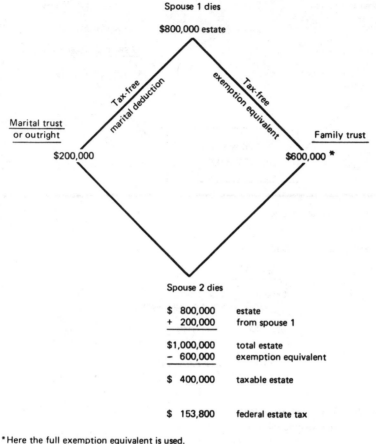

Figure 25-20. Two-trust approach.

Under the two-trust plan, a total federal estate tax of $153,000 was generated. Under the bypass family trust, $150,000 of federal estate tax was generated. The two-trust plan *increased* the total federal estate tax by $3000 ($153,000 minus $150,000).

But you must remember that the two-trust plan actually defers the federal estate tax until the second death. As we discussed earlier, this deferral may be significant. You should also be aware that under our two-trust example, the minimum-to-spouse motive was used. If it is not used, the second spouse to die has a higher estate for federal estate-tax purposes, and taxes increase significantly. You can see that as estates increase in size and assets are owned in each spouse's name, the estate-planning possibilities and variables increase significantly.

In this chapter, we have highlighted some basic planning techniques that you should be familiar with in planning for your family under ERTA tax laws. These techniques are not, however, exhaustive. The number of planning alternatives that are available to you and your professional advisers is staggering. It is critical that you seek out professional estate planners to assist you in planning your estate.

26

Life Insurance

"Estate-Planning Fuel"

To discuss life insurance in a book on estate planning should not come as a surprise to anyone. Life insurance and estate planning go hand in hand. Life insurance very often represents a major building block in the estate-planning process. We will devote Chapters 26, 27, and 28 to the relationship between life insurance and the planning process. This chapter will discuss the basics with regard to the role life insurance plays in the estate-planning process. Subsequent chapters will discuss its application under ERTA and how to keep insurance proceeds free of federal estate tax.

A majority of our clients have evidenced a sincere desire to know more about life insurance and how its proper purchase facilitates the accomplishment of their estate-planning objectives. Many of our clients have been and continue to be confused as to the amount of life insurance they should purchase. They also do not know what type should be purchased. They do not understand its pricing and have a very difficult time comparing product costs between companies and even between products offered by the same company. They do understand that life insurance costs money and does not represent a current benefit to them or their families. They are often reluctant to make a purchasing decision and are concerned that they may be overinsured. They then turn to the noninsurance estate-planning professionals for guidance and information.

Within the estate-planning process, life insurance should be purchased for two reasons: to create an estate that does not exist or to protect an existing estate from losses that will be sustained through death taxes and the probate process.

Life insurance purchased to create an estate should be looked upon as casualty insurance — insurance purchased to replace economic loss resulting from the death of the family bread-earner. The problem resulting from a bread-earner's death is the replacement of lost income over a period of years. The solution that life insurance provides is to create a fund of cash dollars that can be used to sustain family members who do not have an alternative source of income for a projected period of time.

The amount of life insurance so purchased should be tailored to the family's lifestyle as it existed before the bread-earner's death. The amount of insurance that is purchased should be tempered with the income the proceeds will generate after death to living beneficiaries. The income that will be generated from prudent investment of life insurance proceeds should be calculated by using a conservative interest factor. Unreasonably high estimates of income resulting from the investment of insurance proceeds generally result in inadequate insurance portfolios.

In our experience, most clients who need casualty or estate-creation (income-replacement) life insurance are significantly underinsured. They do not realize the value of their income contribution to their dependents. They do not consider the present dollar value of their income over the period of years required to care for those dependents. They do not consider inflation and place too much emphasis on a social security system they do not understand. Many of our clients who do understand social security benefits believe them to be too little for too much cost. They are concerned that our social security system will not survive, and if it somehow does survive, they are pessimistic about the amounts that will be derived by their family members. Many of our clients believe that the social security system is bankrupt and that prudent planning dictates it be ignored.

Life insurance is not affordable in the minds of many people. These people are trying to build their estates and, at the same time, are trying to maintain a reasonable standard of living — a standard, we might add, which appears difficult to sustain, much less improve upon, given the inflationary reality of rising prices of goods and services. Most clients we have talked to prefer to maintain their lifestyles at the expense of realistic insurance portfolios. They are betting that they will survive, at least for the foreseeable future. Their mentality suggests: "I'll buy it when I can afford it" or "I'll go without it and use my surplus funds to create an estate which will care for my family after my death."

Good estate planning dictates that all reasonably foreseeable needs must be planned for on a current basis. Clients betting that they will survive are betting against themselves, in our opinion. Fortunately, most of our clients who find themselves in the situation we have been discussing do have life insurance, but it is often the wrong kind. These clients usually have two or three small policies that augment their employer-sponsored group policy. In our experience, most clients have insurance programs that represent, in sum total, less than five years' gross income.

We strongly believe that maximizing life insurance coverage should be the goal of clients who need estate-creation life insurance. This belief dictates that the clients buy as much coverage as possible within their premium budgets.

Life insurance that is purchased to protect an estate from losses sustained as a result of death taxes or probate requires a planning process unique to the economics of that specific situation.

In this area, insurance should not be purchased without first calculating what those death costs are likely to be. The calculation of projected costs is essential to the estate-planning process. Many people who do not have an estate plan purchase life insurance to cover costs that could be avoided at a fraction of the life insurance premium being expended.

Every person whose motivation in purchasing life insurance is to protect the estate should first plan that estate to reduce or avoid every cost possible. After projected costs have been reduced to the lowest dollar possible, life insurance should be purchased to cover the remaining costs. The estate-planning process creates the car, gas tank, and gasoline gauge. Life insurance is the gasoline, in the right amount and in the right octane, that should meet the designer's specifications.

Often clients who have an estate of the size that will generate tax and other death expenses believe, incorrectly, that they have no need for life insurance. They envision that their property will be sold to pay the estate bills and that the balance of the property will be sufficient in value to accomplish their planning objectives. Too often clients believe that their estate assets can be sold at their fair market value to pay death costs when due. In our experience, this assumption is not practical and seldom occurs.

We have previously discussed the fact that federal estate taxes are due and payable nine months from the date of death in cash. Nine months does not represent a great deal of time, particularly when the survivors have other matters on their minds. Death's aftermath is always frenetic, even with the best of estate plans. Buyers are usually aware of the time constraints placed on estate sellers. The more aware the buyer, the more likely the price offered will be reduced. Panic sales are seldom fair market value sales. They are usually distress sales.

Prudent estate owners should always plan to pay their estates' debts with cash. Estate property should be sold at the highest price, and that price should be negotiated without timing constraints. Life insurance should be considered as a planning alternative to create instant estate cash. This entire discussion, and the problems it describes, is referred to by estate planners as the liquidity problem. The more nonliquid the estate, the greater the potential need for life insurance.

There is a panoply of insurance products in the marketplace, and more are coming on-stream every day. There are term policies and permanent policies and policies that cover everything in between as well. Like all other estate-planning techniques, life insurance involves specialized knowledge. Most non-life insurance advisers are not experts in life insurance. Many life insurance salespeople are estate-planning professionals; they are experts on the products within their industry. These insurance professionals are knowledgeable on comparing products in terms of cost, deductibility of those costs, benefits provided, and a host of other life insurance-related issues that are critical to the total estate-planning process.

Our belief is, "If you do not know jewels, know your jeweler." You should take the time to interview and select an insurance professional who is knowledgeable. You should select an insurance professional you like and one who will work comfortably with your other estate-planning advisers. Once such an individual is found, you can test your preliminary feelings regarding the expertise of that individual through your other advisers. Attorneys, accountants, and financial advisers may not be insurance experts, but they recognize them when they work with them. Your other estate-planning advisers should give you feedback as to their opinions of your insurance adviser. This professional feedback should be both helpful and reassuring to you.

The following are insurance-related concepts that are critical to the estate-planning process:

Insurance is a third-party beneficiary contract. Leaving proceeds to third parties, whether directly or in trust, removes proceeds from the probate process.

Life insurance owned by the insured is subject to federal estate taxation on the owner-insured's death.

The owner of a policy does not have to be the insured. In fact, the owner should not be the insured if insurance proceeds are designed to avoid death taxes. We have devoted Chapter 28, "The Irrevocable Life Insurance Trust," to this concept.

Most state death taxes do tax life insurance after certain dollar deductibles have been met. Some states do not tax life insurance proceeds at all.

Precisely written beneficiary designations are of critical importance.

Contingent beneficiary designations should always be made.

The estate of the insured should *never* be named as beneficiary; to do so is to subject the life insurance proceeds to the probate process.

Minors should never be named as primary or contingent beneficiaries because they cannot receive the proceeds without court supervision until they are adults.

Insurance proceeds intended to benefit minors should be left to a trust created for their benefit.

Life insurance proceeds left to beneficiaries other than the estate of the insured owner are generally not subject to the claims of creditors. This is true with regard to creditors of the deceased, of the estate itself, and of the beneficiaries.

A life insurance program should always be coordinated with and become an integral part of the total estate plan.

Life insurance recommendations should always be discussed with and reviewed by other members of the estate-planning team. These other advisers and the insurance professional should be encouraged to work closely with one another.

Life insurance can create an estate for loved ones. It can also protect an estate that has already been created. Policy proceeds can provide liquidity and the certainty of knowing that cash will be available to pay estate debts. Life insurance can be purchased in a host of ways to accomplish a host of objectives. It should always be considered in the estate-planning process.

We believe the following analogy will illustrate our concern and feelings with regard to the use of life insurance in the estate-planning process.

> The attorney's job, with the help of the accountant and the client's other financial advisers, is (1) to design an estate plan to enable the client to pass property to whom he or she wants in the way and when he or she wants and (2) to avoid, in addition, every tax dollar, attorney's fee, and court cost possible.
>
> The client, with the help of advisers, designs an automobile he or she wishes to drive. Color, size, and extras should be selected after discussion and thought.
>
> The attorney cannot, and we stress *cannot*, provide the client with the fuel to power that car. The fuel is the client's responsibility.
>
> The insurance professional sells fuel. It is the responsibility of the insurance professional to sell the fuel that will fill the vehicle's tank with the right fuel mixture at a price that is fair in the marketplace.

Attorneys have been accused (mainly by life insurance professionals) of saying: "You don't need life insurance; drop it. Insurance is too expensive, a waste of good money. I've written your will; your wishes have been executed; your planning is now completed."

Life insurance salespeople have been accused (mainly by attorneys) of saying: "Buy my product; I need the commission. Buy insurance, and you will discharge your planning responsibilities to your loved ones. Purchase insurance, and you won't have to worry about those death costs."

Both sets of statements, or others like them, are dead wrong. What good is a vehicle without fuel? What good can come from purchasing fuel without owning a vehicle that can be powered by it? What real good can come from either if it were not designed for the other?

27

Life Insurance Since ERTA

"New Engineering Requires New Fuel"

We have already discussed our belief that life insurance is generally purchased to satisfy one of two estate-planning objectives: to create an estate or to protect an estate that has already been created. *This chapter discusses ERTA as it applies to life insurance purchased to protect an estate that has already been built.*

Prior to ERTA, life insurance was purchased to protect an estate under certain planning guidelines. These guidelines can be summarized as follows:

Life insurance was purchased on the life of the bread-earner spouse when a majority of the family's property was titled in his or her name or when he or she contributed the funds toward the acquisition of jointly held property.

Life insurance was purchased by many individuals to pay death taxes resulting from a spouse's death.

Estates that exceeded $425,000 were subject to federal estate tax when left to a spouse. The more the estate exceeded that amount, the greater the tax on an escalating formula or bracket basis. Life insurance was frequently purchased to cover federal estate taxes.

Under ERTA, people can leave their entire estates tax-free to their spouses. In addition, spouses can leave all or part of their exemption equivalent ($600,000) to nonspouses.

What wonderful news. Now, most planning for U.S.-citizen surviving spouses and other family members results in no tax liability on the death of the first spouse. This is true regardless of the size of the estate. The tax bite may be deferred to the second spouse's death.

Now for the problem. Most existing life insurance policies purchased prior to ERTA with federal estate taxes in mind insure the life of the bread-earner spouse; in our experience, this spouse is usually the husband. Actuarially, if the husband and wife are the same calendar age, the husband is older for insurance purposes (males die younger than females—that is a statistical fact) and is therefore more expensive to insure. If the husband does die first, the purpose for which the insurance was purchased may not materialize. There should be no federal estate tax on his death.

The bottom line with regard to life insurance and ERTA would appear to be this: Do not insure a spouse for purposes of the first death; insure the second death, which is where the taxes will be.

Insuring a second death presents another problem. How are you and your advisers supposed to know with certainty in what sequence death will occur? Obviously, there can be no precise answer to this question. What can be determined, however, is whether you or your spouse is less expensive to insure. The insurance company will tell you.

If your spouse is less expensive to insure than you, why not insure your spouse's life rather than yours? If you, as the older spouse, fulfill the actuarial role and die first, there will be no federal estate tax and no need for life insurance proceeds to pay federal estate tax. On your spouse's subsequent death, there will be taxes, and there will be insurance proceeds.

If, however, your spouse dies first, there will be no taxes but there will be insurance proceeds. Those proceeds could be invested in liquid assets, and on your death, funds would be available to pay taxes. In either case, regardless of the sequence of death, significant premium dollars can be saved by insuring the younger (for insurance purposes) spouse.

By insuring the younger of the two spouses, significant premiums can be saved and, regardless of whose life is insured, the proceeds can be available to pay the taxes resulting from the death of the surviving spouse. This is of massive importance where significant insurance programs are in place or envisioned.

Many insurance companies provide a unique product called a joint and survivor policy. This type of policy insures two lives and pays out death proceeds only on the death of the last of the two insureds to die.

As a method for only insuring the payment of death taxes, joint and survivor policies have merit. However, if life insurance proceeds are needed for any other purpose, insuring the younger spouse may be the better alternative.

The decision whether to insure the younger of the two spouses or to purchase a joint and survivor policy can generally be reduced to an economic decision based on the relative premium costs of each product. In our experience, different companies have different premium structures for each of their insurance products. This will necessitate a comparison between the two alternatives and their costs among companies.

The decision between these two products may not entirely hinge on economics. There may be many spouses who will elect to insure their younger spouses rather than elect the joint and survivor policy just in case those younger spouses do the unexpected and die first. If the younger spouses do die first, the other spouses will have the insurance proceeds to use and invest. What a turn of events; ERTA has certainly changed the rules.

Please remember that this discussion applies only to life insurance purchased solely to protect an estate already created.

Regardless of whether the younger spouse is insured or the joint and survivor policy route is taken, please read the next chapter. In it we discuss how life insurance proceeds can be protected from federal estate tax regardless of the insurance alternative selected.

One problem or concern that will certainly surface as a result of our discussion in this area is, "Can I afford to cash in existing policies that I've been paying on for years?" We do not recommend that existing policies be canceled until the following is accomplished under the direction of your insurance professional:

A complete analysis is made of the relative costs between existing policies and new policies under the format we have discussed.

If the new method is less expensive, truly less expensive, on an apples-to-apples basis, old policies should still not be canceled until the new policies are in force. Too many clients have made this mistake, only to find out that they were then uninsurable or very highly rated due to health problems.

We do know that the insurance industry has gone through a rate revolution these past few years, and from what we see, the revolution is continuing. As a result of interest rates and a host of other economic factors, insurance rates have plummeted. We have been absolutely astounded at the rates many of the insurance professionals we have worked with have been quoting to our clients. We have been equally astounded by the number of new policy formats that have recently been introduced into the marketplace.

The old rule that one should never cancel a policy that has been in existence for a period of years no longer seems to be a good rule of thumb. You should seek out your insurance professional and redetermine whether or not your insurance portfolio is properly structured.

28

The Irrevocable Life Insurance Trust

"Having Your Cake and Eating It Too"

As we have said, life insurance proceeds provide the fuel that powers many an estate-planning car, but most of the time the fuel mixture is taxed at the pump before it finds its way into the estate-planning vehicle.

A disadvantage generally associated with the purchase of life insurance is that the life insurance proceeds usually *increase* the taxable estate of the policy owner. Upon the death of the insured owner, the life insurance proceeds will be included in the insured owner's estate for federal estate-tax purposes. Most people buy life insurance with the belief that insurance proceeds can be used by their beneficiaries federal estate-tax-free. If the insured owns a life insurance policy on his or her life, all the life insurance proceeds will be included in his or her estate for federal estate-tax purposes.

In order to avoid federal estate tax, many people have the life insurance on their lives owned by their spouses or others; then upon the death of the insured, the policy proceeds would be paid to the owner's beneficiary federal estate-tax-free.

There are problems with this cross-ownership technique:

The insured loses control of the life insurance policies.

Proceeds are usually taxed on the death of the policy owner if he or she is the beneficiary and dies after the insured.

181

Few people can plan for the contingency that the owner/beneficiary may die first.

If the proceeds are payable to other than the insured or the owner, there is a gift of the entire insurance proceeds to the beneficiary from the policy owner.

We have discussed these problems at length in Chapter 29, "Some Estate-Planning Solutions: Techniques and Gimmicks That Do Not Always Work."

The goal sought by insurance policy cross-ownership—to avoid federal estate tax on life insurance proceeds—is a noble one. But there is a better way to accomplish this goal. You can use an irrevocable life insurance trust (ILIT) to own life insurance policies that insure your life. (Please refer to Figure 28-1.) By using an ILIT, the insurance proceeds will be federal estate-tax-free on your death. In addition, if you plan for your spouse, the ILIT will keep the proceeds out of your spouse's estate as well.

The ILIT has been used as an estate-planning technique since the federal estate-tax laws were permanently implemented. These trusts were designed to keep life insurance proceeds federal estate-tax-free. Since the government was losing tax revenue, the Internal Revenue Service attacked their use on many grounds, and as a result, the ILIT fell into disuse. Since World War II, however, their use has come back into vogue. Today, they are frequently used and, quite frankly, are in their heyday. It is important that you understand how an ILIT works. Once you understand how these trusts work, you will appreciate why they are in their heyday.

Generally, if a life insurance policy is given away, the value of the life insurance proceeds will not be included in the estate of the person who gave the policy away. Whoever gives a life insurance policy away must be careful not to retain "incidents of ownership" in that policy. This means that the person who gives the policy away must not retain control over the use of that life insurance policy in any way.

The ILIT is used to own an insurance policy, whether it is purchased by the ILIT or given to it. The ILIT, as its name implies, must be irrevocable. Once the trust is drafted and signed, it can never be changed, except by the courts and then only under very special circumstances. If an ILIT is not totally irrevocable or if the maker retains direct control over it, the insurance proceeds will not be federal estate-tax-free.

By using an ILIT, three estate-planning objectives can be achieved:

Insurance proceeds can be kept federal estate-tax-free upon the deaths of both spouses.

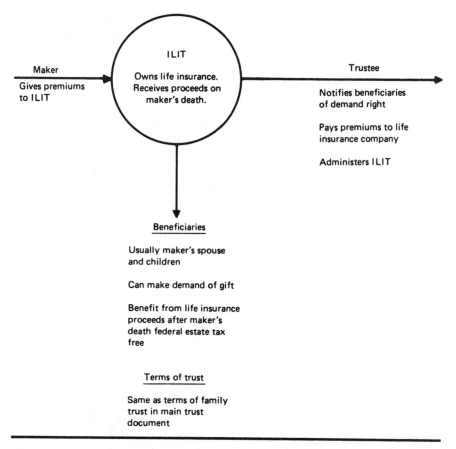

Figure 28-1. How an ILIT works.

Because of the terms provided in the trust document, the trust maker can control the insurance proceeds received by the ILIT to care for the maker's beneficiaries.

The life insurance proceeds received by an ILIT can be used to pay the death expenses, including taxes of both the maker and the maker's spouse.

The beneficiaries of an ILIT are generally exactly the same as the beneficiaries of the maker's revocable living trust. In fact, the terms of the ILIT are almost identical to those of the maker's revocable living trust (main trust), and, believe it or not, the trustees under both the ILIT and the maker's revocable living trust are the same after the maker's death.

As we have discussed, assets receive a step-up in basis at death. To get cash (insurance proceeds) from the ILIT to the maker's main trust, a sale generally takes place. The ILIT buys nonliquid assets from the main trust, using cash provided by the life insurance proceeds. Because of step-up in basis rules, this sale can be accomplished income tax-free. Another technique often used to transfer the ILIT's cash to the main trust is a loan. Regardless of which approach is used, the result is the same. The net result is that the main trust has cash and can pay expenses. The ILIT has the nonliquid property either as collateral for the loan or as the owner after the sale. There are no distress sales or unreasonable borrowing requirements, and since the beneficiaries of the main trust are identical to those of the ILIT, there is no loss of asset value or control.

Too good to be true? Not if the ILIT is properly drafted and implemented by an estate-planning professional. Irrevocable trust drafting is no place for rookies. One small mistake in an ILIT, and all the tax benefits can be lost; remember, irrevocable is irrevocable. Good advice on the front end is essential so that flexibility can be incorporated into the ILIT, making irrevocability less ominous.

Your spouse can be the trustee of your ILIT as long as your ILIT is properly drafted. An ILIT that gives your spouse too much control over the terms of the ILIT may have adverse tax consequences. Some professionals prefer to use an institutional trustee or another family member to alleviate these potential adverse tax consequences. TRA 1986, by changing the income tax rules of trusts, has had great impact on the ILIT. The law surrounding the ILIT is fast-changing and must be double-checked by your estate-planning professional prior to creating one for you.

An ILIT must be irrevocable, but its assets do not have to be. You can name a person other than the trustee, such as an adult child or other family member, as the holder of a special power to remove the life insurance policies owned by the ILIT, as well as any other assets owned by it, and distribute them to the beneficiaries of the trust. This power can be exercised in the holder's discretion, allowing for flexibility in your planning. If your planning objectives change, the assets can be removed from your ILIT. The ILIT will continue because it is irrevocable, but it may not have anything in it. In reality, a properly drafted ILIT may not be irrevocable at all.

How insurance policies find their way into an ILIT and how the premiums are paid on those policies are of critical planning importance.

When an existing life insurance policy is transferred into an ILIT, a gift is made. Whether the gift is subject to federal gift tax or not is another matter. The value of the existing policy determines if it is subject to federal gift tax.

The value of the life insurance policy is sometimes hard to determine and should be done with caution. The value of the life insurance policy is the replacement value of that policy. If you do not know the value of an existing life insurance policy, your insurance professionals can easily tell you.

You can transfer your existing policies into your ILIT, or you can have your ILIT purchase life insurance policies on your life. The latter is easier because you may not have to be concerned with policy values for federal gift-tax purposes or about the three-year gift in contemplation of death rule discussed later in this chapter.

Through gifts of cash from you or others, the ILIT receives funds in order that it can pay premiums on life insurance policies it owns on your life, or it can pay those premiums from the income generated by other property you have already transferred into your ILIT. The federal gift-tax consequences of these transfers must be examined.

The annual exclusion for gifts under ERTA is $10,000 per recipient each year. The annual exclusion can be used only when there is a gift of a present interest in property. A present interest is a gift of which the recipient can have the current use and benefit. A gift of a life insurance policy or the money to pay its premium is generally not a gift of a present interest when given to a trust. If there is no annual exclusion available for life insurance, the use of an ILIT may not be attractive, but this apparent problem has been solved. A man named Mr. Crummey established a special irrevocable trust for the benefit of his beneficiaries. Under his trust, his beneficiaries were to receive property from the trust sometime in the future. Mr. Crummey claimed the annual exclusion for the gifts he made to this trust, and the IRS took him to court. Mr. Crummey beat the IRS. Mr. Crummey won because his irrevocable trust had an added feature. This feature is called a "demand right."

A demand right is the ability, for a limited period of time, of a beneficiary to ask for and receive from a trust the value of the current gifts made to the trust.

For example, on November 1, Dee Fox gives $5000 to her ILIT. The trustee, pursuant to the terms of Dee's trust, notifies the beneficiaries that they have until December 1 to demand their share of the $5000. If they choose not to make this demand, the demand right ends. This demand right can be given even if the beneficiary is a minor because the minor's guardian may exercise the demand right for that minor.

Because of the demand right, a present interest is created in the property given to the ILIT, and the annual exclusion is available. Because of Mr. Crummey, your gifts to your ILIT can qualify for the federal gift-tax annual exclusion.

There may be a practical problem with giving others a demand right. The beneficiaries may demand their share of the premium money; however, in our experience, this has not been a problem. The demand right is refused by the beneficiaries and the money is used to pay life insurance premiums. After all, the beneficiaries are *your* family members.

Despite Mr. Crummey's groundbreaking efforts, when you give money or property to your ILIT, you can use only $5000 of your annual exclusion for each beneficiary of your ILIT. Why? Because of a technical quirk in our federal estate- and gift-tax laws, use of more than $5000 of annual exclusion per beneficiary in an ILIT does create gift-tax problems. There are ways to circumvent the $5000 limitation. An understanding of these methods, however, is beyond the scope of this book. If you want to exceed the $5000 limitation, see your planning professionals.

If the terms of an ILIT require that the gift of the premium be used only to purchase life insurance on the maker's life, then any income or available deductions of the ILIT are included on the maker's income tax return. This rule is just one example of the income tax rules associated with the ILIT.

TRA 1986 has changed a number of the income tax ramifications of trusts, many of which affect the ILIT. For example, if you name your spouse as a trustee or beneficiary of your ILIT, the income of the trust will be taxed to you. Usually, this does not present a problem, since an ILIT is generally not designed to create taxable income. However, this change, as well as others, may have an effect on your planning. TRA 1986 is another good reason to check with an experienced professional before establishing an ILIT.

Having a friendly trustee is important. A second reading of Chapter 19, "Trustees," is probably a good idea. Trustees and their successors must be provided for in the original ILIT trust document and cannot be changed.

There is one last pitfall in giving life insurance to an ILIT. If a life insurance policy is given to your ILIT within three years of the date of your death, the life insurance proceeds are brought back into your estate for federal estate-tax purposes. This could also be true for insurance policies purchased directly by your ILIT. It is best for the trustee to apply for the life insurance policy as the owner to reduce the risk that the insurance policies will be included in your estate if you died within three years of the date the insurance policy is effective.

Almost any type of insurance can be used in an ILIT. Term, whole life, group, annuities, or corporate insurance, properly structured, can all be used.

Creating an ILIT that will meet your objectives and really work requires the hands of both an expert estate-planning attorney and an expert insurance professional. To use less than the best is to invite disaster. If you use competent advisers, your ILIT will allow you to have your tax cake and eat it too.

An Irrevocable Life Insurance Trust

Keeps life insurance proceeds federal estate-tax-free upon the deaths of both spouses.

Allows the maker to control life insurance proceeds.

Allows the life insurance proceeds to pay death expenses and taxes of both the maker and the maker's spouse.

29
Some Estate-Planning Solutions

"Techniques and Gimmicks That Do Not Always Work"

There are many estate-planning techniques that do not always work. There are also some estate-planning gimmicks that never work. In this chapter, we will discuss both the techniques and gimmicks that are too frequently tried as solutions in the estate-planning process. They are as follows:

Techniques

Cross ownership of life insurance

Joint tenancy

Uniform Gifts to Minors Act custodial accounts

The general power of attorney

Gimmicks

Hiding property in a safe-deposit box

The Dacey forms

Do-it-yourself estate planning

The constitutional trust

Cross Ownership of Life
Insurance

The proceeds of life insurance are subject to federal estate tax in the estate of the owner of the policy. They are not necessarily subject to federal estate tax in the estate of the insured. As a result, many insurance salespeople suggest that spouses purchase and own insurance policies on each other. For example, the husband is the owner of the insurance policy insuring the wife and vice versa. By doing this, each spouse is the beneficiary of the death proceeds from the policy he or she owns on the other spouse's life. On the death of a spouse, the insurance proceeds are paid to the other spouse free from federal estate tax.

Let us take a closer look at this technique. Under current law, the proceeds going to a U.S.-citizen spouse would be tax-free anyway because of the unlimited marital deduction. On the second death, the entire amount of the remaining insurance proceeds will be included in the estate of that spouse and will be subject to federal estate tax.

The tax consequences of cross ownership are even worse if the insurance proceeds are payable to someone other than the spouse who owns the policy. If this occurs, there is a gift under federal law of the entire insurance proceeds to the beneficiary from the spouse who owns the policy.

Cross ownership is not a good technique for avoiding federal estate tax. In reality it does not accomplish a thing for spouses. There are better techniques available to avoid death taxation on insurance proceeds, techniques that can keep the proceeds federal estate-tax-free on *both* deaths.

Cross ownership also results in loss of control over the policy and the proceeds. The owner of the policy, not the insured, controls the policy. What if a divorce occurs? The insured may be left without insurance. On the death of the insured, the owner/beneficiary will have the proceeds without any requirement as to how, why, or for whom the proceeds should be used.

Cross ownership between nonspouses is equally dangerous. Here, though, the benefit is potentially greater: there will be no federal estate tax on the death of the insured where there might otherwise be if the insured was the owner. But remember, the insured loses all control in the policy and its proceeds. The better technique to avoid federal estate tax is an irrevocable life insurance trust, which can keep control of the policy and its proceeds in the insured. This technique was just discussed in the last chapter.

Joint Tenancy with Right of Survivorship

Because of its importance and frequent use as an estate-planning technique, we have discussed joint ownership in several other chapters. A summary of its weaknesses is apropos here, however.

Putting property in joint ownership with a nonspouse creates a gift for federal and some state purposes. This is true when one party paid for the property or already owned it.

Joint ownership results in loss of control of the joint property because the other owner can require that it be split up or sold. On death, there is no control; it is a mini-estate plan. The entire property could be subject to the other owner's creditors. The property cannot be planned. There is a loss of step-up in basis which is particularly detrimental in spousal planning.

Joint tenancy is an estate-planning technique that should be avoided, because other techniques can accomplish the estate-planning goals far better.

Uniform Gifts to Minors Act Custodial Accounts

Uniform gifts to minors custodial accounts can be created in all our states. Uniform Gifts to Minors Act legislation was essentially passed to allow an adult to give stock to minors; some states' acts apply them to savings accounts and annuity contracts. The gifts-to-minors law allows an account to be created for the benefit of a minor child in the name of an adult and, in some states, in the name of a bank or trust company. The adult or institution in whose name the account is created is called a custodian.

Gifts-to-minors laws allow certain property to be given to minor children without necessitating the creation of a trust. When a child reaches the age of twenty-one, the account is closed and the property transferred to the child.

Many states have adopted a newer version of the Uniform Gifts to Minors Act called the Uniform Transfers to Minors Act. This newer version is aimed at eliminating some of the shortcomings of the older Uniform Gifts to Minors Act. Essentially, the new law allows all types of property to be held in the custodial account, rather than the limited types allowed under the older act, and the new version broadens how custodial accounts can be established and used. In most other respects both versions of the law are the same, with almost the same problems and pitfalls.

The problems resulting from these accounts can be weighty:

> If the dividends or other income generated by the stocks are used to support the child and the person who created the account is legally obligated to support the child, the income will be taxed to the person who created the account.

> If the person making the gift is the custodian of the account, the entire value of the account will be taxed in that person's estate on death.

> The custodian cannot invest in property other than stock in many states but may put the income in a savings account for the benefit of the child. There is very little investment flexibility in these accounts.

> The custodian is liable to the child for the negligent handling of these accounts and must, on the child's request, make a complete accounting with respect to the transactions in the account.

> The child must receive the account property, including the income earned from the account, on the child's twenty-first birthday. What the child does with the account proceeds thereafter is the child's business.

> The creation of these accounts is a gift under both federal and state gift-tax laws. If the value of the gift to a minor exceeds $10,000 in any given year, gift tax may have to be paid.

We believe, more often than not, that this technique does not accomplish the objectives of the account creator. Too often these accounts are abused, cannot be controlled sufficiently by their makers, and result in adverse tax consequences.

A better way to accomplish your objectives in this area is a minor's trust. Estate-planning professionals call this a 2503(c) trust. The use of this trust provides much greater flexibility as to the investment of your funds because the trust investments are not limited to just stock and the trust property is not included in your estate on death. Gifts to a minor's trust, like gifts under the Uniform Gift to Minors Act, qualify for the annual exclusion under federal gift-tax law. In addition, the 2503(c) trust allows the maker more control over the property in the trust and the income it earns.

You should always be wary of making gifts under the Uniform Gifts to Minors Act and, where appropriate, use the 2503(c) trust as a potentially better alternative.

General Powers of Attorney

Many older people concerned about their ability to conduct their affairs grant a general power of attorney to loved ones. By giving their loved ones a general power of attorney, these mature adults hope to avoid the confusion that could occur should they become ill or mentally incompetent. They want their children or other loved ones to be in charge of their affairs, not attorneys or courts of law. Their objectives are sincere and patently reasonable.

However, a general power of attorney generally does not accomplish the objectives of its maker. Under the laws of most states, a general power of attorney is invalid upon the death or adjudicated incapacity of its maker. Thus when the event the maker feared occurs, the solution that was envisioned will not work.

The granting of a general power of attorney is exceedingly dangerous. The person who has a general power of attorney can control all the property of the maker. This means the holder can spend or dispose of the property for the holder's own benefit.

The concerns that motivate individuals to use these general powers of attorney are real, however, and should be addressed. If you are concerned about your affairs, you should create a revocable living trust, spelling out how you wish to be taken care of in case of your incapacity. You should name a trustee you can trust, whether child, friend, or adviser. If these alternatives are not available or acceptable to you, name an institutional trustee.

By using a revocable living trust, you can reduce the likelihood that others will appropriate your property for nonauthorized purposes. This alternative is discussed at great length in Chapter 17, "The Revocable Living Trust."

General powers of attorney should not be confused with limited or durable special powers of attorney. A discussion of these powers can be found in Chapter 18, "Funding a Revocable Living Trust."

Hiding Property in a Safe-Deposit Box

We have found that many of our clients believe that if assets are placed in safe-deposit boxes, family members can go in after their deaths, take the assets out, and nobody will be the wiser.

This kind of thinking could not be further from the truth. Our public officials are not so naive. The first public act, generally through each state's death-tax division, is to lock or freeze a safe-deposit box upon the death of the owner. The box stays frozen until the proper public official can inventory every asset in that box.

On being so informed, many clients do not relent but become even more creative: "I'll put my assets in someone else's box so that the state won't know about it." Not a bad idea except for the fact that a gift has been made without a receipt, total control over the contents has been lost, and a potential fraudulent transaction has been entered into. Not reporting assets for federal estate-tax purposes is like not reporting income; it is a crime. Need we say more?

The Dacey Forms

In 1965, Norman F. Dacey authored *How to Avoid Probate*. The book was a national bestseller. In it, as we have indicated elsewhere, Mr. Dacey made a vicious attack on attorneys and the probate process. His thesis was that probate should be avoided.

Most of the Dacey book represented his views and suggestions—complete with tear-out forms—on how probate should be avoided and how estate plans should be drafted. Mr. Dacey is not an attorney; his forms were to be filled in and used by the readers of his book to effectuate their estate-planning goals. Mr. Dacey did not encourage his readers to seek the advice and counsel of attorneys, accountants, insurance professionals, or other estate-planning advisers in using his forms.

We partially agree with Mr. Dacey. Probate should be avoided. We do not believe, however, that his "forms" approach represents a sound estate-planning process. We do not believe that the reading of one book (including this one) qualifies anyone to properly estate plan without the additional help and knowledge of experts in the field. We believe that filling out forms is a gimmick that should be avoided.

Do-It-Yourself Estate Planning

An extension of the Dacey forms is the growing industry of buying estate plans through the mail or having advisers other than lawyers prepare estate plans. This is a gimmick that should be avoided at all costs.

Wills, trusts, and all other aspects of estate planing almost invariably involve legal and tax rules. These rules apply in certain ways based on an individual's particular personal and financial situation. For an individual to plan his or her estate without legal counsel is akin to a person performing brain surgery without the aid of a physician.

Mail-order planning and planning provided by those who are not lawyers may sound attractive, but it is a big mistake. Lawyers are the only professionals who can, by law, draft legal documents and render legal advice. They are trained in what information is critical to perform certain legal tasks.

Some of the people who sell forms to nonlawyers or who provide mail-order planning make the claim that their documents have been drafted and reviewed by lawyers. This is a weak and misleading statement. For a lawyer to draft a form for a particular fact situation without having any specific information about the client's family, financial situation, and particular wants and needs is unethical in every state in the United States. These boilerplate plans that have not been tailored to the needs of a client do not result for the most part in responsible planning.

The definition of estate planning is giving what you have to whom you want, the way you want and when you want, and, if possible, saving every fee and tax possible. Mail-order planning and estate plans sold by nonlawyers do not even begin to meet that definition.

To attempt to circumvent lawyers in estate planning may cost more money in the short run — many mail-order trusts are more expensive than those drafted by lawyers. It may cost more in the long run, too. When do-it-yourself plans, mail-order plans, or plans drafted by nonlawyers are put to the test because of disability or death, it may well be that undoing one of these plans is much more expensive than doing the right plan. Do yourself and your loved ones a favor. Use a lawyer as well as other professionals and form an estate-planning team that will clearly meet your planning needs.

The Constitutional Trust

Many of the techniques we refer to in this chapter do have some basis in fact and in law. They are honest attempts at planning.

The constitutional trust does not fall in this category. The constitutional trust, or, as it is sometimes referred to, the pure equity trust, is out-and-out fraud. It is a hoax being promulgated by hucksters masquerading as professionals.

These hucksters claim that by using a constitutional trust, estate tax can be avoided and no gift-tax liability will be incurred if their trust is used. They even claim that income tax will be avoided through the use of their technique. Can you believe it? A triple play! They are selling these trusts and the planning kits that go with them at prices ranging from $4000 to $25,000 or more. Generally they have been presenting or selling their package to professionals, with some emphasis, it seems, on the medical profession.

This scheme does not work, nor does it accomplish any of the benefits claimed. The Internal Revenue Service has watched these trusts for some time and has been coming down hard, very hard, on the oftentimes innocent participants who were taken in by this hoax. *Time Magazine* exposed these devices. These trusts are shams and nothing more than page after page of nonsense.

If you have been taken in by this type of hoax, we strongly suggest you seek out competent counsel immediately, or, if you prefer, your local district or prosecuting attorney.

30
Freezing Techniques

"Putting Your Estate in Cold Storage"

ERTA has reduced the number of estates that will be subject to federal estate taxation. Many estates, however, will continue to qualify for federal estate tax, and it is probable that inflation and real growth will push estates that currently are not taxable into the realm of taxability. This chapter deals with traditional techniques that stop or at least control the growth of your estate through passing that growth to other family members and how these traditional techniques have been radically altered by Congressional attempts to prevent their abuse. These techniques are known as freezing techniques.

By using a freezing technique you can accomplish the following with respect to your assets:

Transfer future appreciation from your estate to your children and grandchildren while you are alive with little or no federal gift-tax implications.

Keep control of your assets during your life.

Continue to receive income from your assets.

Traditional Freezing Techniques

Prior to 1988, freezing techniques could be used for almost any asset, such as stock of closely held corporations, partnership interests, sole proprietorships, and real estate. Beginning in 1987, Congress began to enact tough legislation to address what was considered the abusive use of a tax-avoidance measure. Since 1987 Congress has made two major revisions to the tax laws, enacting in quick succession two completely different methods to discourage the use of freezing techniques.

The Revenue Act of 1987 introduced a new section 2036(c) to the Internal Revenue Code. That section substantially eliminates many of the freezing techniques used prior to 1988 by bringing the value of certain transferred interests back into the federal taxable estate of the person who made the transfer. Section 2036(c) was very complex. It covered a broad spectrum of transactions, not just traditional freezing techniques, and was very difficult to administer. In response to these problems, the IRS provided guidance on the administration of section 2036(c), but this was not sufficient. There was still broad opposition to the new section 2036(c) by taxpayers and tax and estate practitioners and many difficulties remained.

In the Revenue Reconciliation Act of 1990, Congress completely repealed section 2036(c), but did not abandon trying to limit the use of freezing techniques. The 1990 Act replaced section 2036(c) with an entirely new set of rules. These new rules focus more on the valuation of transfers for gift-tax purposes, rather than on those interests retained under section 2036(c) that were taxed at the donor's death. The new provisions have a substantial effect on the use of traditional freezing techniques.

In order to understand the freezing techniques that are still available, it is important to understand the traditional freezing techniques. After an explanation of freezing techniques as they were used prior to 1988, we will briefly discuss repealed section 2036(c). We will then explain the new valuation rules introduced by the Revenue Reconciliation Act of 1990.

One of the most popular freezing techniques was called a "recapitalization." A recapitalization restructures stock ownership in a corporation. A corporation is restructured by exchanging growth stock for nongrowth stock.

There are two types of corporate stock—common stock and preferred stock. Common stock is the growth stock. As a corporation prospers and grows in value, so does the common stock of the corporation. And if the value of the corporation goes down, so does the value of the common stock. Owning common stock is risky.

Preferred stock is nongrowth stock. Its value is fixed when it is issued.

As a corporation prospers and grows in value, the preferred stock does not grow in value, and if the value of the corporation goes down, the preferred stock does not necessarily go down. Preferred stockholders get the first right to receive dividends paid by the corporation. If the corporation is sold or liquidated, preferred stockholders have the right to get paid for their stock before common stockholders. When preferred stock is issued by a corporation, it has a predetermined dividend. For example, 15 percent preferred stock with a face value of $100 means that if a corporation pays a dividend, the preferred stockholders will receive $15 of dividend income for each $100 of preferred stock they own.

Preferred stock can be issued so that the corporation is required to pay the agreed-upon dividend, or it can be issued so that the payment of the dividend is left to the corporation's discretion. If the preferred stock is "cumulative preferred stock," the corporation must pay the agreed-upon dividend every year. If the corporation cannot afford to make a dividend payment to cumulative preferred stockholders, then it must make up these missed dividend payments in future years.

If the preferred stock is "noncumulative preferred stock," the corporation may or may not pay dividends each year. If these dividends are not paid, they do not have to be made up in later years.

If a corporation is sold or dissolved, the preferred stockholders receive all the proceeds, after all creditors are paid, until the face value of their preferred shares, plus any dividends owed, is paid. Preferred stockholders get paid before common stockholders.

A corporate recapitalization occurs when a common stockholder exchanges common stock for shares of preferred stock. While there are many variations on how one of these tax-free trades is made, one of the more common types that was used prior to 1988 is described as follows:

The existing common stock was valued by an independent appraiser.

The corporation issued preferred stock to the common stockholder in exchange for all or part of the common stock owned by that stockholder.

The corporation issued new common stock to the preferred stockholder's children or grandchildren or other designated individuals. Or the original stockholder gave the common stock to his or her children or grandchildren or to other designated individuals.

The recipients of the common stock paid for their common stock if it was issued by the corporation. Since the corporation was only worth the value of the preferred stock, the price of the common stock would be very low.

The end result of this stock trade (recapitalization) was that the children or grandchildren had all the growth (common) stock. The original stockholder had no-growth (preferred) stock and had removed the future growth of the corporation from the stockholder's estate.

The most difficult and risky aspect of a corporate recapitalization is how the preferred stock is valued. Because preferred stock in a closely held corporation is often structured in such a manner as to make its value problematical, it is not uncommon to have it valued significantly below the value of the corporation as a whole. When this occurs, the common stock is worth more, which may result in federal gift-tax implications when the common stock is given to children or grandchildren. The IRS, in 1983, issued some guidelines as to how preferred stock is to be valued in a corporate recapitalization. These guidelines should be adhered to in a recapitalization to avoid later problems.

Following is an example of how a recapitalization worked prior to 1988:

John Walls, a man in his late sixties, and his wife Betsy, who is the same age, have spent all their lives accumulating an estate. They own a small print shop that designs and produces a line of greeting and Christmas cards. Their business was incorporated years ago. All the corporation's common stock is in John's name.

John and Betsy have three children. Their son, Dave, works for the corporation. Their two daughters, Sally and Betty, have never worked in the business. Sally is a successful businessperson, Betty a homemaker.

John and Betsy depend on their corporation for their livelihood.

Both John and Betsy want their son, Dave, to operate and own the business upon their deaths. They also want to be fair to their daughters. If John dies, Betsy needs to receive cash from the business. If the estate continues to grow at its present rate, the federal estate taxes that will ultimately have to be paid by the children may force the sale of the family business.

John and Betsy's advisers recommend a recapitalization to them. A report is issued by a professional appraiser stating that the common stock of the family's business is worth $750,000. After conferring with their appraiser and tax advisers, they agree that the preferred stock can be valued at $710,000. This will leave $40,000 worth of common stock to divide among Dave, Sally, and Betty.

John trades $710,000 worth of his common stock for $710,000 worth of 15 percent noncumulative preferred stock. The preferred stock has the right to vote on all corporate matters. John, however, still owns $40,000 worth of common stock, which he can divide up among Dave, Betty, and Sally in any manner he and Betsy decide. John and Betsy can give up to $20,000 a year to each of their children federal gift-tax-free. If they want to give Dave more than $20,000 worth of stock, either they can use up part of the exemption equivalent, or they can make a $20,000 gift in the current year and the remainder the next year. No matter how the gifts are made, any future growth in the value of the corporation will be passed on to John and Betsy's children free from federal gift, estate, or income tax.

Under our example, John transferred the future appreciation of the corporation to the children in the percentages that he and Betsy desired, federal income-tax- and gift-tax-free. John and Betsy also retained control of the corporation because the preferred stock had voting rights. John and Betsy continued to work in the family corporation and continued to take their salaries. They have also assured themselves that if the business does well, they can receive dividend payments upon retirement. On John's death, he can leave the preferred stock to Betsy so that she may continue to enjoy all the ownership benefits. On Betsy's death, Dave will own and control the family corporation, fulfilling John and Betsy's desires.

Figure 30-1 will help you understand our example.

The example of John and Betsy is illustrative of how a recapitalization used to work. A recapitalization could be structured to accommodate almost any family situation that involved a family-owned corporation. This was not a technique that was commonly used because only trained tax advisers understood it and knew how to implement it.

There is a second freezing technique known as a partnership freeze. It is used to freeze assets other than corporate stock. This technique accomplishes all the objectives that are accomplished by a recapitalization. It is more advantageous than a recapitalization. Since no corporation is involved, many of the valuation problems encountered in a recapitalization are avoided. In addition, there is no double tax on income when using a partnership.

The definition of a partnership is any endeavor entered into by two or more people with a view to making a profit. Profit can be made through operating a business, or it can be made by investing in assets for a later sale. Either way, the business or assets can be placed in a partnership. A partnership may either be a general partnership or a limited partnership. In a general partnership, all partners have an element of control and therefore have unlimited liability. A limited partnership has both general and limited partners. The general partners control a limited partnership and have the same liability as they would in a general partnership. The limited partners do not have control and are liable only to the extent of their partnership investment.

Either a general partnership interest or a limited partnership interest can be frozen for estate-planning purposes. Just like no-growth preferred stock, partnership ownership can be established in such a manner that its value does not increase. Any nonfrozen partnership owner-

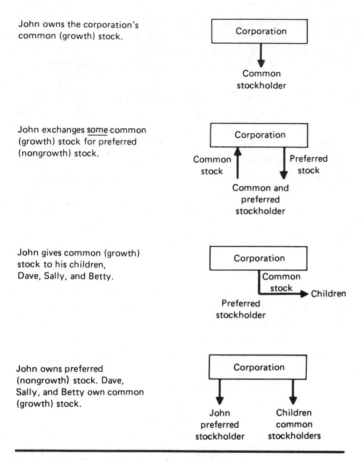

John owns the corporation's common (growth) stock.

Corporation

Common stockholder

John exchanges some common (growth) stock for preferred (nongrowth) stock.

Corporation

Common stock   Preferred stock

Common and preferred stockholder

John gives common (growth) stock to his children, Dave, Sally, and Betty.

Corporation

Common stock → Children

Preferred stockholder

John owns preferred (nongrowth) stock. Dave, Sally, and Betty own common (growth) stock.

Corporation

John preferred stockholder   Children common stockholders

Figure 30-1. Recapitalization of corporation.

ship will then be growth ownership. To illustrate this concept, we will continue the example of John and Betsy.

John and Betsy own a building in a joint tenancy. It, like the corporation, is increasing in value. John and Betsy want the building's appreciation out of their estates but want to keep the income they receive from the building.

John and Betsy have the building appraised. It is worth $650,000. John and Betsy then form a limited partnership and transfer the building into the partnership in exchange for a 50 percent general partnership interest for each of them.

John and Betsy each owned 50 percent of the building *before* the partnership was formed, and nothing has changed except they have a new name on the deed—the name of the partnership.

The formal partnership agreement states that upon the sale of the building or the liquidation of the partnership, the general partners,

John and Betsy, will receive the value of the building as it was appraised when put into the partnership. The value at that time was $650,000. Thus the most John and Betsy could receive in the future is $325,000 each. The value of the building is frozen in the same manner as a corporate recapitalization.

After the partnership is formed, Dave, Betty, and Sally will buy limited partnership interests of the partnership. The price for these limited partnership interests would, however, not be high because, as in the recapitalization of the corporation, the amount each can purchase will be decided by John and Betsy. If John and Betsy decide to sell $10,000 worth of limited partnership interests, $4000 worth each may go to Betty and Sally and $2000 to Dave. Betty and Sally would each have 40 percent of the future growth of the building, and Dave would have 20 percent.

John and Betsy can retain the income from the building. The partnership can provide an income to them before any of that income is paid to the children.

Under the example of a partnership freeze, John and Betsy transferred the future appreciation of their building to their children in the percentage that John and Betsy decided, federal income-tax- and gift-tax-free. John and Betsy also retained control of the building because they became general partners. As general partners, they control the partnership. John and Betsy continued to receive the income from the building. On either John's or Betsy's death, the survivor will continue to receive income from the building. On the deaths of both John and Betsy, Betty, Sally, and Dave will own the partnership and therefore will own the building. The partnership freeze, like the recapitalization, has accomplished all of John and Betsy's planning objectives.

This second example involving John and Betsy illustrates one of the many ways that a partnership freeze was used prior to 1988. Like the recapitalization of a corporation, a partnership freeze was understood and properly used only by trained tax advisers. Figure 30.2 will help you see how this concept worked.

Changes in Freezing Techniques Made by Section 2036(c)

Once section 2036(c) became effective in 1988, the rules for freezing techniques were changed substantially. This antifreeze law stated that for virtually all purposes, traditional freezing techniques would have no effect. The appreciation of the property transferred to a family member was to be included at death in the estate of the person who attempted to transfer it.

A transfer of property fell under the provisions of section 2036(c) if the following elements were present:

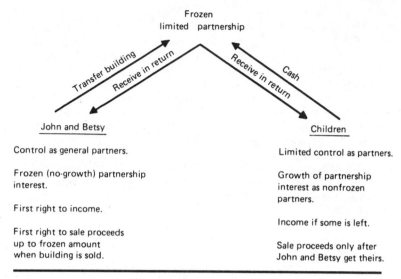

Figure 30-2. Frozen limited partnership.

A person who owned a substantial interest in an enterprise transferred part of it.

The person making the transfer kept or retained an interest in the enterprise.

The part of the enterprise transferred represented a disproportionate part of the appreciation in the enterprise.

A substantial interest in an enterprise under section 2036(c) meant that a person had 10 percent or more control of the enterprise, its income, or both. For purposes of determining 10 percent control, all ownership by a family was lumped together. For example, if Ken Dole owned part of a building, his wife owned part, his father owned part, and his children and their spouses owned part, but only Ken made a transfer, for purposes of section 2036(c) Ken was considered to own the whole building.

The control element was only one part of the scope of section 2036(c). It applied to any property that was considered to be an "enterprise." An enterprise included just about any business or property that might produce income or some other form of gain. There was much confusion as to exactly what an enterprise was, something that was never really resolved.

It was clear that, under section 2036(c), our earlier examples of freezing techniques would no longer accomplish the desired result. Because

John owned a substantial part of the enterprise and he transferred part of it—the common stock—which had the potential to appreciate in value, the entire value of the common stock would have been included in his estate. Section 2036(c) completely defeated the attempted freeze.

The same would have been true of the partnership freeze example. The limited partnership interests held by Dave, Betty, and Sally would have been included in John's and Betsy's estates when they died.

Section 2036(c) was so broad that it was applicable to almost every transaction between family members where the person who made the transfer kept some income or control and the recipients received the appreciation in value. The law was so all-encompassing that it could apply even if a family member bought property from another family member and paid full fair market value for it! All in all, because of its broad application and complexity, it simply did not work.

Changes in Freezing Techniques Made by the Revenue Reconciliation Act of 1990

Congress, in the Revenue Reconciliation Act of 1990 (which we will shorten to 1990 Act), repealed Code section 2036(c) retroactively to the date of its enactment and replaced it with a new set of rules. Every transaction that has the potential to freeze an estate must be analyzed in light of these new rules.

As explained earlier, the focus of section 2036(c) was to include any appreciation in the value of property after its transfer in the estate of the person who transferred it. This made it virtually impossible for an individual to freeze the value of the property; the value was taxed for federal estate-tax purposes in the transferring person's estate.

Traditional freezing techniques were based on the assumption that the value of future appreciation is very low and that the value of the retained interest is very high. Under our earlier example of a traditional recapitalization, when John transferred common stock to his children, his advisers valued it at a much lower value than the preferred stock that John retained. By doing this, the cost of transferring the future appreciation of the business to John's children was very low.

The new rules take a different approach. Instead of allowing the taxpayer to value the property, the new law sets out how property is to be valued. In addition, instead of imposing federal estate tax at the death of the person who makes the transfer, the new rules immediately subject the transfer to federal gift tax.

The new rules, in most situations, require John to value the preferred stock at a low or no value. Under John's plan to recapitalize the corporation, federal gift tax may well be generated when he gives the common stock away to his children because it will be valued at a substantially higher value than it would have been prior to the new rules.

The same is true in a traditional partnership freeze. Again, under the new rules the value of the general partnership interest is valued lower and the limited partnership interests are valued at a higher amount. This allows Uncle Sam to subject the property to his federal gift tax immediately, rather than waiting to collect the federal estate tax as was the case under section 2036(c). It also makes a recapitalization much less attractive from a planning point of view.

Under the new rules, some of these valuation issues are addressed under certain distribution rules for corporations and partnerships. Now, if an individual transfers an interest in a corporation or partnership and retains a right to distributions from a corporation with respect to its stock or a right to distributions from a partnership with respect to a partner's interest in the partnership, that distribution right is given a zero value. The transferred interest—the part that will appreciate—is thus deemed to have all the value.

These distribution rules also apply to persons who "control" an entity immediately prior to the transfer. Control is defined as holding at least 50 percent, by vote or by value, of the stock of a corporation or at least 50 percent of the capital or profits interests in a partnership, or having any interest as a general partner in a limited partnership. As with section 2036(c), the ownership of certain family members are lumped together for purposes of the 50 percent requirement.

For transfers of other types of interests, the valuation rules apply regardless of whether the person making the transfer or family members have control. Some of these types of interests include rights upon liquidation and conversion, and puts and calls.

The new rules recognize that a retained interest is not always worthless. If a corporation, for example, is paying periodic dividends under cumulative preferred stock at a fixed rate, and that stock is the retained interest, then the zero-value concept does not apply. These payments are called "qualified payment" rights under the new law. By properly structuring a recapitalization by including qualified payment rights, the value of the gift may be decreased to such an extent that the recapitalization may be attractive. There are other exceptions to the zero-value rule for other types of interests.

As usual, the new law comes with its own baggage of complexities. For example, the 1990 Act introduces special valuation rules for different types of transactions. One set of rules applies to transfers of certain types of interests in corporations or partnerships. Another set of special valuation rules applies to transfers of interests in trust. Still another set of rules provides that the value of property is determined without regard to certain rights, options, or restrictions; this set of rules applies to buy–sell agreements. And, a set of rules deals with the valuation of rights that terminate or lapse.

For transfers in trust, the valuation rules disregard the value of any retained interest which is not a qualified interest. A qualified interest is the right to receive fixed amounts, payable not less than annually, or the right to receive amounts which are a fixed percentage of the fair market value of the property, not less than annually, and any remainder interest which is not contingent on some event occurring in the future. Thus if an interest retained by a person making a gift to a trust is not a qualified interest, the retained interest is treated as having no value and does not decrease the value of the gift. This concept is much like the "qualified payment" right for recapitalizations.

There are other exceptions to the valuation rules for transfers in trust. These valuation rules do not apply if there is no completed gift. This would include the situation where a maker funds a revocable living trust. There is no gift made when transferring one's property to one's revocable living trust; it is an incomplete gift. Another exception applies to the holding of a personal residence in a trust.

Similarly, in the context of buy–sell agreements, the value of property being transferred is determined without regard to any option, agreement, or other right to acquire or use the property at a price less than the fair market value of the property or without regard to any restriction on the right to sell or use the property. This means that a price established in a buy–sell agreement to purchase the stock of a shareholder will not be binding for estate, gift, or generation-skipping transfer tax purposes unless the buy–sell agreement is a bona fide business arrangement and is not a device to transfer property to members of a person's family for less than full market value. Also, its terms must be comparable to similar agreements entered into by persons in arms-length transactions.

The valuation rule for lapsing rights provides that if a person who makes a transfer fails to exercise any retained voting or liquidation rights in a corporation or partnership, then that failure to exercise lapses and is treated as a transfer by the individual by gift or it may be included in the person's estate for federal estate-tax purposes.

The new rules introduced by the 1990 Act was extremely complex, and we have only touched the surface of many of the provisions contained in the law. The implication of the new valuation rules are not clear and will likely not be for some time because of its broad scope and its lack of history in terms of court cases and IRS rules explaining its effects. The general provisions of our federal tax laws have now changed several times in the last several years and have made it much more difficult to freeze estates and pass on any future appreciation in a business or other enterprise. The only good news is that section 2036(c) has been repealed and the traditional estate freezing techniques are once again available, subject to the new valuation rules.

One of the most effective methods for avoiding the new rules and shifting appreciation to family members is to plan ahead. Creating more than one class of stock in a new corporation may allow you to steer clear of these estate freezing rules.

For example, Tammi had decided to begin a new basket-decorating and gift business. Her children, Shayna, David, and Brian, will be running the business with her and Tammi hopes they will take over the business one day.

Typically, prior to section 2036(c) and the new rules, if Tammi incorporated her new business, she would own all the common stock. Now it may be appropriate to have preferred stock issued to Tammi and common stock issued to Shayna, David, and Brian before the business begins, especially if Tammi has a large estate. This would keep the growth in the value of the corporation out of Tammi's estate and there should be no gift-tax consequences, assuming Tammi and the children each contributed their own funds to the business.

Putting your estate in cold storage has traditionally been a most effective estate-planning tool. In certain situations it is still possible to freeze the value of property. The advice of your estate-planning experts in the planning and implementation of these family freeze techniques is of critical importance if you wish to put your estate in cold storage.

31

Loans to Family Members

"It's Hard to Be Your Family's Banker"

Loans to family members have been one of the most popular—and safe—methods of freezing the value of an estate and shifting income to family members in lower tax brackets. Unfortunately, the Supreme Court and the Tax Reform Act of 1984 have done a great deal to discourage the use of loans to family members. As a matter of fact, not only are the rules for such loans made after June 6, 1984, totally different from the rules prior to that date, but loans made in the past, which many, if not most, tax practitioners felt were gift-tax-free, may now be subject to the gift tax.

In the past, two types of intrafamily loans have been used for estate and income tax planning purposes. These are the below-market loan and the interest-free loan.

The *below market loan* is a loan made by one family member to another for less than the going interest rate. For example, a child could go to a bank and borrow money at 12 percent interest, but a parent could lend the child the money for 6 percent. Under prior law, the effect was twofold. The child only had to pay 6 percent interest, which represented a substantial economic savings. The child, however, received an income tax deduction for the interest, and the parent only paid income tax on the 6 percent received.

The *interest-free loan* was based on the same principles, except no interest was charged. There was no payment of interest by the child, and there was no income to the parent.

For many years, the IRS felt that if a parent made a below-market or interest-free loan to a child, a gift had been made. The amount of the gift, according to the IRS, was the difference between the prevailing market rate of interest and the interest, if any, charged by the parent. In our example above, the gift was considered by the IRS to be 6 percent of the amount loaned if a below-market loan was made, or 12 percent if an interest-free loan was made.

Whether or not a gift was made was generally inconsequential to most Americans. Since every American can give away $10,000 each year to as many people as the giver desires, and a husband and wife can team up to give away $20,000, most loans were not big enough to generate a gift tax. For a $100,000 loan, where the going interest rate was 12 percent, the gift on a below-market loan at 6 percent would be $6000 per year; the difference between $12,000 if full market interest rates were charged and the $6000 actually charged. On an interest-free loan, the difference would be $12,000 per year.

A $6000 gift would be below the $10,000 annual exclusion, making it gift-tax-free. A $12,000 gift could be made gift-tax-free by having both parents make the gift. Thus, the gift tax, even if the IRS contention was correct, would only come into play on very large interest-free or below-market loans.

For those Americans who made large interest-free or below-market loans, demand loans were used to avoid the gift tax. A *demand loan* is a loan which can be called or demanded by the lender at any time. This type of loan does not have a fixed due date. Since interest-free or below-market demand loans had no actual due date, the theory was that the amount of a gift could not be computed.

When the IRS contested this theory in the courts, it invariably lost. The courts agreed that the amount of the gift could not be computed and, in addition, held that a gift had not really been made.

The courts did hold, however, that if a below-market or interest-free loan was made and a demand note was not utilized, a gift did occur. For example, a note for five years at no interest had a gift element. The market interest rate on the note for a five-year term, which was easily computed, was the amount of the gift. The only difference between this transaction and a demand note was that the demand note was not fixed as to time of payment.

The Supreme Court, in an historic 1984 decision, held that interest-free or below-interest loans, whether on a demand basis or for a fixed term, were subject to the gift tax. Worse, the Supreme Court overturned court cases which untold numbers of tax advisers and their clients had relied upon for many years. This decision allows the IRS to assess gift taxes for loans made prior to the Supreme Court's decision, even though a vast majority of lower courts had come to an opposite conclusion for years.

Congress got into the act, too. In the Tax Reform Act of 1984, all interest-free and below-market interest loans were addressed. Massive changes were made which have severely curtailed interest-free and below-market loans as viable planning devices.

Any interest-free or below-market loan is considered as a whole economic package, encompassing not only gift tax but also income tax.

The amount of interest which is not charged, that is, the difference between the amount charged and the amount of the market rate of interest, is considered a gift from the lender to the borrower. The gift is computed on an annual basis, or for the term of the note, if less than a year. For term loans over a year in duration, the interest is compounded semiannually. The market rate of interest is determined by the Treasury Department, and the amounts are announced periodically.

Under TRA 1986, interest deductions for personal interest are phased out and then completely denied beginning in 1991. Personal interest is interest that is not related to a trade or business; is not investment interest; is not interest considered in computing income or loss from a passive activity; is not interest from any qualified primary or secondary residence; or is not interest on certain estate-tax payments. Now, interest-free or below-market loans are even more unattractive, given that it will be more difficult to take a deduction for the interest without securing the loans with the residence of the individual who receives the loan.

The difference between the interest rate charged and the government-imposed rate will be considered income to the lender and an income tax deduction to the borrower, assuming the borrower can itemize his or her deductions. The effect is to recharacterize the family loan as a true business transaction. The assumption is that the lender really did charge interest, the borrower really did pay interest, and a gift was made.

For example, if the prevailing federal rate is 10 percent and an interest-free loan of $100,000 is made from a grandparent to a grandchild for the term of six months, the transaction would be viewed as a gift loan. The grandparent would have income of $5000, representing the income that the grandparent would have earned on the money in 6 months at the federal rate. The grandchild may have a tax deduction of $5000—if the loan is secured by the grandchild's home or second home, or is otherwise not personal interest, and the grandchild can itemize deductions. There also is a gift of $5000 from the grandparent to the grandchild.

There are two additional rules that may aid taxpayers who are considering a below-market or interest-free loan to a family member. The first is that for all loans that are less than $100,000, the amount considered as income to the lender and a deduction by the borrower cannot exceed the investment income of the borrower. If the borrower does not invest the loan proceeds in an income-producing investment or does not have other investment income, generally the income tax provisions will not apply. This leaves the opportunity for below-market interest or interest-free loans for college, buying a house, or other non-income-producing uses. The loan cannot be one which is aimed at tax avoidance, however, and it must be secured by the borrower's primary or secondary residence for the interest to be deductible.

The second rule deals with loans of less than $10,000 per year. As long as the proceeds from these interest-free or below-market loans are not used to buy or carry income-producing property, these loans do not fall under the otherwise complex rules.

Below-market or interest-free family loans are not viable planning tools in most situations. The complex gift-tax and income tax rules make them economically unattractive and difficult to use. Avoid them, unless you are well advised to the contrary by a tax expert.

Below-Market Rate or Interest-Free Loans to Family Members

Create income to the lender

May allow a deduction to the borrower if secured by a residence or is not otherwise considered personal interest

Are gifts to the extent that market interest is not charged

Are only free from complex rules if less than $10,000

32

Sales to Family Members

"Caveat Emptor"

It is possible to freeze the value of certain assets in an estate by selling them to family members on an installment basis. Just like a loan, an installment sale appears to be easy on its face. Also, like a loan, this technique, in order to work, has to be implemented properly. Because of the changes in laws affecting freezing techniques in the Revenue Reconciliation Act of 1990, discussed in Chapter 30, these rules must be carefully reviewed by estate-planning professionals to determine their effects on a particulat sale.

As a result of inflation, most assets are continually going up in value. As we have discussed, inflation forces taxpayers and their estates into higher tax brackets.

Giving an appreciating asset away may not be feasible because either the annual exclusion may not be sufficient to prevent federal gift tax or the exemption equivalent may not be available. Also, many of us are reluctant to give away assets because we want to make sure we have our assets to provide for our security and comfort as we grow older. Under these circumstances, an installment sale to a family member can be an attractive planning alternative.

A sale to a family member is the same as any other sale. A decision is made by the seller as to what asset or assets are to be sold and for what price and under what terms they are to be sold. The sale is then consummated.

A sale to a family member eliminates an appreciating asset from the estate of the seller. The gift- or estate-tax consequences of such a sale will have to be determined under the new valuation rules introduced by the Revenue Reconciliation Act of 1990. The asset is replaced by a promissory note. A promissory note, as we discussed earlier, has a calculated time value. Whatever this calculated value is determined to be at the death of the note owner is the value that is included in the estate for federal estate-tax purposes. Thus the value of the promissory note is less than the value of the asset it replaced in the estate of the seller.

By selling an asset on the installment basis, you may convert a non-income-producing asset to an asset which can provide you with income. Many older taxpayers who are asset rich but cash poor can use this technique to generate needed income and remove the appreciating value of an asset from their estates, subject to the valuation rules contained in the Revenue Reconciliation Act of 1990.

An installment sale to a family member is a transaction that should not be entered into without a great deal of thought because of the tax and the economic results that can occur.

The profit from an installment sale is subject to income tax. TRA 1986 eliminated the favorable maximum capital gains rate of 20 percent and lowered income tax rates in general. The Revenue Reconciliation Act of 1990 made some changes in those income tax brackets. Now, the profit may be taxed as high as 31 percent, although the maximum rate is 28 percent for property held for more than one year. The interest will be taxed as ordinary income and can be taxed as high as 31 percent.

The type of property chosen for sale is an important consideration for sales between family members. Sales between family members of property subject to depreciation do not qualify for installment sales. TRA 1986 excludes installment sales for publicly traded securities.

TRA 1986 severely curtailed deductions for interest payments. On most installment sales, the interest will not be deductible, at least fully. From 1987 to 1990, the amount of interest deductible declines each year, and, in 1991, most interest deductions are prohibited. Interest deductions for loans secured by a primary or secondary residence are fully deductible, but structuring an installment sale to meet this requirement is difficult. The deductibility of interest is clearly a tax and economic factor that must be considered before an installment sale is entered into.

When you sell an asset to a family member, you must be sure that the family member has the economic ability to make the installment payments to you. This is a problem that is oftentimes overlooked. If, after a sale is made, your loved one is financially unable to meet the payments, what are you going to do? Are you going to foreclose on the note? Probably not. You will probably be inclined to forgive the note. If you do, you will not have the income you need nor the asset you sold. Worse yet, you will have made a gift and may have to pay federal gift tax to boot.

If an asset is sold to a family member at a price below its fair market value, the difference between the fair market value of the asset and the actual price paid for it is a gift. Fair market value, remember, is the value for which a willing buyer would sell an asset to a willing seller when neither is subject to any compulsion to buy or sell and both are aware of the facts relevant to the sale.

The best way to determine an asset's fair value is by professional appraisal. If this is not accomplished, be ready to defend the purchase price used. If there is an IRS audit as to the sale and the asset was not valued by a professional, the price will be scrutinized by the IRS. Under our tax law the burden of proof as to the asset's value is always on the taxpayer. This means the IRS can disagree with your sales price and make you prove that it was the fair market price.

The interest rate that you use in your installment note can be of tax consequence. Earlier, we discussed that a note for a fixed term can be valued in terms of present value. If a note has an interest rate which is lower than prevailing market rates, the difference between the value of the property and the time value of the note can be construed as a gift for federal gift-tax purposes. In addition, the rules for below-interest loans discussed in the previous chapter may apply to the transaction.

What constitutes a favorable interest rate is a matter of conjecture. The Internal Revenue Code states that installment sales must carry certain minimum interest rates. These rates vary depending on the type and the amount of a particular installment sale. The different rates, required under complex rules introduced by the Tax Reform Act of 1984, make it all but impossible to come up with an accurate prevailing market interest rate. To avoid a gift, it is best to charge the interest rate that your bank would charge under similar circumstances.

ERTA provided, and the Tax Reform Act of 1984 retained, a major benefit to real estate owners who would like to sell their land to their family members. On these sales the interest rate is 6 percent, and may be lower if prevailing rates are lower than 6 percent. This special provision applies only to sales totaling $500,000. After all sales exceed $500,000, the general rules apply. Remember, this provision applies only to sales of land. It does not apply to buildings or other improvements on the land.

You can combine a gift and a sale if you choose. If you sell an asset to a family member, you may forgive any installment payment as it becomes due. For example, if you sell property to your two children for $50,000 at 15 percent interest over 10 years in equal payments of principal plus any interest due, the first payment would be $12,500. Of that amount, $5000 is principal ($50,000 divided by 10 years) and $7500 is interest ($50,000 multiplied by 15 percent). Because you have two children, you have two $10,000 annual exclusions available, a total of $20,000. Thus the whole $12,500 payment (or any part of it) can be waived. Because the amount waived is less than the combined annual exclusions, there is no federal gift tax.

Before you waive an installment payment, be aware of the income tax ramifications. The $12,500 is still income to you, and any income tax you would have paid had the installment actually been paid to you will still be due. Your children will still have the advantage of deducting the interest as if it were paid.

The advantage of the gift-sale technique is twofold. The children may not have to come up with cash to make the installment payment, and the $12,500 you would have received (*less* income taxes, of course) is not added to your estate.

The courts have held, however, that if there was no intent that the note be paid because the sale was really a plan to avoid paying federal gift tax, the sale can be defeated and the entire sales price treated as one big current gift.

Family members who buy property under this technique receive a step-up in basis for income tax purposes. For example:

> Sandy and Rich buy a piece of property from their parents for $100,000. Their parents paid $10,000 for the property. If Sandy and Rich sell it for $110,000, only $10,000 ($110,000 less $100,000) is subject to federal income tax.

The family-installment-sale technique has been used so creatively that, in the eyes of Congress, it has been abused. The most common abuse involves a two-sale method. In this method, dad and mom own a second home worth $100,000. They bought it for $20,000. They now wish to sell it. If they sell it for cash, $80,000 (the difference between the selling price of $100,000 and their cost of $20,000) will be income taxable to them, and as a result, if the potential buyer wants to pay cash, dad and mom will have all the gain in the year of the sale. So, dad and mom sell it to the kids for $100,000 for 10 years at a fair interest rate. The kids sell it immediately to the real buyer for cash. The result of the transaction appears to be a good one for everyone. The kids bought the house for $100,000 and sold it for $100,000. They have no taxable gain. Mom and dad pay tax over ten years as opposed to one year. The kids put the money in the bank and draw interest. They use this same interest and some of the principal each year to pay mom and dad. What a great method to save taxes.

In 1980, Congress closed this tax-avoidance door. Today if the kids were to sell the house within two years of buying from mom and dad, mom and dad cannot pay their taxes over ten years; they will pay their total tax in the year the kids sell the house. The solution, of course, is for the kids to wait two years and then sell the house.

Another loophole that Congress closed under ERTA was forgiving an installment note on the death of the note owner. Before ERTA, a parent could, at death, leave an installment note owed by a child to that child. The result was that the installment note was forgiven with no income tax consequence.

This technique is no longer effective. Income tax *will* be due if this technique is used. In our experience, many estate plans use this outdated device. If your planning includes this device, you should amend your plan.

Installment sales are complicated. By way of review, look at the following lists.

Installment Sales Help Sellers Because

They can get appreciating assets out of sellers' estates.

Non-income-producing assets can be favorably converted to an income-producing asset.

Installment Sales Help Buyers Because

Buyers get appreciating assets at a fair price on favorable terms.

Buyers receive a step-up in basis when they buy the asset.

Family installment sales may accomplish some of your estate-planning objectives. They have been abused in the past and may not be as attractive as they once were, but they still represent a viable planning tool. Let your professional estate-planning advisers guide you in their use.

33
Private
Annuities

"The Ultimate Gamble"

The private annuity has long been a favored estate-planning technique. It is discussed by many but, in our experience, understood by few.

A private annuity has three elements. An individual called an "annuitant" (seller) transfers property to a family member called an "obligor" (buyer). The buyer promises to pay the seller certain payments. These payments are paid to the seller for the duration of the seller's life. Sounds like a sale? It is, but this sale has several unique twists which we will examine.

An installment sale, as we discussed earlier, can eliminate an appreciating asset from your estate; however, the asset removed from your estate is replaced by a promissory note. Because of this asset replacement, the installment sale converts appreciating assets to a nonappreciating asset. The value of the nonappreciating installment note, however, still remains in your estate. The installment note creates income to the seller and may create interest deductions for the buyer. The installments are paid for a definite period of time no matter what happens to either the buyer or the seller.

A private annuity is designed so that the value of your appreciating asset and the value of the promissory obligation are *both* totally eliminated from your estate.

An annuity is a promise by the buyer to pay the seller fixed payments *for the life of the seller*. When the seller dies, the buyer owns the asset and does not have to make any more payments. If the buyer dies before the seller, the buyer's heirs must continue the payments.

Annuities are governed by the Internal Revenue Code. Its regulations provide a method to value a private annuity and spell out what the payments for the annuity must be. This method must always be used.

The value of the annuity and the payments resulting from its value are based on two factors. The first factor is how long the seller is expected to live. The number of years that any seller is expected to live is written in the regulations of the Internal Revenue Code in the form of actuarial (life expectancy) tables. The second factor is the interest rate which must be charged. The interest rate is equal to 120 percent of the federal midterm rate in effect for the month in which the annuity is being valued. Your estate-planning adviser can help you calculate this rate.

If you place a value on the property you sell through an annuity and that value is not fair market value, you will also make a gift subject to the federal gift tax. Does this sound familiar?

Using a private annuity is a little bit like gambling. If the seller dies before he or she statistically is supposed to, the buyer wins because the payments end. In addition, the seller's estate wins because the annuity is not includable in the seller's estate. On the other hand, if the seller lives longer than predicted, the buyer continues to make the payments for as long as the seller lives. Remember, an annuity is an agreement by the buyer to pay fixed payments to the seller for the seller's life no matter how long or short the seller's life is.

There is *no* requirement that the seller be in good health. If the seller, however, has a terminal illness, a private annuity cannot be used. An individual who is in poor health but does not have a terminal illness is an excellent candidate for a private annuity.

Care must be taken when an older person contemplates using a private annuity. As age increases, life expectancy decreases. That means that the number of annuity payments decreases and the value of the payments increases. If there are fewer payments to pay for an asset, it necessarily follows that each payment will be higher. These payments may be so high that the buyer cannot afford to make them, particularly if the seller fools everyone and turns into Methuselah.

The income tax ramifications of a private annuity may be disadvantageous. The federal income tax treatment of the payments made to a seller is similar to that afforded installment sales. A portion of each payment is a return of the seller's original adjusted cost basis, which is tax-free. Another portion of each payment is the capital gain element, which is the difference between the fair market value of the asset transferred under the annuity and the asset's original cost to the seller, as adjusted for depreciation and other factors. The remainder of each payment is the interest factor.

A private annuity is an estate-planning technique that allows a seller to remove an asset completely from the seller's estate, still maintain an income stream from that asset, and assure the buyer that all payments cease on the seller's death.

The new valuation rules in the Revenue Reconciliation Act of 1990 do not necessarily apply to private annuities, except in situations where the annuity is used to transfer certain types of property for less than full value. For the transfer of an interest in a personal residence, the new valuation rules do not apply if the seller retains an interest in the residence for life or a term of years. Every private annuity transaction should be reviewed by estate-planning professionals to determine whether the new valuation rules apply.

Annuities, properly drafted and implemented, still represent the ultimate gamble. Will the seller live longer—or shorter—than he or she is supposed to?

34

Installment
Payment
of Estate Taxes

"The Easy-Payment Plan"

A problem which has existed since the advent of federal estate tax is the inability of nonliquid estates to pay their federal estate tax when due. Closely held businesses and farms have been especially vulnerable to this problem.

The federal tax is ordinarily payable in cash nine months after date of death. If there is not enough cash available to pay the tax, a problem arises. Needless to say, the Internal Revenue Code gives the IRS power to make sure the taxes are paid by enforcing the collection of the federal estate tax. Simply put, the IRS can seize and sell assets of the estate in order to raise the cash needed to satisfy the tax. When faced with this alternative, the agent of the estate may choose to sell assets instead of facing IRS "help." Often the effect of a forced sale of assets can be devastating to the estate. Distress sales usually bring lower purchase prices.

If the agent of the estate does not feel selling estate property would be prudent, borrowing to pay the tax may be a solution. Borrowing may not be a viable method of raising cash for payment of federal estate taxes. The assets of the estate may already be mortgaged and lenders may be reluctant to advance additional funds. Interest rates could be prohibitive. Borrowing is not an automatic process in most situations.

The Internal Revenue Code provides some relief for all estates which lack liquidity to pay estate taxes. If the agent of an estate can show reasonable cause, the IRS can allow the estate a deferral on estate-tax payments of up to ten years. However, the estate will have to pay interest on the estate tax due at then current market rates, but the interest is deductible to the estate even under TRA 1986. The IRS can also require that the estate post a bond as security. Bonds are not cheap. Whether the agent of the estate chooses to borrow from the IRS or traditional sources will depend upon the rate of interest and terms required by each.

While lack of liquidity can be a problem in all estates, those which consist primarily of a closely held business, farm, or ranch are particularly vulnerable. This vulnerability arises from the fact that these business interests are extremely difficult to sell or borrow against. A closely held business is normally owned by a family. Even if owned partially by a family, family involvement is usually intense. If federal estate taxes force a family to sell all or part of its business, the family may lose its source of livelihood.

In recognition of these hardships, Congress has passed certain federal estate-tax rules to ease the burden of federal estate tax on family business survivors.

Congress has long allowed the estate of a business owner to pay federal estate tax on an easy-payment plan. Historically, qualification for this easy-payment plan was not so easy. This was because the value of the business interest had to be 65 percent of the value of the total estate after it was reduced by debts and expenses.

As a result of ERTA, the value of the business interest has to be only 35 percent of the value of the total estate *less* debts and expenses to qualify for the federal estate-tax easy-payment plan. If an estate meets this test, the agent of the estate can pay the estate's federal estate tax attributable to the business interest over a fourteen-year period.

If an estate qualifies, the benefits can be substantial. The first four years of payments are interest only. The interest rate is an incredibly low 4 percent for the portion of the estate tax attributable to the first $1,000,000 of closely held business property. Interest on deferred estate tax in excess of the 4 percent portion is subject to the regular rate of interest contained in the Internal Revenue Code. That part of the estate tax subject to the 4 percent rate is the lesser of $345,800 or the estate tax attributable to the closely held business.

It is probably advantageous to attempt to qualify for the easy-payment plan whether an estate is liquid or not. Clearly, an interest rate of 4 percent is extremely favorable. Even if an estate has liquidity, the agent of an estate can probably invest those liquid dollars at a higher interest rate than the 4 percent that must be paid to the government.

The difference between the rate received on an investment and the 4 percent interest that must be paid to the government can return a significant profit to the estate beneficiaries.

The easy-payment plan is not a panacea. Here, too, there are traps for the unwary taxpayer. For example, a gift which is made within three years of the death of a business owner will be brought back into the estate for purposes of calculating the 35 percent requirement. A large gift within three years of death can nullify use of the easy-payment plan, especially if the reason for the gift was to qualify the estate for the easy-payment plan.

Because Congress has provided the easy-payment plan to the families of business owners, many family businesses may survive the death of their principal owners.

35

Using Assets
of a Corporation
to Pay Death Costs

"Trading Dollars for Stock"

Many of our clients own all or part of the stock of a successful corporation which has cash or assets that can be readily converted to cash. Their estates consist primarily of their corporate stock. This stock may be hard to sell or may be difficult to borrow against at their deaths. The money needed by their beneficiaries to pay death taxes and expenses is, unfortunately, in the wrong place; it is in the corporation, not the estate.

The federal government has long recognized the difficulty of using corporate assets to pay personal death taxes and, as a result, passed section 303 of the Internal Revenue Code. Section 303 is a provision which allows corporations to provide their assets to pay the federal and state death taxes, funeral expenses, and other death expenses of deceased stockholders. Professional estate planners refer to this technique as a section 303 redemption.

A section 303 redemption is merely the purchase by a corporation of enough of a deceased stockholder's stock of that corporation to pay all or part of the deceased shareholder's state and federal death taxes, funeral expenses, and administrative expenses. Administrative expenses include expenses involved in the operation and maintenance of an estate.

For example, a deceased businessperson owned 1 million shares in XYZ Corporation worth $1 million, or $1.00 per share. The state and federal death taxes and the funeral and administrative expenses of the estate total $325,000. Assuming the stock meets all of the technical requirements of section 303, the estate may sell $325,000 worth of stock (325,000 shares) back to XYZ Corporation. The cash received by the estate in exchange for the stock *must* be used to pay the deceased stockholder's death expenses. As a result, cash or other liquid assets in the corporation have been successfully exchanged for the "nonliquid" stock.

An additional reason why section 303 is a benefit to a corporate owner is because of the income tax savings it can generate. Generally, a stockholder who sells only part of his or her stock in a corporation back to that same corporation will be subject to federal income tax on the sale proceeds as if those sale proceeds were a dividend. A dividend is a terrible way to be taxed—a dividend creates two federal income taxes.

Double taxation occurs with a dividend because the money that a corporation uses to buy its own stock is usually money that has already been subject to corporate federal income tax. For example, assume that a corporation is in the 34 percent tax bracket, the maximum corporate tax bracket under TRA 1986. A dollar of profit is made and the corporation pays $0.34 on that $1. This is the first tax. The $0.66 left is then used by the corporation to purchase its stock from the selling stockholder. The selling stockholder receives the $0.66 for his or her stock and, under TRA 1986 and the Revenue Reconciliation Act of 1990, if the stockholder has held the stock for more than one year, the $0.66 will likely be taxed at 28 percent. The result is that the selling stockholder has $0.48 of the dollar that was originally profit in his or her corporation. This represents, because of the double tax, a combined income tax rate of 52 percent. It used to be even worse. Before TRA 1986, the double tax was as high as 75 percent, and prior to ERTA it was as high as 85 percent!

On the death of a stockholder, the stock's cost basis is increased, or "stepped up," to its value as of the day of the stockholder's death. We have discussed step-up in basis rules in other chapters. If the stock is sold back to the corporation, there should be little if any income tax. An example will help you understand:

> The deceased stockholder originally paid $100,000 (cost basis) for 325,000 shares of stock that the estate sold back to the corporation. If the stockholder sold that same stock to a third party before death, the gain would have been $225,000 ($325,000 less $100,000). If the stock was worth $325,000 on death, however, the step-up in basis rule gives the stock a new cost basis of $325,000. As a result, if the stock was sold for $325,000 back to the corporation under section 303, there would be no gain or federal income tax at all.

Now that we have explained the advantages section 303 allows the estates of corporate owners, we will discuss some of the requirements that must be met in order to use it. (Please refer to Figure 35-1.)

Before ERTA, the value of the stock that was owned by the deceased stockholder had to be 50 percent of the value of the adjusted gross estate to qualify for section 303. Basically, the adjusted gross estate is the value of the estate *less* expenses and debts of that estate. ERTA reduced this percentage to 35 percent. It is much easier for the estate of a corporate business owner to take advantage of section 303 than ever before.

There are other requirements that must be met in order to qualify under section 303. Some of these requirements deal with the time periods under which the stock must be sold. These are complicated and should be discussed with your professional advisers.

There can be disadvantages related to the use of a section 303 redemption. If the corporation does not have liquid assets, section 303 may not be beneficial. The corporation is allowed to distribute property other than money in a section 303 redemption, but if the property distributed cannot be sold by the estate within the time provided in section 303, then the distribution will be taxed as a dividend: a catastrophic result.

Another potential disadvantage of a section 303 redemption is that the deceased stockholder's family may lose control of the family corpo-

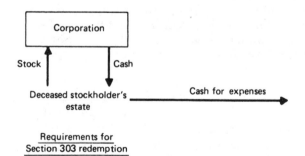

Figure 35-1. Requirements for section 303 redemption.

ration. For example, if the deceased stockholder owned 51 percent of the corporation before death and enough stock is sold back to the corporation under section 303, the family may be left with far less than 50 percent ownership; this can occur when there are stockholders other than family members. When a section 303 redemption is used without proper advice, outsiders can end up controlling a family corporation.

A section 303 redemption usually takes cash out of a corporation. If that corporation needs its cash to survive after the death of its principal shareholder, a section 303 redemption may kill the goose that could lay more golden eggs.

The last disadvantage of section 303 is that it can create a tax trap for the unwary. This section of the Internal Revenue Code is fairly simple when compared to other code sections; however, the technical requirements of section 303 are intricate and, if not thoroughly understood, can result in a tax-planning disaster. The following example should prove our point:

> Bob, a stockholder of Bolt Corporation, reads a book on estate planning and is interested in the chapter on section 303 redemptions. Bob discovers that 35 percent of the value of his estate must be corporate stock to qualify. He calculates the value of his Bolt stock and finds its value is less than 35 percent of the value of his estate. As a result, our self-taught stockholder figures out that if he gives some property (other than Bolt stock) to his spouse, his estate will qualify. He gives property to his spouse and then dies two years later.
>
> Because of one of the intricacies of section 303 and other provisions of ERTA, the amount of the gift Bob made to his spouse is *added back* to his estate. The result is loss of section 303 treatment.
>
> If Bolt Corporation, following the section 303 planning, buys its stock back, all the proceeds received by the estate are taxed *as a dividend.*

Section 303 provides an easy way to convert nonliquid stock into liquid dollars on the death of a stockholder. Used wisely, it can be of great benefit to the beneficiaries of a corporate business owner's estate, but it is a technical section of the Internal Revenue Code, and it should never be used without expert professional advice, both in its conception and in its application.

36

Special Use
Valuation

"Keeping the Farm in the Family"

Farmers and ranchers face unique federal estate-tax problems. Over the years, farm and ranch income has been declining dramatically as a percentage of land value. Thus farmers and ranchers are continually forced into higher federal estate-tax brackets and are unable to generate the income to pay those taxes. This inability to pay can, and often does, force their families to sell all or part of the family farm or ranch.

A family farm or ranch purchased thirty years ago may have cost as little as $10 per acre. During that thirty years, a city and its suburbs might have expanded to within a mile of that farm or ranch. Developers might pay $2000 or $3000 per acre in order to build houses on the farmland or ranchland. The farm or ranch may produce only enough income to feed and provide the basics for the agricultural family. If the land is valued in terms of its ability to produce agricultural income, it will not have a very high value. The difference in values depending on whether the property is valued at its agricultural use or its city use can be staggering. If the federal government used the city value for federal estate-tax purposes, it would force almost every farm and ranch family off their land.

Recognizing this massive problem, Congress, as part of the Tax Reform Act of 1976, passed a relief provision for the special valuation of family farm and ranch property, and for real estate used in other types of family businesses as well. This relief provision is called "special use valuation."

Special use valuation allows farmland and ranchland to be valued at
its agricultural value instead of its value as city property for federal
estate-tax purposes. This valuation method decreases the value of the
farmer's or rancher's estate for federal estate-tax purposes and gives the
farm or ranch family a better opportunity to continue farm and ranch
operations.

Under the Tax Reform Act of 1976, the value of farmland and ranchland in an agricultural estate could be reduced through special use valuation by as much as $500,000. ERTA increased that amount to $750,000.

To qualify for special use valuation, the value of the farmer's or
rancher's assets, including the land and personal property used in the
farm or ranch, *less* the debt secured by that land and personal property,
must be at least 50 percent of the total value of the estate. In addition,
the value of the land itself must be at least equal to 25 percent of the
estate. In qualifying under these percentage rules, the agricultural land
is valued at its city value. The agricultural land must have been used as
farmland or ranchland for a certain period of time prior to the owner's
death and actively managed by the owner or other family members.
The owner must be a U.S. citizen or resident at the time of death.

The land also must pass upon the death of the owner to an heir who
is a close family member. This "qualified heir" then must operate the
farm or ranch for a period of time after the death of the original owner.
All these rules must be met to qualify for special use valuation.

Agricultural property held in joint tenancy or owned in a community-
property state may affect the application of the percentage test. If one-
half of the estate is considered to be owned by the surviving spouse, a
significant portion of the agricultural property will be ignored for purposes of the percentage test.

The property must have been used for farming or ranching for five
of the eight years immediately prior to the owner's death. During this
same period, the owner or a family member had to be actively engaged
in farming or ranching. Under the Tax Reform Act of 1976, this meant
actually being out in the field.

ERTA relaxed this requirement, and the owner or family member
must materially participate in the decision making rather than being out
in the field. This means that they must regularly advise those persons
managing the farm and participate in most decisions.

Farmers and ranchers had a significant problem prior to ERTA with
regard to social security. If farmers or ranchers wanted to qualify for
social security, they could not earn very much income. To be actively
engaged in farming or ranching for purposes of special use valuation,
farmers or ranchers had to work their properties. Thus if a farmer or
rancher was active for purposes of special use valuation, social security

benefits were most likely denied. To qualify for social security meant possible loss of special use valuation. Every farmer or rancher who reached retirement age was caught on the horns of a dilemma.

ERTA has removed this dilemma. A family member can actively manage the farm or ranch on behalf of the owner, special use valuation can be retained, and the owner can qualify for social security benefits.

Upon the owner's death, the property still must pass to a qualified heir. A qualified heir is a family member who will continue to actively manage the farm or ranch. And here, too, active management means decision making, not being out in the field.

Special use valuation does not end with the closing of the original owner's estate. If the heirs dispose of all or part of the property subject to special use valuation within ten years of the original owner's death, the tax savings that originally resulted from special use valuation has to be paid back to the government.

The Internal Revenue Service monitors the ten-year requirement by placing a tax lien on the property which was subject to special use valuation. The IRS, since it has a lien on the property, will know if the property is sold. The seller cannot sell the property until the lien is removed. The IRS gets paid.

A federal tax lien on property makes it difficult for its current owners to mortgage the property. As a result, the family members actively engaged in farming or ranching may find it difficult to borrow money to keep the farm or ranch going.

With the advent of the unlimited marital deduction, the farm and ranch owner will not owe any estate tax if sufficient property passes to the surviving spouse as long as the surviving spouse is a U.S. citizen, or special planning has been done for a non-U.S. citizen. Special use valuation is of no value to the owner under this circumstance because of the marital deduction. However, the special use valuation is available for the surviving spouse's estate provided the surviving spouse actively manages the farm or ranch. This means that the surviving spouse must make some management decisions but does not have to be involved in the day-to-day operating decisions.

Special use valuation is a potential life saver for farm or ranch families. Like many provisions of the Internal Revenue Code, it has its traps. Applied wisely, however, special use valuation can keep our farms and ranches where they belong — in the family.

Requirements for Special Use Valuation

The value of the farm or ranch assets (*less* debts on them) must be at least 50 percent of the deceased owner's estate.

The value of the farmland or ranchland (*less* debts on it) must be at least 25 percent of the deceased owner's estate.

The property must have been actually managed by the deceased owner for five out of the eight years prior to death and must have been used for farming or ranching during the same period.

A qualified heir must actually manage the property after the owner's death.

The land must be used as a farm or ranch for ten years after the owner's death.

The land is subject to a federal tax lien.

The land value can be reduced through special use valuation by as much as $750,000.

Special use valuation also applies to other types of family businesses.

Special use valuation may be particularly valuable to the surviving spouse.

37
Giving It to Charity

"Good Works Deserve Good Benefits"

Methods of charitable giving have been the subject of significant numbers of technical texts. In a society attuned to charity, it is only logical that a myriad of methods is available to all of us to make charitable giving attractive. This chapter is aimed at the person who wants to obtain a rudimentary knowledge of the vast income tax, gift- and estate-tax opportunities afforded by gifts to charity.

Charitable giving falls into a few general categories. These categories include outright gifts, gifts of a part of or an interest in property, and gifts in trust. All these methods can be used during one's lifetime or at one's death; each has separate federal income tax, gift-tax, and estate-tax implications.

Outright gifts of property are probably the most commonly used form of giving. People making an outright gift can make their gifts in money, personal property, or real property.

To receive all the tax benefits that can result from a charitable gift, the gift must be made to an Internal Revenue Code qualified charity. To qualify, the charity must be a public, semipublic, or private foundation which has received special approval from the IRS. When you make a gift, either during lifetime or after your death, it is important that you check with the charitable organization to make sure that it has IRS approval. IRS approval is generally given if the charity is a governmental agency; a religious, charitable, scientific, literary, or educational organization; or a war veterans' or domestic fraternal organization.

A lifetime charitable gift has two distinct tax advantages. The first is that an income tax deduction is generated. The second is that assets, along with their future appreciation, are removed from the value of an estate.

Normally, the income tax deduction that can be taken by the giver is limited to 50 percent of adjusted gross income (AGI). AGI is not taxable income; it is all income *less* certain deductions. The income tax deduction is limited, however, to 30 percent of AGI when the gift is made to semipublic or private charities. These include certain veterans' and fraternal organizations and certain private foundations. When checking to see whether an organization is IRS-approved, you should also check its status as a public, semipublic, or private charity.

There is another income tax deduction limitation that can apply when giving property to charity. It applies generally to property which, if sold prior to TRA 1986, would have been taxed at the now defunct capital gains rate. Even though TRA 1986 eliminated the special maximum capital gains rate of 20 percent, it did not eliminate the special rules that apply when property is given to a charity. The deduction that applies to this type of property is limited to either 50 or 30 percent of AGI when it is given to a public charity and 20 percent of AGI when it is given to a semipublic or private charity.

When giving capital gains property to a public charity, you can elect to have the gift qualify for either the 50 or 30 percent deduction limits. The 30 percent limitation is the simplest. The full fair market value of the property can be deducted from AGI, as long as the deduction does not exceed 30 percent of AGI. If it does, the excess can be used in the next five years.

If you wish to use the 50 percent limitation, then the total amount of the deduction is not allowed. The deduction is limited to the basis or cost of the property. This amount is then subject to the 50 percent limitation. Any excess cannot be carried forward.

These rules can be illustrated as follows:

If your AGI is $100,000 and you give $60,000 in cash to a public charity, then only $50,000 can be deducted in the current year. The remaining $10,000 can be used in the future for up to five years. But if the $60,000 is given to a semipublic or private charity, only $30,000 can be deducted in the current year (30 percent of $100,000). The remainder can be carried forward to the next five years.

Let us assume that your gift is of stock which you bought for $45,000 and that it is currently valued at $55,000. A sale of the stock would create a $10,000 taxable gain.

A gift of the stock to a public charity using the 30 percent rule would result in a $30,000 deduction from your AGI in that current year. The remaining $25,000 could be deducted in a future year, as long as it is deducted within the next five years.

If you choose the 50 percent limitation, then your cost basis, $45,000, is deducted in the current year.

A gift of this stock to a semipublic or private charity will result in a deduction which would be limited to 20 percent of your AGI, or $20,000. The remaining $35,000 can be carried over for the next five years.

There are further limitations on the amount that you can deduct when making a gift of appreciated property to a public charity. One example of the many further limitations can be illustrated as follows: if you give a work of art to a hospital, then your deduction is limited. Since the hospital cannot generally use art work to further its exempt purpose, you can only deduct the original cost of the work of art.

These income tax rules, believe it or not, are not exhaustive. A lot of other income tax rules can come into play, depending on the nature of the property and the type of charity to which you are giving it. For example, under TRA 1986 and the Revenue Reconciliation Act of 1990, giving away real property and some types of personal property owned for less than one year generate another tax called the "alternative minimum tax," which may result in making the gift less attractive. You can see how important it is for you to see a tax adviser before making a charitable gift other than a gift of cash.

While charitable giving almost always has income tax ramifications, direct charitable giving, providing it follows the rules, never results in *gift* taxes. A charitable gift made within three years of your death generally cannot be brought back into your estate for federal estate-tax purposes. An exception to this rule is a gift of life insurance as well as other minor types of gifts.

An outright gift upon death has no income tax advantages or disadvantages. But for federal estate-tax purposes, the value of a gift made to a qualified charity does result in a deduction equal to the fair market value of the gift.

Unlike the income tax deduction rules for charitable gifts, there is *no* percentage limitation for gifts made at death.

If a charitably minded individual is in ill health and may not live, a lifetime charitable gift should be considered instead of a charitable gift on death. A lifetime gift has the potential advantage of reducing income taxes as well as reducing the giver's estate for federal estate-tax purposes, as shown in Figure 37-1.

Many people want to give property to charity at their deaths but want to retain the property for their use during their lifetimes. They would also like, if possible, to receive a current income tax deduction. The Internal Revenue Code allows both these benefits through the use of a gift of a "remainder interest" to charity.

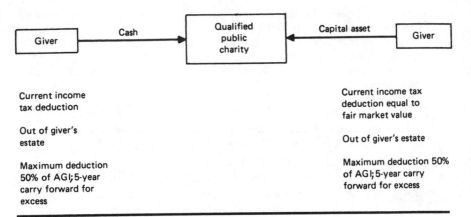

Figure 37-1. Outright gift of cash or capital asset while giver alive.

A gift of a remainder interest that is not in trust is restricted to a farm or a personal residence. This type of gift allows the giver to retain a life estate in the property. Thus the giver can use the property, receive income from the property, and live on the property during life. At the death of the giver, the property automatically passes to the charity.

The value of the remainder interest can be determined under Internal Revenue Code guidelines. Valuation is based on the life expectancy of the giver of the property; if a husband and wife are joint givers, their joint life expectancy can also be calculated. The value of the remainder interest is a deductible expense in the year the remainder interest is given. In addition to this income tax advantage, the asset passes to charity at death and is therefore removed from the estate of the giver. Remember, the gift of a remainder interest that is not in trust is restricted to a farm or personal residence. (See Figure 37-2.)

Gifts to charity from a trust can take many forms. In our experience, the most commonly used charitable trusts are the "remainder trust" and the "lead trust." These vehicles are extremely complex in terms of the rules that govern them. Our discussion is directed toward an understanding of their basic principles.

Charitable Remainder Trust

A charitable remainder trust is a trust to which the maker of the trust transfers income-producing property irrevocably and then retains an income interest in the trust property for the maker or the maker's family. (See Figure 37-3.)

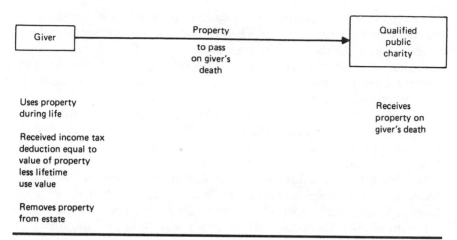

Figure 37-2. Outright remainder interest.

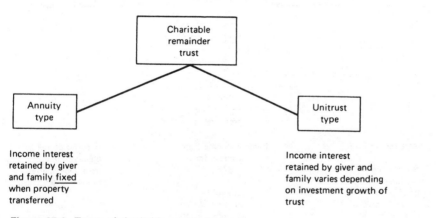

Figure 37-3. Types of charitable remainder trusts.

When the income interest retained by the giver or the giver's family is a fixed amount of the value of the property at the time it is transferred to the trust, the trust is called a charitable remainder annuity trust. When the income interest that is retained by the giver or the giver's family can vary depending on changes in the annual value of the trust fund, the trust is called a charitable remainder unitrust. Regardless of which trust is used, the income must be at least 5 percent of the value of the property in the trust.

A charitable remainder annuity trust is not popular during inflationary times because of its inflexibility. It tends to benefit the charity more than the giver or the giver's family because inflation increases the value of the trust, but the income distributions are fixed as a percentage of the value of the trust property when the property was originally placed in the trust. Thus more of the trust property is left to charity.

A charitable remainder unitrust, however, tends to favor the giver and the giver's family because the income distributions increase as the trust assets increase.

In both these remainder trusts, the beneficiaries of the trusts have a lifetime interest in a percentage value of the assets. At death, the remaining trust assets pass automatically to the named charity or charities. (See Figure 37-4.)

All charitable remainder trusts are similar to remainder interests in property. The income belongs to the beneficiaries, and whatever is left belongs to charity. There is an income tax deduction available to the giver at the time the property is put into the trust in the amount of the

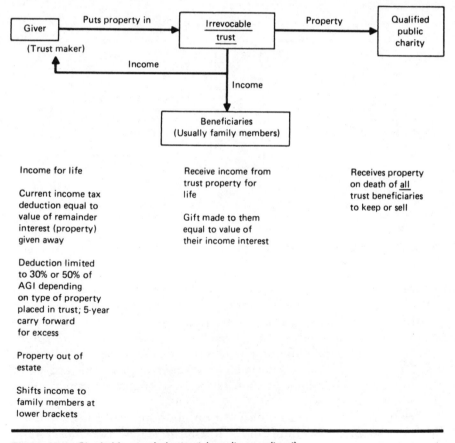

Figure 37-4. Charitable remainder trust (annuity or unitrust).

present value of the remainder interest. This amount can be calculated by using Internal Revenue Code guidelines, as we discussed earlier.

Charitable Lead Trust

A charitable lead trust is the reverse of a charitable remainder trust. Instead of providing income to the beneficiaries and giving the property to charity, a lead trust gives income to charity for a period of time and passes property to the giver's beneficiaries, federal estate-tax-free. (See Figure 37-5.)

A lead trust involves valuing the remainder interest of the property to be placed in trust. As we mentioned, it is possible to value the remainder interest of property. The value of the remainder interest in this

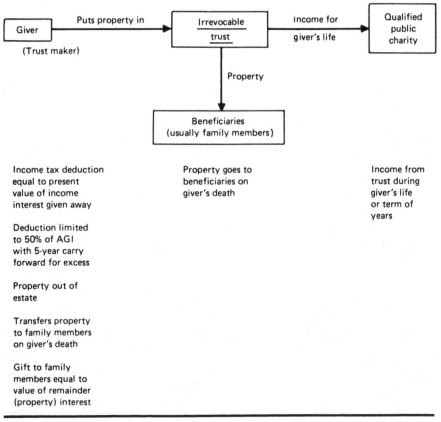

Figure 37-5. Charitable lead trust.

Table 37-1
Gifts to Public Charities

Gift Method	Description	Benefits to Maker or Family	Limitation	Income Tax Consequences	Gift-Tax Consequences	Estate-Tax Consequences	Charity Receives
1. Cash	Outright while giver alive	Tax	50% of AGI; 5-year carry forward for excess	Current deduction	None	Out of	Cash
2. Cash	On death from estate	Tax	None	None	None	Deduction	Cash
3. Capital assets	Outright while giver alive	Tax	30% or 50% of AGI; 5-year carry forward for 30% limit	Current deduction	None	Out of	Capital assets to keep or sell
4. Capital assets	On death from estate	Tax	None	None	None	Deduction equal to fair market value	Capital assets to keep or sell

5. Outright remainder interest	Giver keeps income and use of property for life	Tax and use of property for life	Personal residence or farm only	Deduction equal to value of remainder interest	None	Out of	Property on death of giver
6. Remainder trust	Giver puts property in trust	Tax and family retains income for their lives	50% or 30% of AGI depending on type of property put in trust; 5-year carry-forward for excess	Current deduction equal to value of remainder interest	Gift to family members equal to value of their income interest	Out of	Exclusive control of property on deaths of all trust beneficiaries to keep or sell
7. Lead trust	Giver puts property in trust	Tax and property goes to family beneficiaries when trust terminates	30% of AGI; 5-year carry-forward for excess	Deduction limited to first year, if taken at all	Gift to family members equal to value of remainder interest they will receive	Out of	Income from trust for giver's life or term of years

case, however, results in a taxable gift to the beneficiaries. It is a gift of a future interest and therefore is not eligible for the annual exclusion. If the lead trust is structured properly by a professional estate planner, however, the gift tax, in many instances, can be virtually eliminated.

The value of the income interest in a charitable lead trust must also be valued. The value of the income interest is income tax deductible to the giver in the year that the property is placed in the lead trust. The income tax deduction that the giver can take is limited to 30 percent of AGI. This is true regardless of whether the charity is public, semipublic, or private. The big limitation is, however, that the giver only gets an income tax deduction in the year the property is given to the trust. Worse yet, in future years, the income is taxed to the giver.

Because of this income tax disadvantage, many people elect not to take the income tax deduction. If they so elect, and the trust is drafted correctly, none of the lead trust income will be taxed to them.

A lead trust can be beneficial for several reasons:

The maker removes property from the estate, federal estate-tax-free, while passing it to chosen beneficiaries.

The charity has full use of all the income from the property.

As shown in Table 37-1, charitable giving is a broad area, encompassing not only federal estate- and gift-tax planning but also federal income tax planning. The array of charitable-giving techniques is only limited by one's imagination and, as always, certain provisions of the Internal Revenue Code. If you are genuinely interested in charitable giving, seek expert assistance.

38

An Estate-Planning Summary

"Passing the Bucks"

We know of no average or representative estate-planning situation that could be used as an example or illustration to summarize all the estate-planning principles and techniques that we have discussed. In our experience, people have individual estates requiring individual planning techniques.

There are, however, certain basics or "universals" common to the estate-planning process. We would like to summarize these for you:

Inventory the assets that you own.

Know where all of your title papers are located, and understand how you have taken title.

If title is in your name alone, you own the property in fee simple and can give it away, sell it, or leave it to whom you please. If you own it in tenancy in common, you only own part of it and can only give, sell, or leave your part. If you own property in joint tenancy, you own all of it with someone else. You may give your interest away or even sell it, but you cannot dispose of it on death.

The laws of the state of your domicile will provide an estate plan for you if you do not provide your own.

If you choose to accomplish your planning by using a will, you should remember that wills are only effective on death, and require a public

245

probate process. In addition, your will may not control the passage of all your property. If you move to another state, you should have your will reviewed—each state's laws are different, and it may have to be rewritten.

Probate involves unnecessary red tape and expense; it puts the real control in the judge's chambers. Probate can and should be avoided.

Federal estate taxes are imposed on your right to transfer almost all your property interests on death. It is a tax which is levied on the fair market value of your property and is generally paid within nine months of death; it is paid before your beneficiaries receive their inheritance.

The federal estate-tax rules generally only apply to estates greater than $600,000. In addition, the maximum tax bracket is 55 percent (50 percent beginning in 1993). Spouses in all states can give or leave an unlimited amount of property to their U.S.-citizen spouses tax-free. The only requirement associated with this unlimited marital deduction is that surviving spouses receive all of the income from the property during their lifetimes.

Federal estate tax can be deferred in estates that lack liquidity or in those in which 35 percent of the value consists of closely held business interests. If a family business is incorporated and certain technical tax requirements are met, the surviving family may trade corporate dollars to the estate in return for stock with no adverse tax consequences. Congress has also provided special relief for farm and ranch families who wish to retain ownership of their farms or ranches following the deaths of the farm or ranch owners.

The federal estate- and gift-tax systems have been unified for some time. The $600,000 exemption equivalent and the unlimited marital deduction apply to gifts made during life as well as on death.

The law allows you to make gifts to anyone of up to $10,000 (the annual exclusion) without the requirement of filing a federal gift-tax return. If your spouse chooses to "split" the gift with you, the amount goes up to $20,000. You should exercise care to avoid inadvertent gifts. How you give may be as important as the amount and nature of your gifts.

If you make a gift to your non-U.S.-citizen spouse, the annual exclusion is $100,000 because the unlimited marital deduction only applies to U.S.-citizen spouses.

Most states have their own death and gift taxes. Always consider your state's laws when planning.

Your property interests receive a step-up in basis at your death. This fact should be taken into consideration when structuring your plan.

Trusts are truly the estate planner's golf clubs because they can accomplish just about any of your objectives. Any number of separate trusts can be created in a single trust document. A death trust is called a testamentary trust and can only be created in your will. A living trust is always created during your lifetime. A living trust that allows you the right to change your mind and thereby change the trust is called a revocable living trust; one that cannot be changed is called an irrevocable living trust. A revocable living trust does not involve a gift; an irrevocable trust does.

An irrevocable living trust commonly used to give property to minors is the 2503(c) trust.

A revocable living trust can provide for the control, coordination, and distribution of your property while you are alive as well as on your death. It can also provide for your care and needs as well as those of your beneficiaries. Revocable living trusts are not public and are good in all states. They are extremely difficult for disgruntled heirs to attack.

Your revocable living trust can be unfunded, partially funded, or totally funded during your lifetime. It can also be funded subsequent to your death. Your trust can be funded directly, through the use of a nominee partnership, or, in some states, through other techniques such as unrecorded deeds, POD designations, and postmortem assignments. A properly funded revocable living trust avoids the probate process.

Your trust planning will only be as good as the performance of your trustees. Trustees are totally responsible for expert performance and judgment while following the written instructions provided in your trust document. Trustees have awesome power, accountability, and liability all wrapped together in their roles as superagents.

Both individual and institutional trustees have their strengths and weaknesses. You should select those types of trustees that best serve your planning purposes. Trustees are compensated. Institutional trustees publish fee schedules which are pretty much the same. Individual trustees usually negotiate their fees within parameters set by local state statutes or court rules.

Getting property to a minor can be difficult. Under the laws of most states, in order to make a gift to a minor, you must set up a Uniform Gifts to Minors Act or Uniform Transfers to Minors Act account, establish a Totten trust, or fund a living trust created for the minor's benefit.

Property left directly to a minor will be waylaid in a court-imposed custodianship until the minor reaches legal age. Leaving property directly to a minor involves a great deal of red tape; it depersonalizes the planning process and can create confusion and insecurity for your loved ones while generating substantial expense and delay.

When planning for children, you should provide for a succession of guardians and discuss your situation with the guardians you choose; it is always a good idea to share your planning with them.

How you divide and distribute your property among your loved ones is your business. However, some general rules of thumb would be: Do not divide your property among your children until the youngest of your children is an adult. Once your property is divided, you can provide for different distribution dates for each child to allow for specific thoughts you may have with regard to each. It is important for you to recognize that you *can* control how you wish your property to pass to your children and grandchildren. If you wish to bypass your children in favor of your grandchildren, you must take into account the generation-skipping federal estate-tax rules.

When planning for your spouse, you must consider your own state's law and the rights it gives your spouse to your property regardless of your planning attempts to the contrary. You may, however, avail yourself of two planning techniques—either a premarriage or an after-marriage contract. Given a choice of the two, you should always opt for the former; they are valid and binding if fair and fairly made and have always been favored under the laws of most states.

Planning for a spouse under pre-ERTA law was fairly simple. Today the number of planning possibilities available when planning for a spouse is staggering. There is no hypothetical best or optimum planning approach which can be used when planning for a spouse today. Great care must be taken to analyze all the spousal-planning possibilities before you select that best personal tax choice.

Your life insurance program should be coordinated with, and become an integral part of, your total estate plan. Life insurance that you own on your life will be federal estate taxable on your death and may be taxed by your state as well. It is important for you to properly record both primary and contingent beneficiary designations with your agent. Never make your estate or minors the direct beneficiary of your insurance proceeds.

You should reexamine your life insurance portfolio. Insuring the life of the younger spouse makes excellent sense in light of the federal estate-tax rules.

Life insurance can be purchased and structured to totally avoid federal estate tax. In general, this is best accomplished through the use of an irrevocable life insurance trust. ILITs can be structured by estate-planning specialists to accommodate almost any type of insurance you may own.

There are many estate-planning techniques that are oftentimes not appropriate and that do not always work. These include cross ownership of life insurance policies, joint tenancy, Uniform Gifts to Minors Act accounts, Uniform Transfers to Minors Act accounts, and general powers of attorney. There are also some estate-planning gimmicks that never seem to work. These include forms books, hiding property in a safe-deposit box, and attempting total tax avoidance through the use of a so-called constitutional or pure equity trust.

Both techniques of stock recapitalization freezing and partnership freezing, prior to 1988, allowed you to stop, or at the very least, control the growth of your estate by passing growth to others. In 1987, Congress passed section 2036(c), which substantially curtailed the use of freezing techniques. In 1990, Congress repealed the 1988 version of section 2036(c) and replaced it with another attempt to control the use of freezing techniques.

Installment sales are complicated and have been substantially curtailed under TRA 1986 and may be affected by the new valuation rules introduced by the Revenue Reconciliation Act of 1990. Under some circumstances, they can help you as a seller because they can allow you to get appreciating assets out of your estate and, at the same time, create cash flow. If you are a buyer, an installment sale will allow you to purchase an appreciating asset under favorable terms and provide you with a step-up in basis. As a buyer, however, you will find it difficult to receive a meaningful interest deduction under TRA 1986.

If you like the installment sales law but desire even potentially higher benefits, you may wish to consider the private annuity. A private annuity can be designed so that the value of your appreciating assets and the value of the promissory obligation are *both* totally eliminated from your estate; the danger is the gamble between your real and anticipated life expectancy. Private annuities may also be subject to the new valuation rules introduced by the Revenue Reconciliation Act of 1990 and should be used with caution until the full implications of the effects of the 1990 Act are known.

If you desire to make contributions of cash, or assets other than cash, to qualified charities, either currently or on death, you may receive tax benefits for your good works. The rules surrounding the income tax, estate-tax and gift-tax deductibility of your munificence are extremely complex. You should always seek out expert assistance in conjunction with your charitable desires.

Estate planning is no place for loners. Professional advisers should be selected for the knowledge they possess within their particular disciplines. All your advisers should participate in your estate-planning process and should work well, not only with you, but with each other.

If you properly approach the estate-planning process, you can be assured that you will be successful in "passing your bucks."

Appendix A
Getting Organized

PERSONAL INFORMATION

FAMILY INFORMATION

Name_____ Nickname_____

Home address_____ City_____ State_____ Zip_____

Home telephone_____ Birthdate_____ Social security number_____

Employer_____ Position_____

Business address_____ City_____ State_____ Zip_____

Business telephone _____

Spouse_____ Nickname_____

Birthdate_____ Social security number_____ Business Telephone _____

Employer_____ Position _____

Business address_____ City_____ State_____ Zip_____

Client's Children *(use full name)*   BIRTHDATE

_____ _____

_____ _____

_____ _____

_____ _____

Spouse's Children *(if different from above)*   BIRTHDATE

_____ _____

_____ _____

_____ _____

_____ _____

Advisers   TELEPHONE

Accountant_____ _____

Attorney_____ _____

Primary personal bank _____ _____

Stockbroker_____ _____

Referred to our firm by _____ _____

CASH

Name of Institution   TYPE* ACT. NUMBER OWNER† AMOUNT

_____ ____ _____ ____ _____
_____ ____ _____ ____ _____
_____ ____ _____ ____ _____
_____ ____ _____ ____ _____
_____ ____ _____ ____ _____
_____ ____ _____ ____ _____

*Checking Account (CA), Savings Account (SA), Certificates of Deposit (CD).
†Husband (H), Wife (W), Jointly (JT), Tenants in Common (TC), or Community Property (CP).

Note: If Account is in your name for benefit of a minor, please specify and give minor's name.

NOTES RECEIVABLE

Name of Debtor	DATE OF NOTE	DATE NOTE DUE	OWED TO*	CURRENT BALANCE OWED

*Husband (H), Wife (W), Jointly (JT), Tenants in Common (TC), or Community Property (CP).

BONDS

Description (*U.S. Savings Bonds, corporate, municipal, etc.*)   OWNER†   FACE VALUE

_____ _____ _____
_____ _____ _____
_____ _____ _____
_____ _____ _____
_____ _____ _____
_____ _____ _____
_____ _____ _____

If bond is owned either JT or TC with someone other than spouse, please furnish name and relationship.
†Husband (H), Wife (W), Jointly (JT), Tenants in Common (TC), or Community Property (CP).
Note: Please put ✓ next to Bearer Bonds.

REAL ESTATE

Where you have either a deeded or land contract interest *(land or buildings that you own in partnership with someone else should be listed under the partnership section):*

General description and/or address	OWNER*	FAIR MARKET VALUE	MORTGAGE

*Husband (H), Wife (W), Jointly (JT), Tenants in Common (TC), or Community Property (CP).
If property is owned either JT or TC with someone other than spouse, please furnish name and relationship.
Note: if two or more names are on deed or contract without stating type of ownership, please use "?".

CORPORATE BUSINESS INTERESTS

Privately Owned *(nonpublicly traded)*

Company	NUMBER OF SHARES	BUY/SELL AGREEMENT*	PERCENTAGE OWNERSHIP	OWNER†	VALUE

*Please put if a Buy/Sell Agreement Exists
†Husband (H), Wife (W), Jointly (JT), Tenants in Common (TC), or Community Property (CP).
Note: If stock is owned either JT or TC with someone other than spouse, please furnish name and relationship.

STOCKS

Please list all stock ownership in publicly owned corporations *(stock traded on an exchange or over the counter)*. Stock owned in family or nonpublicly traded companies, should be listed under the corporate business section.

Company	OWNER*	NUMBER OF SHARES	FAIR MARKET VALUE
Total			

*Husband (H), Wife (W), Jointly (JT), Tenants in Common (TC), or Community Property (CP).
If stock is owned either JT or TC with someone other than spouse, please furnish name and relationship.

If any of your shares are held in a street name account with your broker, please furnish us with:

Brokerage firm _____

Broker_____

Exact name and number of account_____

PARTNERSHIP INTERESTS

Partnership Name	PERCENTAGE OF PARTNERSHIP INTEREST		OWNER*	VALUE
	GENERAL PARTNER	LIMITED PARTNER		

Husband (H), Wife (W), Jointly (JT), Tenants in Common (TC), or Community Property (CP).

SOLE PROPRIETORSHIP BUSINESS INTERESTS

Name of Business	DESCRIPTION OF BUSINESS	OWNER*	VALUE

*Husband (H), Wife (W), Jointly (JT), Tenants in Common (TC), or Community Property (CP).

FARM AND RANCH INTERESTS

Description *(livestock, machinery, leases, etc.)*	OWNER*	VALUE

*Husband (H), Wife (W), Jointly (JT), Tenants in Common (TC), or Communioty Property (CP).

OIL AND GAS INTERESTS

Description *(lease, overriding royalty, fee mineral estate, working interest, pooling agreement, etc.)*	OWNER*	VALUE

*Husband (H), Wife (W), Jointly (JT), Tenants in Common, or Community Property (CP).

ANTICIPATED INHERITANCE, GIFT, OR LAWSUIT JUDGMENT

Description_____

_____
_____
_____
_____
_____

Total estimated value _____

RETIREMENT PLANS

Type of Plan	COMPANY	BENEFICIARY UPON YOUR DEATH	PERCENT VESTED	VALUE

*Pension (P), Profit Sharing (PS), H.R. 10, IRA

PERSONAL EFFECTS AND OTHER ASSETS

(Furniture, automobiles, jewelry, collectibles and other personal assets of more than nominal value)

_____
_____
_____
_____
_____
_____
_____
_____
_____
_____

*Total estimated fair market value*_____

LIFE INSURANCE POLICIES

Policy Number and Company_____

_____

Type*_____   Insured _____

Owner _____

Primary beneficiary _____   Secondary _____

Who pays premium† _____   Cash value _____

Amount of loans on policy _____   Face amount _____

*Term, whole life, split dollar, group life, annuity.
†Husband (H), Wife (W), Corporation (C).

Policy Number and Company_____

_____

Type*_____   Insured _____

Owner _____

Primary beneficiary _____   Secondary _____

Who pays premium† _____   Cash value _____

Amount of loans on policy _____   Face amount _____

*Term, whole life, split dollar, group life, annuity.
†Husband (H), Wife (W), Corporation (C).

Policy Number and Company_____

_____

Type*_____   Insured _____

Owner _____

Primary beneficiary _____   Secondary _____

Who pays premium† _____   Cash value _____

Amount of loans on policy _____   Face amount _____

*Term, whole life, split dollar, group life, annuity.
†Husband (H), Wife (W), Corporation (C).

Policy Number and Company_____
_____

Type*_____   Insured _____

Owner _____

Primary beneficiary _____   Secondary _____

Who pays premium† _____   Cash value _____

Amount of loans on policy _____   Face amount _____

*Term, whole life, split dollar, group life, annuity.
†Husband (H), Wife (W), Corporation (C).

Policy Number and Company_____
_____

Type*_____   Insured _____

Owner _____

Primary beneficiary _____   Secondary _____

Who pays premium† _____   Cash value _____

Amount of loans on policy _____   Face amount _____

*Term, whole life, split dollar, group life, annuity.
†Husband (H), Wife (W), Corporation (C).

Policy Number and Company_____
_____

Type*_____   Insured _____

Owner _____

Primary beneficiary _____   Secondary _____

Who pays premium† _____   Cash value _____

Amount of loans on policy _____   Face amount _____

*Term, whole life, split dollar, group life, annuity.
†Husband (H), Wife (W), Corporation (C).

SUMMARY OF VALUES

ASSETS

AMOUNTS*

	HUSBAND	WIFE
Cash	$_____	$_____
Notes receivable	_____	_____
Bonds	_____	_____
Real estate	_____	_____
Corporate business interests	_____	_____
Stocks	_____	_____
Partnership interests	_____	_____
Sole proprietorship business interests	_____	_____
Farm and ranch	_____	_____
Oil and gas	_____	_____
Anticipated inheritance, gift, or lawsuit judgment	_____	_____
Retirement plans	_____	_____
Personal effects and other assets	_____	_____
Life insurance face amounts	_____	_____
Total assets	_____	_____

*Joint Tenancy (JT), Tenancy in Common (TC) and Community Property (CP)
values go half in husband's column, half in wife's column.

LIABILITIES

AMOUNTS

	HUSBAND	WIFE
Loans payable	$_____	$_____
Accounts payable	_____	_____
Real estate mortgages payable	_____	_____
Contingent liabilities	_____	_____
Loans against life insurance	_____	_____
Unpaid taxes	_____	_____
Other obligations	_____	_____
_____	_____	_____
_____	_____	_____
Total liabilities	_____	_____

Net Estate

_____   _____

Federal Estate- and Gift-Tax Tables

1987–1992

Taxable Estate, in $	Federal Estate Tax, in $
600,000*	—0—
750,000	55,500
850,000	94,500
1,000,000	153,000
1,250,000	255,500
1,350,000	298,500
1,500,000	363,000
1,750,000	475,500
2,000,000	588,000
2,250,000	710,500
2,500,000	833,000
2,750,000	965,500
3,000,000	1,098,000

55% on the excess over $3,000,000; the tax becomes 60% for the portion of an estate between $10,000,000 and $21,040,000, and reverts to 55% for amounts in excess of $21,040,000.

*Exemption equivalent; maximum under ERTA.

1993

Taxable Estate, in $	Federal Estate Tax, in $
600,000*	—0—
750,000	55,500
850,000	94,500
1,000,000	153,000
1,250,000	255,500
1,350,000	298,500
1,500,000	363,000
1,750,000	475,500
2,000,000	588,000
2,250,000	710,500
2,500,000	833,000

50% on the excess over $2,500,000; the tax becomes 55% for the portion of an estate between $10,000,000 and $18,340,000, and reverts to 50% for amounts in excess of $18,340,000.

*Exemption equivalent; maximum under ERTA.

Appendix **C**
Spouses Have Rights Too

Throughout the United States, the law has evolved to protect the interests of a surviving husband or wife. Depending upon the state involved, these spousal rights are called a "right to elect against the will," a "dissent from the will," or by other terms. Their purpose remains the same, regardless of terminology. As a matter of public policy, based in an historical context, society has decided that it serves the public good by preventing husbands and wives from completely disinheriting their spouses.

Following is a brief explanation of the terms used in this appendix and a state-by-state synopsis of the spousal rights and obligations on death. Remember that state legislatures meet at least every other year; therefore, it is imperative that you contact your estate-planning professional to ascertain the current law in your state.

The concept that husbands and wives should receive at least a minimum amount of their spouses' property on death is based on English common law. The English common law is that body of principles and customs which developed in England and was brought to this country at the time of its settlement.

Historically, the first terms used to describe these spousal rights were "dower" and "curtesy." Dower is the wife's right to participate in the husband's estate; curtesy is the entitlement of the husband to share in his wife's estate. Usually these represented limited rights, most commonly, "life estates." To have a life estate in property means that you are entitled to all income from that property for your life.

A life estate cannot be transferred by will. After the death of the surviving spouse, the property usually reverts, or goes back, to the descendants of the deceased person (decedent). Frequently life estates are expressed in terms of a fraction of the estate; for example, a wife would receive a life estate in one-half of her husband's property. If personal property is involved, it might be placed in a trust by law with income going to the surviving spouse. Where real estate is involved, a deed for the life of the survivor would usually be prepared.

In the past there was frequently a distinction between the rights of the husband and the wife. These differences were based on the way society viewed the roles of men and women at that time. For the most part these distinctions have been removed, but some states still retain vestiges of this type of sex discrimination.

As the law changed, more and more states decided that the dower and curtesy rights were either outdated or insufficient to protect the interests of the surviving spouse. The right of spouses to elect against the will or to dissent from the will of their spouses was then created by state legislatures. In some states these new laws did not always replace dower and curtesy, but merely supplemented them.

To elect against or dissent from the will (synonymous terms) means that the surviving spouse chooses to take what the law provides in lieu of the deceased spouse's will. It is not possible to take under the will and also dissent from it; you cannot have both.

The amount that a spouse receives through a "will election" will vary depending upon the state involved. There are two terms with which you should become familiar. The first term, "augmented estate," is used in those states that have adopted the Uniform Probate Code (UPC). The augmented estate generally includes all property in which the deceased spouse retained any ownership as well as certain types of gifts. In UPC states, the electing spouse receives a fraction of the augmented estate, usually one-half or one-third.

Another term that is used when the surviving spouse elects against the will is the "intestate share." This term is derived from the word "intestacy," which means to die without a will. If intestacy occurs, the law provides the specific share of the estate that the wife or husband receives. This varies depending upon the number of children and a host of other factors. In some states, if a spouse dissents against the will, it is as if the decedent left no will. The dissenting spouse receives an intestate share of the estate as prescribed by state law.

Other states use neither the augmented estate nor the intestate share. They may rely solely upon forms of dower or curtesy, or they provide what essentially are the same rights by their law.

If a spouse elects against the will, the election is against probate assets. A probate asset is property the passage of which must be proved in court. In fact, the word "probate" has its roots in the Latin term for proof or truth. Whether or not the election will reach nonprobate assets is frequently an open question. Examples of nonprobate assets are life insurance policies, pension plans, funded living trusts, and jointly held property.

One type of trust is the revocable living trust. The person who creates the revocable living trust (the settlor or maker) can cancel, alter, or revoke its terms. The trust is called "living" because it exists while the settlor is alive and is funded with assets, directly or indirectly. This is to be contrasted with the testamentary trust, which does not exist until after death. This latter type is virtually always included in the elective share. Whether the revocable living trust is included in the elective share or not depends upon the state involved. In almost all UPC states this type of trust would be part of the elective share because the maker retains the right to revoke it as well as other powers.

In addition to the right to take against the will, most states also provide allowances for the surviving spouse. These are generally *in addition* to the right to elect against the will. These allowances are taken off the top before computing the elective share. In some states these allowances are substantial and frequently are exempt from other claims against the estate.

The homestead allowance or exemption is based on a legislative desire to preserve the family home. In many states these homestead allowances are inadequate and have been outdated by inflation. For example, a state might permit $10,000 for a homestead exemption. If creditors demand it, there could be a forced sale of the family home; the first $10,000 would go to the spouse and/or children of the decedent. The balance of the proceeds would be subject to the claims of creditors.

The surviving spouse may be entitled to an allowance intended to support that spouse as well as surviving minor children during the administration of the estate. These allowances are usually restricted to one year but can be extended by court order. The amount and frequency of payment differs from state to state. Sometimes this allowance is intended solely for the spouse. Occasionally, it is a lump-sum payment. This allowance is called a maintenance, family, or support allowance.

Many states provide an exempt personal property allowance which can cover everything from sentimental objects and the decedent's clothing to household furniture and even the family car. This allowance is a fixed amount and it is usually in the $3000 to $5000 range.

It is not necessary to elect against the will in order to be entitled to these allowances; they are in addition to either the elective share or the share under the will. Proper procedure must be followed to file claims for these allowances.

In most states it is required that the decedent be domiciled in the state in order for the allowance provisions to apply. Domicile is a legal term having a different meaning than residence but one which does not lend itself to a particular definition. If there are any doubts, one should always consult an attorney to verify the question of domicile.

Frequently, a person will have already made a will prior to marriage. If there is no provision in that will for a spouse, the spouse may receive a share of the estate anyway. This is known as the "omitted spouse" provision; however, in almost all states, if the person making the will specifically states that the omission is intentional, this law will not apply.

The rules in community-property states are different. Most property owned by spouses in a community-property state is marital property; however, community-property spouses may have separate property. This is usually property that was acquired before the marriage. If a community-property spouse attempts to dispose of more than his or her community-property interest, the other spouse can usually elect against the will.

In reading the material in this appendix, you will frequently note that the word "descendant" is used. Generally, a descendant is the child of the decedent, or the grandchild or great-grandchild, etc. People in *previous* generations are referred to as ancestors. People in *subsequent* generations are referred to as descendants.

Now that you have read this material, locate your state in this appendix and determine what your spousal rights and obligations are. You should, however, always seek the advice of a knowledgeable professional before utilizing any of these concepts in your estate plan.

Alabama.   In the state of Alabama, a surviving spouse has a right to the *lesser* of (1) all of the estate of the deceased spouse, reduced by the value of the surviving spouse's separate property, or (2) one-third of the estate of the deceased spouse. The surviving spouse's separate property includes all lifetime transfers from the deceased spouse to the surviving spouse, as well as property the surviving spouse may have received from other sources.

The surviving spouse and minor children whom the deceased spouse was obligated to support or children who were in fact being supported by the deceased spouse are entitled to a reasonable allowance in money from the estate during the period of administration. This allowance applies whether or not the spouse has elected against the estate.

The surviving spouse has a homestead allowance of $6000, a personal property allowance of $3500, and rights to miscellaneous other personal property. A spouse may waive the right to the elective share, the homestead allowance, and the family allowance before or after marriage.

Alaska.   The Alaskan augmented estate statute provides for the surviving spouse, husband or wife, to take one-third of the augmented estate. This is all that he or she would receive regardless of whether there were children. The remaining two-thirds would be divided among the children or, if none, to other family members as provided by law. Since the Alaskan code incorporates, generally, the UPC definition of augmented estate, this would seem to include trust property as well as property owned outright. This is true because the UPC refers to all assets which are transferred gratuitously, and in which the transferring spouse retained an interest, as part of the augmented estate. There are no sex distinctions in Alaska's election provisions.

There are also various types of family allowances in Alaska. There is a homestead allowance of $27,000 available to protect the family home. There is also a personal property allowance available of up to $10,000. Finally, there is a family allowance, which is defined as a reasonable sum for the family, not to exceed $15,000, for a period of up to one year. The probate court can, in its discretion, modify this family allowance.

Arizona.   Arizona is a community-property state. In a community-property state, one-half of the property acquired during marriage belongs to the surviving spouse.

Arizona has general allowance provisions. The homestead allowance is $12,000. There is a personal property allowance of $7000 which is intended to protect such items as furniture. There is a standard family allowance permitting a reasonable amount for care of the family up to one year. There is no distinction between the sexes under Arizona law as concerns these rights. As in most community-property states, the right of the decedent to dispose of his or her property is limited to one-half.

Arkansas.   The laws of Arkansas which protect the surviving spouse are generally based in dower rights. By amendment in 1981, sex distinction was removed as concerns the election.

The dower right (which would apply to the husband as well) consists of one-third life estate of the part of the land which the deceased spouse owned and one-third full ownership in the personal property. Again, there is terminology which would include property owned "for his use," which would seem to include living trust property. One-third of the personal property is also given to the surviving spouse if a child or children survive.

If there are no surviving children, the surviving spouse can receive up to one-half of the real and personal property as against the other heirs but only one-third as against creditors.

A somewhat unique provision in Arkansas is that the surviving spouse also receives one-third of the mineral rights.

The homestead provision in Arkansas extends up to $5000 and can be taken from the sale of a qualifying home. Check with your professional advisers for details.

Another allowance provides that in addition to homestead and dower rights, the surviving spouse is entitled to $2000 against other distributees (that is, people who would take under the will) and $1000 against the creditors. There is a living allowance not to exceed $500 per month, usually limited in time to a period set by the court.

One final nuance under Arkansas law is that in order to elect against the will, that is, to receive dower, the surviving spouse must have been married to the decedent for a period of time *greater* than one year.

California.   California is a community-property state. In a community-property state, one-half of the property acquired during the marriage belongs to the surviving spouse.

Upon the death of a married person domiciled in California, one-half of the property, under their community-property system, automatically belongs to the surviving spouse. The other half is subject to the will of the decedent; if he or she leaves no will, the surviving spouse will receive the property subject to the general intestacy provisions.

It is important to know that California uses the concept of quasi-community property as well. Quasi-community property is that property which was acquired elsewhere while the person was not domiciled in California but which, if they had been domiciled in California at the time of acquisition, would have been considered community property. The effect this has on the estate can be complicated; therefore, it should be investigated early.

There is a homestead provision which apparently has no dollar limitation to it. It offers a protection for the family home. There is also a standard family allowance which is intended to provide reasonable support for up to one year.

Colorado.   Colorado is a UPC state. Either the husband or the wife can elect against the will; such election would include trust property. The share received would be one-half of the augmented estate which is the net estate with certain prescribed additions. This is the share regardless of whether there are children.

The exempt property allowance is $15,000 to cover personal property. There is also a reasonable family allowance which is limited to one year, or longer if the court deems it necessary. Under Colorado law, these allowances are in addition to the elective share.

Connecticut.   Under Connecticut law, the surviving spouse is entitled to the use for his or her life of one-third of the value of all property, whether it be real or personal, owned by the decedent. It is important to know that the statute refers to property owned legally or equitably and thus would appear to include living trust assets. The share is the same whether or not there are children.

There is a support allowance provided for the surviving spouse or the family as is deemed necessary by the court. The amount is intended to cover living expenses during administration.

Delaware.   Under Delaware law, the surviving spouse can receive one-third of the elective estate less the amount of certain transfers of property that are made to the surviving spouse by the deceased spouse by virtue of his or her death (including beneficial interests in a trust created during the decedent's lifetime). Elective estate means the adjusted gross estate as that term is used on the federal estate-tax return, after subtracting all transfers which are included on that tax return and which were made with the consent of the surviving spouse. The elective estate in Delaware is highly technical, and you should consult your estate-planning professional for the details. The share is the same whether or not there are children.

Also under Delaware law, the surviving spouse is given an allowance of $2000; this is a one-time fixed amount given to the spouse for his or her use.

District of Columbia.   There is a family allowance provided of up to $10,000; the amounts and time of distribution are decisions made by the court.

The surviving spouse, husband or wife, has a right to elect to take the intestate share against the will. The intestate share is one-third if there are children or descendants. If there are no children, but the deceased had parents, brothers, sisters, nieces, or nephews, the spouse would receive one-half of the estate. The spouse could receive all the estate if there are no descendants, parents, brothers, sisters, nieces, or nephews. He or she may take dower rights in the real estate of the decedent, if desired, in lieu of the intestate provisions affecting real estate. This would mean that the surviving spouse, if taking dower rights, would receive one-half of the personal property outright and a dower interest in the real estate.

Florida.   The surviving spouse in the state of Florida may elect against the will and receive 30 percent of the fair market value of those assets in the estate. This does not include real estate located outside the state of Florida. This share is the same whether or not there are children.

The homestead provision in Florida consists of a life estate if survived by surviving spouse and children and the homestead was not held as tenants by the entirety, which is a special type of legal title to real estate which exists only between husbands and wives. A surviving spouse is entitled to household items up to a value of $10,000, as well as all automobiles in the decedent's name and regularly used by the decedent or the decedent's immediate family. Finally, there is a standard family allowance which appears to have a ceiling of $6000. The latter amount is for living expenses during administration.

Georgia. The Georgia code apparently does not have any provision for an election against the will. There are provisions to give up to one year's support for living expenses to the surviving spouse, for which a minimum figure of $1600 is set.

Dower rights were repealed in Georgia as of 1969.

Hawaii. Under Hawaiian law, the surviving spouse, husband or wife, receives one-third of the net estate if he or she elects against the will. Net estate means the estate to be disposed of under the decedent's will and therefore appears not to include living trust property. The share is the same whether or not there are children.

There is a homestead allowance of up to $5000 for the protection of the family home. There is an exempt property allowance of $5000 for personal property items.

There is also a family allowance for support of the surviving spouse and any children which the deceased was obligated to, and in fact did, support.

Idaho. Idaho is a community-property state. In a community-property state, one-half of the property acquired during the marriage belongs to the surviving spouse; however, if a transfer is made of quasi-community property without adequate consideration, it can be included under the augmented estate provisions of the Idaho law. It should not be assumed that quasi-community property means the same in each community-property state, as there are variations. One should always consult an attorney before making a decision in this regard. If the election is made, it covers one-half of the property which was transferred and in which the decedent has retained certain types of interests. The share is the same whether or not there are children.

There is a homestead provision which varies: $4000 if there is only a surviving spouse but $10,000 if there is a surviving spouse and there are children living with that surviving spouse. There is a family allowance to provide for the living expenses of the family for up to one year. There is also a $3500 exempt property allowance to cover personal property items and other protected assets.

There appears to be no sex distinction in Idaho concerning the election. The issue of living trust property does not seem to be addressed.

Illinois.   Illinois law provides a spousal support allowance for up to nine months. This amount is not less than $10,000, together with an additional sum of not less than $2000 for each dependent child.

The surviving spouse may also elect against the will. If he or she does so, one-third of the entire estate is given if there are descendants; or one-half, if there are no descendants. Remember that descendants include children and their children, etc.

Under case law, it appears that revocable living trusts would not escape the augmented estate provisions.

Indiana.   The election against the will in Indiana applies equally to both men and women. The electing spouse receives one-half of the net personal property and real estate, but if there are children from a prior marriage surviving and the surviving spouse has no children from the second marriage, the following provisions apply: The survivor would receive one-third of the net personal property and a one-third interest in the real estate for life only.

The statute says that the net estate shall consider only property that would have passed under the laws of descent and distribution, which would appear to exclude living trust property.

There is a special personal property allowance of $8500 under Indiana law. If there is not $8500 in personal property, the remainder can be taken from the proceeds of any real property.

Iowa.   There is a general personal property exemption which appears to cover personal effects and household goods. There is also a standard family allowance of up to one year to provide for the living expenses of the family. The amount involved may vary with needs.

If the surviving spouse, husband or wife, elects against the will, the following provisions are applicable. He or she would receive one-third interest in all legal or *equitable* estate assets, except that all personal property held by the decedent as head of the family would also be given to the electing spouse. Thus living trust property seems to be included.

Kansas.   Kansas has a homestead allowance of up to 160 acres if the property is outside the city limits and 1 acre if within the city limits. This helps to protect the family home. There is a personal property allowance which varies in amount depending upon circumstances, which cannot be less than $1,500 nor more than $25,000. See your professional planner for the details.

The surviving spouse may elect against the will and receive an intestate share, which will vary depending upon whether there are children.

If there are no children, the spouse receives all; if there are one or more children or their issue, the spouse receives one-half.

Kentucky.   In Kentucky, when a husband or a wife dies intestate (without a will), the surviving spouse has a dower right, which is a one-half interest in all "surplus" real estate, and a life estate in one-third of any real estate owned by the decedent during marriage, but not at death. The surviving spouse would also receive a one-half interest in all surplus personalty. A surviving spouse who elects against a will can take a modified dower share, which is identical to the intestate dower share, except that the one-half interest in surplus real estate is reduced to one-third.

There appear to be no sex distinctions under the Kentucky election law. The issue of living trust property is not specifically addressed.

There is a $7500 personal property exemption to cover household effects, etc., which is available when the deceased spouse dies without a will or when the surviving spouse renounces the will. There is also a $1000 spousal allowance to any surviving spouse (except that it will be treated as a charge against the exempt property).

Louisiana.   Louisiana is a community-property state. In a community-property state, one-half of the property acquired during the marriage belongs to the surviving spouse.

Unlike any of its forty-nine co-jurisdictions, it is under a civil code that is extremely intricate and quite different from any other state's law. Generally speaking, there is no right to elect against the will.

It is specifically noted in an introduction to this portion of the Louisiana law that the surviving spouse can be deprived of any property by will.

Maine.   Under Maine law, the surviving spouse is entitled to one-third of the augmented estate, which is the net estate with certain additions. The share is the same whether or not there are children. Since Maine uses the UPC language, including gratuitous transfers with retained interests, it would appear to include living trusts. Further, Maine, in its official comments to the law, refers to New York law, which itself does include living trusts but *excludes* insurance, pension plans, and other assets payable to a designated person.

There are also a homestead provision in the amount of $5000 to protect the family home; an exempt property allowance in the amount of $3500 for household furniture, etc.; and a family allowance to provide for the reasonable living expenses of the family. It is limited in duration to one year.

Maryland.   The elective intestate share in Maryland is as follows. The surviving spouse, husband or wife, may receive one-third of the net estate if there was issue from the marriage. If there is no issue, the surviving spouse receives one-half of the net estate.

Net estate is defined to mean property of the decedent exclusive of allowances and claims. It is therefore uncertain as to whether or not Maryland would include a revocable inter vivos trust as part of the elective share.

There is also a family allowance in the amount of $2000 to provide for living expenses plus $1000 for each unmarried child under the age of eighteen.

Massachusetts.   There is a homestead allowance of up to $100,000 in Massachusetts to protect the family home.

Curtesy, the husband's equivalent of dower, has been abolished in Massachusetts, but dower is expressed in terms applying to both sexes. The "dower" provisions of Massachusetts permit the surviving spouse to take one-third of all land owned by the spouse for life. This is referred to as tenancy by dower. There is apparently no discrimination between land owned outright and land owned in a living trust.

There are also other allowances. There is a personal property allowance to cover such items as furniture, plus the right to live in the house for six months with no rent. Additionally, there is an allowance for necessities, apparently as the court orders.

The elective share in Massachusetts is as follows: If there is issue surviving the decedent, the surviving spouse is entitled to elect one-third of the personal property and one-third of the real estate. If there is no issue surviving but there are kindred (defined below), the surviving spouse receives $25,000 plus one-half of the estate. Finally, if there are no issue and no kindred, the surviving spouse receives $25,000 plus one-half of the real estate and personal property absolutely, and not as a life estate.

It should be noted that in the first two categories above, if either amount exceeds $25,000, the surviving spouse receives only a life estate and the share of the excess.

Kindred is generally defined in Massachusetts as those members of the family computed according to the rules of civil law and apparently includes most major family members.

There is no distinction between husband and wife provided under Massachusetts law.

Michigan.   The elective share is *one-half* of the amount which the surviving spouse would have received in an intestate estate, reduced by one-half the value of all property derived from the deceased spouse upon his or her death by any means other than testate or intestate succession. The intestate share for a surviving spouse is *normally* the entire estate or, if there are parents or there are issue who are also issue of the surviving spouse, the first $60,000 plus one-half of the balance. If one or more of the issue are not the issue of the survivor, the normal share is one-half. Remember that these amounts are halved under an election against the will.

Since Michigan law speaks in terms of an intestate share, the applicability toward living trusts is questionable.

The homestead allowance in Michigan is $10,000. This serves to protect the family home. The personal property allowance is $3500 for assets such as furniture. Finally, there is a maintenance allowance intended to give a reasonable amount of support to the family for living expenses.

Minnesota.   Minnesota has adopted the Uniform Probate Code, with several modifications. The surviving spouse has the right to take one-third of the augmented estate of the deceased spouse. In addition, the family residence passes to the surviving spouse, unless the surviving spouse specifically consents that the residence can pass elsewhere. If there are children of the marriage, then on the death of the surviving spouse, the residence passes to the children in equal shares.

The following allowances are available to the spouse: a $6000 furniture and household goods allowance; $3000 in additional personal property; one automobile under certain conditions; and, finally, a family allowance for a period varying from twelve to eighteen months, or longer, at the court's discretion.

Mississippi.   In Mississippi the elective share is the intestate share, not to exceed one-half of the estate. It can be less than one-half if there are children of the decedent. Again, since the statute speaks in terms of an intestate share, one might conclude that living trust property is not included, but there is no solid foundation for this.

There is also a separate estate provision in Mississippi law. If the spouse has a separate estate equal to the elective share, he or she will receive nothing. If there is a difference, the elective share will be made up accordingly.

The homestead provision in Mississippi is $30,000; this is intended to protect the family home. The spouse is allowed personal property of the deceased spouse up to $10,000.

There is also a support provision for the surviving spouse of one year; it gives him or her a living allowance for reasonable needs.

Missouri.   The surviving spouse in Missouri is entitled to elect against the will and receive the following assets. One-half of the estate goes to him or her if there are no lineal descendants, one-third of the estate goes to the surviving spouse if there are lineal descendants. In determining the surviving spouse's share, all property is considered, even if it is not subject to probate. This includes trust property, proceeds of life insurance, and other nonprobate assets.

The homestead allowance is $7500, but is offset against the elective share of the surviving spouse. There is an exempt personal property allowance and a family allowance of $6000 for one year, which can be increased by the probate court.

Montana.   Montana is a UPC state, and therefore it would appear that the elective share would include living trust property. The elective share consists of one-third of the augmented estate. The augmented estate is defined as including all property the affairs of which are subject to the code. The share is the same whether or not there are children. Since there are provisions in the UPC which deal with trust assets, this is further support for the inclusion of living trust assets in the augmented estate.

The homestead allowance is $20,000 to protect the family home; the exempt property allowance is $3500 for personal property; and a family allowance is also provided. The family allowance is for reasonable living expenses.

Nebraska.   In Nebraska, the elective share is one-third of the augmented estate. Again, the augmented estate is defined as including those assets subject to the codes, which probably includes living trust assets. The share is the same whether or not there are children.

The homestead provision in Nebraska is $7500; the exempt personal property allowance is $5000; and a family allowance is also provided for under law. That allowance gives a reasonable amount to the family for living expenses.

The general comments to the Nebraska law imply that the views of New York and Pennsylvania toward will substitutes, that is, that they should be included in the augmented estates, are viewed favorably under the Nebraska law.

Nevada.   Nevada is a community-property state. In a community-property state, one-half of the property acquired during the marriage belongs to the surviving spouse.

It has no elective share provision.

There is a homestead allowance of $90,000 to protect the family home, plus a certain amount of personal property reserved to the surviving spouse. There is a family allowance at the discretion of the court.

New Hampshire.   The elective share for the surviving husband or wife in New Hampshire varies widely depending upon the other survivors. It ranges from one-third of the estate to a one-half interest. If there are children, he or she would receive one-third. There is no men-tion of living trust assets as includable or excludable from the elective share; however, there is case law that indicates that transfers to a living trust will defeat the statutory rights of a surviving spouse unless it can be shown that the transfers were made for that purpose.

There is a reasonable allowance provision for present support *which the court may, in its discretion, count as part of the elective share.* This contrasts with most other states' handling of the support allowance.

The surviving spouse is permitted use of the family dwelling for a period of forty days after death at no rent.

New Jersey. Under New Jersey law, the surviving spouse has a right of election to take one-third of the augmented estate, which is patterned after the Uniform Probate Code's definition of "augmented estate." There is a right to up to $5000 worth of personal property by the surviving spouse, provided the decedent's will does not state otherwise. No other allowances are available, except for the right to the decedent's wearing apparel and $5000 worth of personal property.

New Mexico. New Mexico is a community-property state. In a community-property state, one-half of the property acquired during the marriage belongs to the surviving spouse.

It has no elective share at the present time.

There is a family allowance of $10,000 to provide for living expenses. A personal property allowance of $3500 is also available.

New York. Under the New York law, the surviving spouse has an elective share provision as follows. He or she may receive one-third of the net estate if issue survive; one-half of the net estate is the provision if there is no issue.

New York is the only state that has specifically addressed the issue of the living trust, as it relates to the election against the will. The matter is divided depending upon when the will was executed. If the will was signed after August 31, 1930 (the beginning of the elective share period), but before September 1, 1966, the statute does not apparently reach living trust assets. The law was amended for wills executed after August 31, 1966, to include living trust assets. The same fractions are involved, that is, one-third or one-half of the net estate, regardless of the date of the will.

The surviving spouse has the right to certain items of personal and household property of the deceased spouse, limited by various dollar amounts.

North Carolina. In North Carolina, a surviving spouse has the right to dissent against an estate where the surviving spouse has received less than one-half of the value of all property passing on the death of the deceased spouse. The statute concerning surviving spouses sets out a complete definition of "property passing at death."

Upon making a dissent, the surviving spouse has the right to receive up to a maximum of one-half of the deceased spouse's estate, depending on the number of children of the marriage and other factors. The amount received by the surviving spouse is the same as the surviving spouse would have received had the deceased spouse died intestate.

The surviving spouse can get an allowance of up to $5000 for support for a period of one year after the death of the deceased spouse.

North Dakota.   In this state, the surviving spouse, husband or wife, may receive one-third of the augmented estate. There are notes accompanying the North Dakota statute which indicate that at least Totten trust funds would be included. These are bank accounts which are set up in the name of one individual in trust for another. Whether or not North Dakota would include "regular" living trusts is uncertain, although they do note with approval the New York law on trusts. The share is the same whether or not there are children.

There is a homestead allowance of $80,000 in North Dakota to the surviving spouse for life estate or until remarriage. There is also a family allowance of a reasonable amount for up to one year to provide for the family's living expenses. The exempt property allowance is $5000 for personal property.

Ohio.   In Ohio the surviving spouse can elect to receive the amount of $60,000 plus a share of the balance of the estate depending upon the children or descendants who survive the decedent. The spouse receives one-half of the net estate unless there are two or more descendants surviving, in which case the spouse receives one-third. The $60,000 is reduced to $20,000 if the surviving spouse is not the natural or adoptive parent of the surviving children.

A living trust can probably be used to defeat rights of the surviving spouse in Ohio. State law provides that the surviving spouse has no dower in the corpus of a living trust and cannot reach the living trust as part of the spouse's distributive share or election to take against the will.

The support allowance in Ohio is $25,000 for the living expenses of the family and is deducted before computing the elective share. The surviving spouse may elect to take certain types of personal property not to exceed $2500.

Oklahoma.   In Oklahoma, a surviving spouse can elect to take an interest in one-half of the property acquired by the joint industry of the husband and wife during marriage, a concept somewhat akin to community property.

The surviving spouse has a life estate in the entire homestead subject to various conditions. The surviving spouse also has a right to certain personal property. In addition, if the homestead and personal property amounts are not sufficient for the care of the surviving spouse, the court can award a reasonable family allowance.

Oregon.   Here, the surviving husband or wife may elect against the will and receive one-quarter of the net estate. The share is the same whether or not there are children. It is uncertain whether trust property is included.

The allowances for the spouse permit him or her to occupy the dwelling for one year after the death for no rent and to receive reasonable support.

Pennsylvania.   The surviving spouse in Pennsylvania may elect against the will and receive one-third of the estate.

There is a family exemption of $2000 in real or personal property; this amount is exempt from creditors' claims.

The position of Pennsylvania toward trust property is not exactly clear, but there are some oblique references to the fact that they might include it in the elective share.

Rhode Island.   The surviving husband or wife may elect a life estate in all real estate instead of receiving property under the will. The share is the same whether or not there are children. Where a will fails to indicate an intention that it has made provisions for the surviving spouse in lieu of the statutory life estate in real estate, then the surviving spouse gets the life estate in real estate in addition to the provisions in the will.

There are also family allowances of varying amounts; they cover support for the family and wearing apparel. Also included is the generous provision which permits real estate to go to the spouse as is necessary and deemed suitable by the court if there are no issue.

South Carolina.   South Carolina has adopted its own version of the Uniform Probate Code. A surviving spouse has the right to one-third of the decedent's estate. This right does not seem to include property passed by will substitutes, including living trusts, but the commentary on the law seems to indicate that the courts may take a different view.

The law allows waiver of the right to elect either by a pre- or post-marital agreement.

There is a homestead exemption of $1000 and a provision for personal property, both of which can also be waived by agreement of the spouses.

South Dakota.   South Dakota adopted the UPC for a brief period of time, approximately six months, and then repealed it. They now have their own original Probate Code.

The homestead allowance in South Dakota is limited to $30,000 in most cases (it is unlimited for those over age 70 or their unremarried spouse). There are certain minimal personal property allowances and a family allowance at the court's discretion.

Tennessee.   Both dower and curtesy have been abolished in Tennessee.

There are personal property allowances and a one-year support allowance for living expenses, and the surviving spouse is entitled to at least $1000 of the final wages of the decedent.

There is also a homestead allowance in Tennessee of up to $5000 to protect the family home.

The surviving spouse may elect to take a share in lieu of the will equal to one-third of the net estate. The share is the same whether or not there are children. The position of Tennessee on living trust property is unclear.

Texas.   Texas is a community-property state. In a community-property state, one-half of the property acquired during the marriage belongs to the surviving spouse.

In Texas if the deceased spouse attempts to dispose of more than his or her interest in the community property, the surviving spouse may elect his or her interest in the community property. The share is the same whether or not there are children.

There are homestead provisions designed to protect the family home or a part of it; there is a personal property allowance covering such things as furniture, clothing, etc.; or, there is a cash allowance in lieu of exempt property not to exceed $1000, and a cash allowance in lieu of homestead not to exceed $10,000. The cash allowance is a one-time allotment.

Utah.   Utah has a somewhat complicated mathematical formula for computing the elective share. The husband or wife can take one-third of the augmented estate multiplied times a certain fraction which is determined under that formula. The share is the same whether or not there are children.

The homestead allowance in Utah is $10,000 for the surviving spouse. There are a personal property allowance of $5000 and a family allowance of up to one year. The family allowance is limited to $6000.

The matter of living trust property is not specifically addressed.

Vermont.   Under Vermont law, the dissenting husband or wife can elect against the will and receive one-third of the value of all real estate or one-half if the decedent left only one heir who is also the child of the surviving spouse or was adopted by both. Apparently both these provisions are outright and not life estates.

There are a personal property allowance and a provision for support during the administration of the estate, including living expenses of the spouse and children. There is also a homestead allowance of $30,000 to protect the family home.

Although Vermont does not specifically address the issue of trust property, the above-referenced election does address all real estate and does not seem to distinguish between that which is held in trust and that which is held outright.

Virginia. If a surviving spouse renounces the will of a deceased spouse, the surviving spouse takes one-third of the estate if there are surviving children, or their descendants. Otherwise, the surviving spouse takes one-half.

A surviving spouse can elect a one-third dower or curtesy right in real estate instead of renouncing the will.

There is a $5000 homestead allowance, which reduces any other amounts received by the surviving spouse. In addition, there is a personal property allowance of up to $3500. A reasonable family allowance can be awarded by the court in its discretion, but is not to exceed the amount of $6000.

Washington. Washington is a community-property state. In a community-property state, one-half of the property acquired during the marriage belongs to the surviving spouse.

It permits the surviving spouse to elect *his* or *her* interest in the community property if the deceased spouse attempts to dispose of it.

There is a homestead allowance up to $30,000; the allowance helps to protect the family home.

West Virginia. The surviving husband or wife may elect his or her intestate share in lieu of the interest under the will. The intestate share is as if the decedent had left children, regardless of whether that actually occurred. There is also a provision for dower in West Virginia. It appears that this is a neutral statute and would apply to either a husband or a wife, since curtesy was abolished. The surviving spouse may take one-third of all real and personal property for life; this includes property in a living trust.

The statutes also seem to say that one cannot both take the dower interest and elect against the will.

Wisconsin. Wisconsin has adopted the Marital Property Act, which is somewhat similar to the community-property concept. A surviving spouse may elect to take one-half interest in all "deferred" marital property, including property not subject to probate. Deferred marital property is defined in a relatively complex manner, but generally includes all property acquired during a marriage, excluding individual property. Certain effective dates apply, so see your adviser for details.

There is a generous personal property allowance that includes clothing, jewelry, an automobile, and certain other property. It will be limited to $3000 only if claims cannot be paid in full. Property up to an amount of $10,000 can be advanced for support of the family. The court has the discretion to provide allowances for support during administration or a longer period of time depending on circumstances.

Wyoming.   The Wyoming surviving spouse, husband or wife, may elect against the estate and receive from one-fourth to one-half of the estate depending upon the number of the surviving descendants. If there are no descendants or if the spouse is the parent of the children, the spouse receives one-half; if there are surviving children or descendants and the surviving spouse is *not* the parent, the spouse receives one-fourth.

There are a homestead allowance to protect the family home and a maintenance allowance also. A maintenance allowance provides for the reasonable living expenses of the family unit.

The issue of living trust property is not specifically addressed in Wyoming.

Puerto Rico.   Puerto Rico has a version of community property. A surviving spouse has a legal share in community property and a life estate in a portion of the remaining estate that varies with the number of children.

There are homestead protections for the surviving spouse, children, and other relatives. There is certain exempt personal property, but there are no other exemptions or allowances.

Virgin Islands.   Dower and curtesy are abolished. The surviving spouse may elect to take an intestate share, but if so, it is limited to no more than one-half of the net estate.

The intestate share of the surviving spouse is one-third if there are issue of the decedent. If there are no issue but there are surviving parents, siblings, nieces, or nephews, the share can be greater than one-half by certain amounts depending on which of these relatives survive. If none of these relatives survive, the surviving spouse receives the entire estate.

There are provisions for homestead and an allowance for family support. There are also exempt property and personal property allowances.

Index

About the Authors

Robert A. Esperti and Renno L. Peterson are tax attorneys, lecturers, and consultants. They frequently lecture on business, estate, and Loving Trust planning to Fortune 500 companies and professional associations throughout the United States. They have written extensively about these subjects for both professionals and the general public. Their *Handbook of Estate Planning*, Third Edition specifically addresses the comments and questions they most frequently encountered while planning thousands of estates and businesses—both large and small. Mr. Esperti and Mr. Peterson have previously collaborated on such widely acclaimed books as *Incorporating Your Talents, A Guide to the One-Person Corporation, Loving Trust, A Loving Trust Compendium, Creating a Loving Trust Practice*, and the *Irrevocable Life Insurance Trust*.